MEAN Cookbook

The meanest set of MEAN stack solutions around

Nicholas McClay

BIRMINGHAM - MUMBAI

MEAN Cookbook

First published: September 2017

Production reference: 1250917

Published by Packt Publishing Ltd.
Livery Place
35 Livery Street
Birmingham
B3 2PB, UK.

ISBN 978-1-78728-657-3

www.packtpub.com

Credits

Author
Nicholas McClay

Reviewer
Joel Holmes

Commissioning Editor
Ashwin Nair

Acquisition Editor
Larissa Pinto

Content Development Editor
Onkar Wani

Technical Editor
Akhil Nair

Copy Editor
Dhanya Baburaj

Project Coordinator
Devanshi Doshi

Proofreader
Safis Editing

Indexer
Pratik Shirodkar

Graphics
Jason Monteiro

Production Coordinator
Shraddha Falebhai

About the Author

Nicholas McClay is a software developer and designer with over a decade of JavaScript experience in both corporate and startup technology companies. He is an avid Node.js and JavaScript enthusiast and the founder of the greater Pittsburgh region's Node.js and Angular meetups. A self-described *user experience developer*, he balances using both design and development disciplines to solve problems.

He is a graduate of the Art Institute of Pittsburgh, where he acquired a bachelor's of science degree in Game Art and Design, a passion that springboarded him into a career of interactive experience design.

His previous work experience includes Autodesk, where he worked on next-generation integrated cloud services. His current role is as the UX Lead of Wombat Security Technologies, where he helps bridge the gap between the customers' user experience and the underlying technology and product decisions that deliver it.

He enjoys video games, tinkering and creating things, and lives with his loving wife, son, and daughter in Pittsburgh, Pennsylvania.

Acknowledgement

Writing a book about JavaScript web development wasn't something I was planning, at least not in the manner that it happened.

Like some of my favorite things in life, it was a surprise opportunity, which I feel very lucky to have had.

However, actually making this book was also a lot of hard work, so I want to thank those who helped me do it.

I want to thank Joel Holmes for his careful technical consultation and review for this book as well as the editing and publishing staff at Packt; without your careful attention, this book's content would not have been nearly as good or as readable; it was very much appreciated!

I want to thank my grandfather for introducing me to my passion for technology, and a love of learning new things.

You gave me a great gift that I hope I can teach and share with others, like you did for me.

I also want to thank my mother, who raised me to be creative, curious, and independent. Your son is a huge nerd who wrote a programming book, and he would never have had the talent to pull it off without you.

And finally, I want to thank my wife for supporting me through this whole endeavor and making sure my love of run on sentences didn't contaminate the contents of this book, no matter how much unreasonable stress it might have caused, and also for encouraging me to keep going even when it seemed hard and I wanted to quit; thank you for being my partner though this and every other piece of luck we find together!

About the Reviewer

Joel Holmes (`@Joel_Holmes`) is a graduate from the University of Pittsburgh and is a full stack developer at Wombat Security Technologies. He enjoys learning new technologies and their applications in business. When not working, he enjoys spending time with his wife, Chelsea, and his two children, Eli and Abel.

www.PacktPub.com

For support files and downloads related to your book, please visit www.PacktPub.com. Did you know that Packt offers eBook versions of every book published, with PDF and ePub files available? You can upgrade to the eBook version at www.PacktPub.com and as a print book customer, you are entitled to a discount on the eBook copy. Get in touch with us at service@packtpub.com for more details.

At www.PacktPub.com, you can also read a collection of free technical articles, sign up for a range of free newsletters and receive exclusive discounts and offers on Packt books and eBooks.

https://www.packtpub.com/mapt

Get the most in-demand software skills with Mapt. Mapt gives you full access to all Packt books and video courses, as well as industry-leading tools to help you plan your personal development and advance your career.

Why subscribe?

- Fully searchable across every book published by Packt
- Copy and paste, print, and bookmark content
- On demand and accessible via a web browser

Customer Feedback

Thanks for purchasing this Packt book. At Packt, quality is at the heart of our editorial process. To help us improve, please leave us an honest review on this book's Amazon page at https://www.amazon.com/dp/1787286576. If you'd like to join our team of regular reviewers, you can e-mail us at customerreviews@packtpub.com. We award our regular reviewers with free eBooks and videos in exchange for their valuable feedback. Help us be relentless in improving our products!

Table of Contents

Preface

This book is a collection of recipes targeted at building modern, all-JavaScript web applications using MongoDB, Express, Angular, and Node.js. Using this **MEAN stack**, we will configure everything from the frontend of our application's user interface to the backend API and database in an easy-to-follow, project-based fashion. Follow along from the beginning as we build our knowledge of technologies and techniques to scaffold a blogging application, or choose your area of interest and dive deep into the various layers that make up a MEAN stack web application.

You'll find opportunities to learn the latest JavaScript language enhancements, including working with ES2017 and TypeScript to make your application's code more expressive and modular. We'll also explore the latest versions of popular JavaScript frameworks, including the newly released Angular 4, for frontend application development. The recipes and examples in this book also provide detailed references and documentation explaining the various APIs and tools you'll use in your MEAN stack application.

For developers building a MEAN stack experience, this book will call out common pitfalls and fixes for issues you might encounter along the way. Expert developers will find advanced topics that are not often covered in-depth. No matter what your experience level is, you will find practical, realistic examples of building real MEAN stack web applications.

What this book covers

Chapter 1, *Working with Angular 4*, begins by exploring the frontend layer of our MEAN stack using Angular 4. We'll cover the basics of working with Angular and scaffold out a new application using Angular-CLI. The reader will learn to use Angular-CLI to create components and modules as well as serve the development build of an application to a web browser.

Chapter 2, *Enhancing Your User Interface*, covers using frontend frameworks such as Sass, Bootstrap, and Font-Awesome. This chapter explores how to add some style to our Angular web application. We'll also look at advanced topics such as component styles and working with Bootstrap components inside an Angular application.

Chapter 3, *Working with Data*, explains that our Angular application's relationship with data is key to leveraging it in our MEAN stack application. Here, we'll review the basic mechanisms behind data binding inputs and forms within Angular to models. This includes more advanced topics such as working with data services and validating it, using promises to create asynchronous services, retrieving and querying API data, and handling API errors and invalid responses.

Chapter 4, *Using Express Web Server*, turns our attention to the backend of our MEAN stack web application; we will explore setting up an Express web server using Node.js. This chapter covers the basics of serving assets and routing with Express as well as an exploration of securing an Express web server in production environments.

Chapter 5, *REST APIs and Authentication*, continues with building our Express web server; we'll build our own APIs for serving resources to our frontend Angular application. The reader will learn how to structure APIs using JSON API to send data and errors to our client. We'll also explore the intricacies of implementing authentication and authorization in our application.

Chapter 6, *Cloud Service Integrations*, covers the various types of cloud service integrations for our backend Express webserver, including handling images with Cloudinary and implementing a payment gateway using Stripe. We'll also implement a credit card payment user interface with Angular using Stripe.

Chapter 7, *MongoDB and Mongoose*, explains how to use MongoDB as our database for our Express application. This chapter will cover configuring MongoDB as well as using Mongoose to manage models between an Express web server and a database.

Chapter 8, *Relationships*, focuses on structuring relationships between our documents in MongoDB. We'll cover the most common types of document relationships, including validation, virutals, subdocuments, and document population with Mongoose.

Chapter 9, *Build Systems and Optimizations*, dives deep into using the WebPack build system for both Angular and Express. This chapter discusses advanced optimization strategies to increase the loading speed and performance of our web applications.

Chapter 10, *Debugging*, explores the myriad of options available for debugging a MEAN stack web application. We'll cover the built-in debugger tools of Node.js as well as configuring IDE debuggers such as JetBrain's WebStorm. The chapter will also cover how to set up production error logging for Angular using the error logging service Sentry.io.

`Chapter 11`, *Automated Testing*, concludes the book with a review of the range of testing options within our MEAN stack web application. We'll cover writing unit and integration tests for our Express web application using Mocha and Chai. The reader will also be introduced to how to configure ESLint as a Node.js project linter, and use BrowserSync for cross-browser testing.

What you need for this book

To implement the recipes described in this book, you will need a desktop or laptop computer with at least 2 GB of available memory, running a Mac OS, Windows, or a Linux operating system of your choice. You'll need to have installed Node.js version 6 or greater with NPM version 4 or greater:

`https://nodejs.org/en/download/`

You will also need a text editor to follow along with the examples and recipe source code in this book. Also required is a modern browser with an integrated web developer toolkit such as Google Chrome, Mozilla Firefox, or Internet Explorer 11.

Who this book is for

If you are a JavaScript developer who wants to create high-performing, modern web applications with the MEAN stack, this is the book for you. Web developers familiar with some parts of the MEAN stack will find this a comprehensive guide to fleshing out the other technologies and skills they need to build all JavaScript web applications. Developers interested in transitioning from other web application stacks to an all-JavaScript environment will find a wealth of information about how to work in a MEAN stack environment.

To get the most from this book, you should have a general understanding of web servers and web applications. You are expected to have a basic understanding of running JavaScript, both in a web browser and outside it, using Node.js and the NPM package manager.

Sections

In this book, you will find several headings that appear frequently (Getting ready, How to do it..., How it works..., and There's more...). To give clear instructions on how to complete a recipe, we use these sections as follows:

Getting ready

This section tells you what to expect in the recipe, and describes how to set up any software or any preliminary settings required for the recipe.

How to do it...

This section contains the steps required to follow the recipe.

How it works...

This section usually consists of a detailed explanation of what happened in the previous section.

There's more...

This section consists of additional information about the recipe in order to make the reader more knowledgeable about the recipe.

Conventions

In this book, you will find a number of text styles that distinguish between different kinds of information. Here are some examples of these styles and an explanation of their meaning. Code words in text, database table names, folder names, filenames, file extensions, pathnames, dummy URLs, user input, and Twitter handles are shown as follows: Start the web server by calling the `serve` command.

A block of code is set as follows:

```
{
    ...
    "project": {
     "name": "my-angular4-project"
    },
    ...
}
```

Any command-line input or output is written as follows:

```
ng get project.name
```

New terms and **important words** are shown in bold like this: However, **Component, Directive, Pipe, Service**, and **Guard** also scaffold out additional useful files.

Words that you see on the screen, for example, in menus or dialog boxes, appear in the text like this: We will see our post template rendering on the page with the **post works - 123** text.

 Warnings or important notes appear like this.

 Tips and tricks appear like this.

Reader feedback

Feedback from our readers is always welcome. Let us know what you think about this book-what you liked or disliked. Reader feedback is important for us as it helps us develop titles that you will really get the most out of. To send us general feedback, simply e-mail feedback@packtpub.com, and mention the book's title in the subject of your message. If there is a topic that you have expertise in and you are interested in either writing or contributing to a book, see our author guide at www.packtpub.com/authors .

Customer support

Now that you are the proud owner of a Packt book, we have a number of things to help you to get the most from your purchase.

Downloading the example code

You can download the example code files for this book from your account at `http://www.packtpub.com`. If you purchased this book elsewhere, you can visit `http://www.packtpub.com/support` and register to have the files e-mailed directly to you. You can download the code files by following these steps:

1. Log in or register to our website using your e-mail address and password.
2. Hover the mouse pointer on the **SUPPORT** tab at the top.
3. Click on **Code Downloads & Errata**.
4. Enter the name of the book in the **Search** box.
5. Select the book for which you're looking to download the code files.
6. Choose from the drop-down menu where you purchased this book from.
7. Click on **Code Download**.

You can also download the code files by clicking on the **Code Files** button on the book's webpage at the Packt Publishing website. This page can be accessed by entering the book's name in the **Search** box. Please note that you need to be logged in to your Packt account. Once the file is downloaded, please make sure that you unzip or extract the folder using the latest version of:

- WinRAR / 7-Zip for Windows
- Zipeg / iZip / UnRarX for Mac
- 7-Zip / PeaZip for Linux

The code bundle for the book is also hosted on GitHub at `https://github.com/PacktPublishing/Mean-Cookbook`. We also have other code bundles from our rich catalog of books and videos available at `https://github.com/PacktPublishing/`. Check them out!

Downloading the color images of this book

We also provide you with a PDF file that has color images of the screenshots/diagrams used in this book. The color images will help you better understand the changes in the output. You can download this file `https://www.packtpub.com/sites/default/files/downloads/MEANCookbook_ColorImages.pdf`.

Errata

Although we have taken every care to ensure the accuracy of our content, mistakes do happen. If you find a mistake in one of our books-maybe a mistake in the text or the code-we would be grateful if you could report this to us. By doing so, you can save other readers from frustration and help us improve subsequent versions of this book. If you find any errata, please report them by visiting http://www.packtpub.com/submit-errata, selecting your book, clicking on the **Errata Submission Form** link, and entering the details of your errata. Once your errata are verified, your submission will be accepted and the errata will be uploaded to our website or added to any list of existing errata under the Errata section of that title. To view the previously submitted errata, go to https://www.packtpub.com/books/content/support and enter the name of the book in the search field. The required information will appear under the **Errata** section.

Piracy

Piracy of copyrighted material on the Internet is an ongoing problem across all media. At Packt, we take the protection of our copyright and licenses very seriously. If you come across any illegal copies of our works in any form on the Internet, please provide us with the location address or website name immediately so that we can pursue a remedy. Please contact us at copyright@packtpub.com with a link to the suspected pirated material. We appreciate your help in protecting our authors and our ability to bring you valuable content.

Questions

If you have a problem with any aspect of this book, you can contact us at questions@packtpub.com, and we will do our best to address the problem.

1
Working with Angular 4

This chapter is an in-depth guide to configuring the front-end application of our MEAN stack web application using the Angular 4 JavaScript framework. We will explain how to upgrade from an existing Angular 2 application to Angular 4, as well cover how to generate components and routes using Angular-CLI.

In this chapter, we will cover the following recipes:

- Upgrading from Angular 2 to Angular 4 using NPM
- Generating a new Angular project using Angular-CLI
- Configuring Angular-CLI project settings
- Working with generators in Angular-CLI
- Ejecting Angular-CLI from your project
- Generating new routes in Angular-CLI
- Defining a home page in your Angular routes
- Handling 404 errors in an Angular project
- Creating nested routes in Angular
- Creating sibling routes in Angular
- Programmatic page redirection in Angular
- Route preloading with Angular modules
- Running tests in Angular-CLI

Introduction

The revolution in JavaScript over the past 10 years has brought web applications leaps and bounds ahead of the preceding generation. These gains are perhaps most clearly visible through the use of JavaScript web application frameworks, such as Angular.

Angular is already considered to be the most popular and widely deployed web application framework to date. As a robust and fully featured framework, Angular provides a comprehensive approach to web application development that can be very appealing for developers looking a convention oriented JavaScript development environment. Angular's reliability, modularity, and the ease with which it extends the web client experience are many of the reasons why developers choose Angular for the frontend layer of their web application stack.

The popularity of Angular is easy to find in large-scale developer community surveys, such as those provided by GitHub's most popular frontend JavaScript frameworks showcase and StackOverflow's 2017 developer survey results for top frameworks.

"Node.js and AngularJS continue to be the most commonly used technologies in this category."

2017 Stack Overflow Developer Survey - Top Frameworks

You can visit the following links to learn more about about Angular's popularity compared to other frameworks:

- `https://github.com/showcases/front-end-javascript-frameworks`
- `https://stackoverflow.com/insights/survey/2017/?utm_source=so-owned utm_medium=blogutm_campaign=dev-survey-2017utm_content=blog-link#technology-frameworks-libraries-and-other-technologies`

Upgrading to Angular 4 using NPM

For folks with existing Angular 2 applications, we will discuss the upgrade process to move from Angular 2 to Angular 4, which we will use for the rest of the recipes covered in this book. If you are starting from scratch with a new Angular 4 project, you may wish to skip this recipe and instead start with the *Generating a new Angular project using Angular-CLI* recipe. If you are interested in a comprehensive list of detailed changes that come with upgrading to Angular 4, please refer to the *What's New in Angular 4 Appendix* in the back of this book.

Getting ready

Unlike some frameworks, there is no explicit upgrade command in Angular-CLI to move from Angular 2 to 4. Instead, the actual upgrading is done via updating the underlying NPM dependencies in our web application's `package.json` file. We can do this upgrade manually, but the simplest method is to use the NPM CLI to tell it exactly what packages we want it to install and save them to our project's `package.json` file.

How to do it...

Let's take a look at the NPM commands for upgrading to Angular 4 in different environments:

1. On the Mac OSX and Linux environments, the following is the NPM command to upgrade to Angular 4:

   ```
   npm install @angular/{common,compiler,compiler-
   cli,core,forms,http,platform-browser,platform-browser-
   dynamic,platform-server,router,animations}@latest typescript@latest
   --save
   ```

2. On the Windows environment, the following is the NPM command to upgrade to Angular 4:

   ```
   npm install @angular/common@latest @angular/compiler@latest
   @angular/compiler-cli@latest @angular/core@latest
   @angular/forms@latest @angular/http@latest @angular/platform-
   browser@latest @angular/platform-browser-dynamic@latest
   @angular/platform-server@latest @angular/router@latest
   @angular/animations@latest typescript@latest --save
   ```

How it works...

The commands mentioned in the preceding section may seem very different, but in reality they both do exactly the same thing. Both install all the Angular 4's libraries to your `node_modules` directory and save the dependencies in your `package.json` file.

This installation command may take a few minutes to complete, but after it is done, your `package.json` file will be only file that's updated by this process:

An example of the package.json file showing difference before Angular 4 upgrade with NPM

The amazing thing about this upgrade process is that this is pretty much all there is to it. Upon restarting your Angular application, you should now have your legacy Angular 2 application running on Angular 4. If your application leveraged any of the deprecated or changed APIs mentioned in the *What's New in Angular 4 Appendix*, you may see a compiler error at this time. You will need to review the change list and find the deprecation that is the closest match to the exception you are encountering and resolve that before trying again.

There's more...

Working with dependencies in Angular can be tricky if you haven't had to manage a web application framework as robust as Angular before. Let's look at few of the most common types of dependency and package-related issues developers can get stuck on when upgrading their Angular applications.

Taking advantage of optional dependencies

One of the best parts about removing libraries, such as animations, from Angular 4's core dependencies is that we can now decide whether we want to or not. If our application doesn't need any animation capability, it is completely safe for us to not include it as a dependency in our `package.json` or as a part of our NPM install upgrade command. If we change our mind later, we can always install the animation library when the need arises. Depending on the functionality of your web application, you may also be able to do without the router, forms, or HTTP libraries.

Once your upgraded Angular 4 application successfully compiles, ensure that you take time to check that all your existing automated tests and the application functionality itself continue to function as expected. Assuming that your application is functioning properly, you will be enjoying an approximately 25% smaller generated file size as well as access to the new APIs and features.

Peer dependency warnings after upgrade

Angular 4 also depends on a number of other JavaScript libraries to function; some of those libraries are `peerDependencies` within Angular's own dependencies. That means that they must be fulfilled by your application in order for Angular to function. Some of these dependencies, such as `TypeScript`, were actually provided in the NPM `install` command; however, some of them, such as `Zone.js`, are not. These `peerDependencies` can vary even between minor version differences of Angular, so if you do see one of these warnings, your best bet is to manually update your `package.json` dependency for that library and try again:

```
my-angular-project@0.0.0 /Users/nmcclay/WebstormProjects/my-angular-project
├── @angular/animations@4.0.1
├─┬ @angular/cli@1.0.0-rc.4
│ └── typescript@2.1.6
├── @angular/common@4.0.1
├── @angular/compiler@4.0.1
├─┬ @angular/compiler-cli@4.0.1  invalid
│ └─┬ @angular/tsc-wrapped@4.0.1
│   └── tsickle@0.21.6
├── @angular/core@4.0.1
├── @angular/forms@4.0.1
├── @angular/http@4.0.1
├── @angular/platform-browser@4.0.1
├── @angular/platform-browser-dynamic@4.0.1
├─┬ @angular/platform-server@4.0.1
│ ├── parse5@3.0.2
│ └── xhr2@0.1.4
├── @angular/router@4.0.1
├── typescript@2.2.2  invalid
└── UNMET PEER DEPENDENCY zone.js@0.7.8

npm WARN @angular/core@4.0.1 requires a peer of zone.js@^0.8.4 but none was installed.
```

An example of an unmet peer dependency warning during Angular 4 upgrade

Now that our Angular application is upgraded to Angular 4, we will move on to using Angular 4 for the rest of this book's Angular content. From now on, when I use the term Angular, it is specifically in reference to Angular 4. This conforms with Google's own usage of the name, always using Angular generically to be the latest major SemVer version of the Angular framework.

Official Angular guidelines: Google has actually gone to great lengths to provide developers, bloggers, and the press with detailed examples of a proper usage of Angular terminology and the reasoning behind it. You can find more information about these guidelines on the official Angular blog, including a link to the official press kit: `http://angularjs.blogspot.com/2017/01/branding-guidelines-for-angular-and.html`
`https://angular.io/presskit.html`.

Generating a new Angular project using Angular-CLI

For developers starting with Angular 4 from scratch, this section will cover how to use the Angular-CLI utility to generate a new project. There are many ways to create a new Angular project, but a very popular convention for getting started is to use a dedicated CLI utility. Angular-CLI is an all-in-one new project initializer and everything that we will need to run our new application locally. It includes a standalone web server, live reload server, and test runner to use in local development. We will use Angular-CLI in many of the examples throughout this book when working with Angular. There are also many useful features in Angular-CLI besides creating new projects, which we will discuss later in this chapter.

Getting ready

To create a new Angular project, we will use the Angular-CLI command-line utility. To install this utility, you must first have Node.js version 8.4.0 or greater installed locally as well as NPM version 4 or greater. You can check your local Node.js and NPM versions with the following commands:

```
node --version
npm --version
```

Using a node version mangement tool:
Node.js version management can be an important aspect of maintaining consistent application builds, especially in a team environment. Angular-CLI doesn't come with a predefined Node.js version management system, so adding a configuration file to your project for a Node.js version management utility, such as *NVM*, *Nodenv*, or *Nodist*, to your project early can help you solve configuration headaches down the road.

How to do it...

Let's look at the following steps to create an Angular project:

1. To install Angular-CLI, simply run the following command:

   ```
   npm install -g @angular/cli
   ```

2. This may take several minutes to install Angular-CLI locally and make it ready and available to use in your project. Wait until the command prompt is ready, before proceeding to generate a new Angular project using Angular-CLI.

3. To create a new Angular application, simply type ng new, followed by the name of your new application--in this case, I am using my-angular-project:

   ```
   ng new my-angular-project
   ```

4. This will create a new project folder called my-angular-project and preinstall everything that we need to run our new Angular application locally.

How it works...

There are many options available when working with commands in Angular-CLI. For example, let's look at what other options are available for the new command:

```
ng new --help
```

This will show you all the available optional flags you can pass when initializing your project.

Whenever you are trying out a new command, passing the `--help` option can be a handy way to learn what options are available before running the command.

Now that we have our new Angular project set up, we can start the application locally using the built-in web server capability of Angular-CLI. Start the web server by calling the `serve` command:

```
ng serve
```

After running this command, you can actually see Angular compile all the default modules necessary to run your new application, including a message that tells you where to find your project in your local web browser:

```
** NG Live Development Server is running on http://localhost:4200 **
```

There's more...

NPM scripts are a great way to run common actions in your Angular application. In fact, Angular-CLI sets up your project with some predefined scripts tailored for it. By opening the `package.json` file in your project, you can find the scripts configuration, which should look very similar to this:

```
"scripts": {
    "ng": "ng",
    "start": "ng serve",
    "build": "ng build",
    "test": "ng test",
    "lint": "ng lint",
    "e2e": "ng e2e"
},
```

From here, you can see that `ng serve` is mapped to the `start` command in NPM. The `start` script is a special type of script command that is available by default in NPM, whereas other commands, such as `lint`, are nonstandard, and, therefore, must be called using the `run` command in NPM:

```
npm start
npm run lint
```

Editing these NPM script commands are a great way to automate passing flags to your application configuration. For example, to make Angular-CLI automatically open your default web browser with your application during the startup, you could try updating your start command, as follows:

```
"start": "ng serve --open",
```

Now, whenever you run `npm start`, your Angular application will automatically boot up with your custom options, and a web browser pointing to the correct host and port will open.

> Configuration errors can often cause problems when you start your application. A common configuration error is caused by a missing configuration file:
>
> ```
> Cannot read property 'config' of null
> TypeError: Cannot read property 'config' of null
> ```

> There are many hidden dot-files in a newly created Angular application. If you created a new project and moved its app contents and structure to a new location for reorganization, this error means that you have missed or accidentally deleted the hidden `.angular-cli.json` file. If you are encountering this error after your project creation, it probably means that the project wasn't created in exactly the directory you wanted. Instead of moving the project, an easy fix is to provide the `--directory` flag when you create a new project:
>
> ```
> ng new my-angular-project --directory my-angular-project
> ```

Now that our application is running, let's take a look at the project structure of the newly created Angular application. Your project structure should look very similar to the following example:

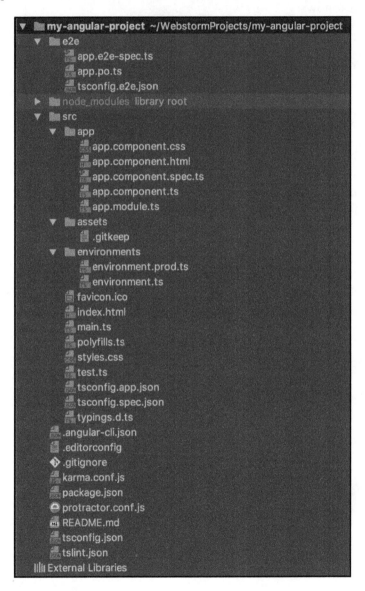

There are a lot of files in a new Angular application. Many are specific configuration files, which we won't touch on in this book. Most of the content we will work with in this book will be focused on the /src directory and the content within it. This directory is the default location for virtually all of our Angular project structures, which we will start stubbing out in the next section.

However, before we continue, you may wish to fulfill the age-old tradition of creating a *Hello World* app. Simply open the /src/app/app.component.ts file to change the title property to 'Hello World!':

```
export class AppComponent {
    title = 'Hello World!';
}
```

After saving, your application will automatically reload using live-reload to show your changes in your web browser. Live-reload is another feature that comes out of the box with Angular-CLI that makes development much easier to iterate and see changes rapidly in the frontend of your application.

Tips for resolving port collision

Port collision is a problem that can happen when the port you are attempting to run your app on is already in use:

```
Port 4200 is already in use. Use '--port' to specify a different port.
```

This often happens if you accidentally leave open a previous instance of your application while trying to start another. On Unix systems, you can find and kill orphaned processes using the ps and grep commands:

```
ps aux | grep angular
```

This will return a process list you can consult to find your rogue Angular-CLI process:

```
nmcclay    88221    0.0  1.8  3398784 296516    ??   S    7:56PM    0:12.59
@angular/cli
```

Now that you have found your process, you can stop it with the kill command:

```
Kill 88221
```

Another common cause of this error can be running multiple different web applications locally. In this case, the best option is to simply change the default port used in the NPM start command of your `package.json` file:

```
"start": "ng serve --port 4500",
```

Configuring Angular-CLI project settings

The `.angular-cli.json` file in the root of our project serves as a configuration file for our Angular-CLI application instance. We can customize these configurations manually by editing the file itself, but we can also read and write from it using the Angular-CLI commands `get` and `set`.

How to do it...

Let's follow the steps below to learn how to read and write from our Angular application's configuration file using Angular-CLI:

1. To get the name of an Angular-CLI application, we would use:

   ```
   ng get project.name
   ```

2. You can see how the `project.name` value maps to the content of our `.angular-cli.json` file:

   ```
   {
       ...
       "project": {
        "name": "my-angular4-project"
       },
       ...
   }
   ```

3. We can also write to this configuration file using the `set` command:

   ```
   ng set project.name=my-awesome-angular-project
   ```

 Note that any configuration changes here will not be picked up by live reload, and will require an entire restart of your Angular-CLI web server to be picked up by your application.

Working with generators in Angular-CLI

We can build many parts of our Angular application using the Angular-CLI utility. Components, views, routes, controllers, and services can all be generated in this manner. Scaffolding out new functionality using a CLI helps us to save time when building our application by automatically creating the required boilerplate content and putting it exactly where we want it in our project.

We will use Angular-CLI as the preferred method for scaffolding out a new Angular functionality through the rest of the book.

How to do it...

Let's follow the steps below to create a new button component in our Angular application using Angular-CLI generate:

1. Angular-CLI's scaffolding command is ng generate, or the alias ng g. The generate command's function is to create stubs of ready-to-customize content for our application from blueprints within Angular-CLI.

   ```
   ng g component my-button
   ```

2. After running generate, the command line will show an output of what content has been added to our project:

   ```
   installing component
   create src/app/my-button/my-button.component.css
   create src/app/my-button/my-button.component.html
   create src/app/my-button/my-button.component.spec.ts
   create src/app/my-button/my-button.component.ts
   update src/app/app.module.ts
   ```

How it works...

If we look at our project, we can see that Angular-CLI has automatically scaffolded out a `my-button` directory that contains stubs for all of the files that make up our button component. This includes its class boilerplate, `my-button.component.ts`, its template, `my-button.component.html`, its style sheet, `my-button.component.ts`, and its test file, `my-button.component.spec.ts`:

```
▼ 📁 my-angular4-project  ~/WebstormProjects/my-angular4-project
    ▶ 📁 e2e
    ▶ 📁 node_modules  library root
    ▼ 📁 src
        ▼ 📁 app
            ▼ 📁 my-button
                📄 my-button.component.css
                📄 my-button.component.html
                📄 my-button.component.spec.ts
                📄 my-button.component.ts
            📄 app.component.css
            📄 app.component.html
            📄 app.component.spec.ts
            📄 app.component.ts
            📄 app.module.ts
```

These stub files are very generic, but they cover virtually all the boilerplate code involved in creating a new component in Angular. Another detail handled for us is the actual importing of the component into our application through `app.module.ts`:

```
...
import { MyButtonComponent } from './my-button/my-button.component';

@NgModule({
...
  declarations: [
    AppComponent,
    MyButtonComponent
  ],
...
})
export class AppModule { }
```

The module declarations section here has automatically been updated for us by the generate command, so all that we need to do is invoke the component within a template of our application:

```
<app-my-button></app-my-button>
```

If we look back at our application, we will see the words **my-button works** printed out from wherever in our app we have invoked the component.

> **Generating content into specific locations**: Angular-CLI's generate command can accept a file path along with a name in order to control where your content will be generated. For instance, if I had an admin module in my Angular application where I organized all the functionalities that are unique to my administrator user experience, I might want to nest an admin unique component there with `ng g component admin/dashboard`. This will create all my component files in a directory under `src/app/admin/dashboard` instead of in my root module space.

We can create many types of content using the generate command. The syntax for scaffolding out a new piece of content is always the same, as follows:

```
ng generate <blueprint> <name>
```

You can find a complete list of all the available blueprints and examples of their usage in the following table:

Blueprint	Angular-CLI
Component	`ng generate component my-new-component`
Directive	`ng generate directive my-new-directive`
Pipe	`ng generate pipe my-new-pipe`
Service	`ng generate service my-new-service`
Class	`ng generate class my-new-class`
Guard	`ng generate guard my-new-guard`
Interface	`ng generate interface my-new-interface`
Enum	`ng generate enum my-new-enum`
Module	`ng generate module my-module`

Many of these generated blueprint types create simple boilerplate files in the root of our app module directory. However, **Component, Directive, Pipe, Service**, and **Guard** also scaffold out additional useful files.

Angular-CLI add-ons: The future of Angular-CLI and its convention-oriented approach to Angular development is evolving very rapidly. One feature on the future roadmap for Angular-CLI that will greatly shape the usage of it by the community is **add-ons**. Add-ons will allow developers to plug in functionality to Angular-CLI through shared modules to enhance their Angular applications. For example, custom blueprints for Angular-CLI could be created through an add-on, and allow developers to scaffold out custom content using the generate command.

There's more...

There are many types of content you can scaffold out with Angular-CLI's generators. Let's take a look at how we can generate new services in our Angular application using Angular-CLI's generate command.

Generating new services with Angular-CLI is very similar to generating components, but with the following few key differences:

```
ng g service my-store
installing service
create src/app/my-store.service.spec.ts
create src/app/my-store.service.ts
WARNING Service is generated but not provided, it must be provided to be
used
```

Scaffolding a new service generates fewer files than a component and also nests the service at the root of our application directory by default instead of nesting it in its own namespace. The warning that is presented after creating our service stub files notifies us that, unlike components, services have to be manually provided to our application. Unlike components that are naturally isolated from each other, services can have explicit dependencies and load order requirements that Angular-CLI is unable to predict. In general, adding these services to your application is easily done by importing and adding the service to the provider list:

```
...
import { MyStoreService } from './my-store.service';

@NgModule({
  ...
  providers: [
    MyStoreService
  ]
  ...
})
export class AppModule { }
```

With the service provided to your application, it is now available for use.

Generating guards: Guards generated with Angular-CLI also show the warning that they are not provided by default. Adding a generated guard to your application is identical to adding a service.

Ejecting Angular-CLI from your project

While the convention-oriented approach of Angular-CLI can be a positive thing for many developers, sometimes, you may find the need to manually take back control of your build process and project configuration. Luckily, there is an easy way to convert an Angular-CLI project to a generic project using the `eject` command.

Getting ready

Let's take back control of our Angular application's build process from Angular-CLI. We may need this to do a variety of tasks, including customizing WebPack builds or just getting more granular control of our local web server runs. Ironically, we will use Angular-CLI to remove our application from Angular-CLI's control.

How to do it...

Perform the following steps to remove Angular-CLI from your project:

1. First, you must remove your `start` script from your `package.json` file, as it will be overwritten in this process.
2. Then, run the `ng eject` command:

```
======================================================================
=======
Ejection was successful.

To run your builds, you now need to do the following commands:
 - "npm run build" to build.
 - "npm run test" to run unit tests.
 - "npm start" to serve the app using webpack-dev-server.
 - "npm run e2e" to run protractor.

Running the equivalent CLI commands will result in an error.
```

```
=====================================================================
=======
Some packages were added. Please run "npm install".
```

How it works...

Your project has been fully converted over to a standard Angular project, with a fully defined build toolchain ready in a new `webpack.config.js` file. Note that this conversion is a one-way process, and should only be done if you are ready to take full control of your application's build process.

The build process that remains is actually a standard WebPack based build. We will discuss WebPack builds and how to customize them for your application more in `Chapter 9`, *Build Systems and Optimizations*.

Generating new routes in Angular-CLI

Now we are ready to start really digging into the details of routing in Angular; how to create new routes and how to redirect to routes in your application, including error handling. We'll also cover how to nest routes and use route preloading to speed up your application navigation.

 Creating new routes: Routing in Angular is handled by the optional Angular router package and must be imported into your application to be used.

Getting ready

To mount the router to the root of our application, we must first import the `RouterModule` from the router and call the `forRoot` method to tell the router that we are setting up routes on the root of our web application:

```
import { NgModule } from '@angular/core';
import { FormsModule } from '@angular/forms';
import { HttpModule } from '@angular/http';
import { RouterModule } from '@angular/router';
import { AppComponent } from './app.component'

@NgModule({
```

```
    ...
    imports: [
    BrowserModule,
    FormsModule,
    HttpModule,
    RouterModule.forRoot([])
    ],
    ...
})
export class AppModule { }
```

With the router set up on the root of our web application, we are now able to provide a mapping between the **Universal Resource Indentifier** (**URI**) of the route that we want to show in the browser and the component we want to be rendered on that route. For the sake of simplicity, we will imagine we are building a simple blog website and will stub out two components: posts and authors. `Posts` will show all the available blog posts on our blog, whereas `authors` will show a list of all authors of blog posts on our blog:

```
ng g component posts
ng g component authors
```

This will scaffold out the two components as well as add them to our app module so that we can start routing to them.

How to do it...

After scaffolding the two components and adding them to our app module, let's follow these steps to add our routes:

1. First, we will need to create the route map between these components and the two routes we want to create: `/posts` and `/authors`. We will do this by passing an array of route configuration objects into the `forRoot` method of our `RouterModule`. This configuration tells the router that the `/posts` route will resolve with the `PostsComponent`, and the `/authors` route will resolve with the `AuthorsComponent`:

   ```
   @NgModule({
     ...
     imports: [
       ...
       RouterModule.forRoot([
         {
           path: "posts",
           component: PostsComponent
   ```

```
        },
        {
          path: "authors",
          component: AuthorsComponent
        }
      ])
    ],
    ...
})
export class AppModule { }
```

2. With our routes and components now properly associated, we just need to provide an outlet, where this content can be presented, and links to make navigating to it more easily. We can add both of these to our `app.component.html` template, as follows:

```
<nav>
  <a routerLink="/posts">Posts</a>
  <a routerLink="/authors">Authors</a>
</nav>
<router-outlet></router-outlet>
```

How its works...

Instead of a traditional `href` attribute, we tell the router to navigate to a route we've configured by attaching the `routerLink` directive to it. This directive takes a path string that matches a path configured with our router. Next, we provide the outlet where our content will be presented through when a route is active with the `router-outlet` directive. With these two elements in place, we can see two folders called `Posts` and `Authors` in our `app` folder; clicking on either link will add the **posts works!** text for `/posts` and **authors works!** for `/authors`.

By updating the template within our components, we can change the content that shows up when the user navigates to the associated route. We can also change the template in `app.component.html` to alter the shared master template that is used by both routes. We will explore this topic more in the next chapter when we upgrade our application's styling.

Defining a home page in your Angular routes

Often, we will want our web application to have a specific home page for our application. We will simply define a home page route in our Angular route configuration.

How to do it...

We can define a home page with our `RouterModule` configuration that will be served when the user loads the top level of our application, as follows:

1. First, we will generate a new component for controlling our home page. We will create this component using the Angular-CLI `generate` command:

```
ng generate component home
```

2. Next, we'll simply add our `HomeComponent` to our `/src/app/app.module.ts` route configuration:

```
...
import { HomeComponent } from './home/home.component';

@NgModule({
  declarations: [
    AppComponent,
    AuthorsComponent,
    PageNotFoundComponent,
    AuthorComponent,
    HomeComponent
  ],
  imports: [
    BrowserModule,
    BrowserAnimationsModule,
    FormsModule,
    HttpModule,
    RouterModule.forRoot({
      path: "",
      component: HomeComponent
    },{
      path: "posts",
      component: PostsComponent
    },{
      path: "authors",
      component: AuthorsComponent
    }),
    PostsModule
```

```
    ],
    providers: [],
    bootstrap: [AppComponent]
})
export class AppModule { }
```

3. Now when we visit `http://localhost:4200` in your local browser, you will see the text *home works!* displayed.

How it works...

By setting the path to an empty string, we will define it as the index route for our router. We can then provide it any component we want to present to the user, but what if we wanted to use a route you have already defined in your application as your home page? For example, in our blog application, we will want to serve the posts component as the home page of our application. This configuration is possible through the use of the `redirectTo` property in the route configuration:

```
RouterModule.forRoot([
    {
        path: "",
        component: PostsComponent
    },
    {
        path: "posts",
        redirectTo: ""
    }
    ...
])
```

With the preceding configuration, the `PostsComponent` will be served for all visitors on the home page of our application, and anyone who navigates to `/posts` will be redirected to our home page. We can also create a link to our home page in the same manner as linking to any other route of our application:

```
<a routerLink="">Home</a>
```

There's more...

When working with multiple modules in your Angular application, you may want to route to a specific module from the home page of your application. To accomplish this, you just need to provide a `redirectTo` route as a string that is registered with your module's route configuration, and the flag `pathMatch: 'full'`:

```
{
  path: "",
  redirectTo: "/posts",
  pathMatch: 'full'
},
```

This flag tells Angular how much of the path has to match before triggering the redirect. In this case, we want it when the path is completely empty to redirect to the `/posts` route.

Handling 404 errors in an Angular project

A common problem with web applications is a user landing on an invalid URI; this error, known as the venerable *404 - page not found error*, is a common fallback error case when the application is unable to redirect or resolve a route in an application. Let's configure our Angular application to handle these error cases.

How to do it...

In Angular, we can use our `RouterModule` configuration to catch any route that doesn't match our configuration by defining a wildcard route in our configuration, as follows:

```
RouterModule.forRoot([
  ...
    {
      path: "**",
      component: PageNotFoundComponent
    }
])
```

How it works...

By setting the path as $**$, we will catch any route that is not first served by the routes defined above this wildcard route configuration. We then direct the user to a new component we generated with `ng g component page-not-found` to serve the user a 404 message informing them that the page they have attempted to reach is not available.

Creating nesting routes in Angular

Having nested children routes in an application is a very common way to present detailed information within a category. Routes inside Angular can be configured to have nested parent-child relationships in your route configuration.

Getting ready

In our case, we may want to have a specific blog post route that is accessible by a unique ID under our `/posts` route. We will also need to provide a way to pass an ID parameter along to our component so that it can look up the details we would want to present to the user for that specific blog post.

How to do it...

To add a child route to our router module, we will need to update its route configuration:

1. First, we must define children routes using the `children` property in the route configuration:

```
RouterModule.forRoot([
    ...
    {
      path: "posts",
      component: PostsComponent,
      children: [{
        path: ":id",
        component: PostComponent
      }]
    }
    ...
])
```

2. Once we have set up our child route, we can retrieve our ID parameter in our new `PostComponent.ts` using the `ActivatedRoute` class from the Angular router:

```
import { Component, OnInit } from '@angular/core';
import {ActivatedRoute} from "@angular/router";

@Component({
  selector: 'app-post',
  templateUrl: './post.component.html',
  styleUrls: ['./post.component.css']
})
export class PostComponent implements OnInit {
  postId = null;
  constructor(private route:ActivatedRoute) {
    route.params.subscribe(
      params =>{
        this.postId = parseInt(params['id']);
      }
    );
  }
}
```

3. Now that we have the ID parameter, we can use it in our template:

```
<p>
  post works! - {{postId}}
</p>
```

4. Finally, we will also need to provide another outlet within the template of `PostsComponent` to surface our specific post template:

```
<p>
  posts works!
</p>

<router-outlet></router-outlet>
```

How it works...

The `children` property of our `/posts` route configuration is itself a new router configuration that we can nest under a specific route in our root router configuration. By setting the path to `:id`, we are declaring that whatever value is passed as the next segment of the URI beyond `/posts` will be made available as a parameter in our controller known as `params['id']`.

We receive the route parameters from the router as an observable that must be resolved before we can retrieve the ID. This sort of asynchronous data handling will be something that we will explore more in Chapter 3, *Working with Data*, but for now suffice to say that this is just a means of resolving this property so that we have it available to our component. Since the ID parameter could, in theory, be any type of data, here we parse it into a number. We will need to add a case to handle when this result is invalid, but we will return to that problem in a future section.

Creating sibling routes in Angular

When we nest a route as a child route, we declare to Angular that it must be surfaced through a `router-outlet` inside our parent component. Depending on the context of our application, that might be what we want, but what if we wanted to render the component at the root level of our application? This is a case where a sibling route with a nested path would be more appropriate.

How to do it...

Let's take a look at the following code to create module with sibling routes:

1. First, we will generate a new module for controlling our sibling routes. This will be useful in future chapters of this book for isolating the routing control for our blog posts:

```
ng generate module posts
```

2. Instead of defining our related route as a child of `"posts"`, we will define it at the same level. To distinguish the route for Angular we will provide the `:id` dynamic segment:

```
...
@NgModule({
  imports: [
    ...
    RouterModule.forRoot([{
      path: "posts",
      component: PostsComponent
    }, {
      path: "posts/:id",
      component: PostComponent
    }])
    ...
})
export class PostsModule { }
```

3. Now when Angular resolves the route, if it doesn't have any dynamic segments it will be served by `PostsComponent`, otherwise it will end up being served by `PostComponent`.

How it works...

Here, we can see that both `PostsComponent` and `PostComponent` are at the root of our router configuration. However, the path for `PostComponent` is nested one level deeper to `/posts/:id`, so it will display as a nested URI in the browser. This approach will only allow `PostComponent` to be served in our root `router-outlet`, instead as a child of `PostsComponent`.

With that, we can now navigate to `/posts/123`, and we will see our post template rendering on the page with the **post works - 123** text. By changing the URL to `/posts/456`, we will see that our `id` parameter updates to show us the text **post works - 456**. However, if we put in `/posts/foobar`, we will see our page render with the text **post works - NaN** due to a type conversion failure. In the next section, we will validate and properly handle this case.

There's more...

Another valid way to approach child routing is through the use of modules and the `forChild` method of the `RouterModule`. This approach lets any given module manage its own child routing tree under the root module's router:

```
...
RouterModule.forChild([
  {
    path: 'posts',
    component: PostsComponent,
    children: [{
      path: ':id',
      component: PostComponent
    }]
  }
])
...
```

A good reason to choose modular routing over simply nesting child routes in your root module is to keep your routing configuration clean and decoupled from the deep nesting of routes. Modular routes are easier to refactor and manage as your application grows, whereas simple nested children route configurations are a bit easier and faster to implement.

Programmatic page redirection in Angular

In our preceding example, we passed a dynamic parameter from a route to a component. However, because this parameter can be anything that is provided as the URI segment after `/posts`, we will need to handle the error case for what happens when this value is invalid. The easiest thing to do here is to check whether the value is indeed a valid number, and if it is not, redirect the user to the 404 page we created.

How to do it...

Let's add a 404 page to our application for when a user attempts to access an invalid route:

1. We can redirect a user to our 404 page using the Angular router's `navigateByUrl` method:

```
...
export class PostComponent implements OnInit {
```

```
    postId = null;
    constructor(private route:ActivatedRoute, private router:Router)
{
    route.params.subscribe(
      params =>{
        this.postId = parseInt(params['id']);

        if (isNaN(this.postId)) {
          this.router.navigateByUrl("/404")
        }
      }
    );
  }
}
```

2. To prevent the browser's URL from showing the /404 route name, we will provide the skipLocationChange flag:

```
...
if (isNaN(this.postId)) {
    this.router.navigateByUrl("/404", { skipLocationChange: true })
}
...
```

3. Now when we land on an invalid route, we will see the 404 page content without updating the browser's URL.

How it works...

Since /404 isn't a defined route in our application, it gets picked up by our wildcard path route configuration. Additionally, it exhibits an unintended behavior; the URL in the browser points at /404. Even worse, if the user navigates back to their browser from this page, they will re-trigger the logic that redirected them and will not be able to easily return to their preceding page. Yikes!

We generally don't want 404 errors to appear to have redirected the user at all, so we need to tell the router to not update our router location for this transition. We can do that by passing along the skipLocationChange option in our navigateByUrl redirect.

Route preloading with Angular modules

Angular's route loading is considerably optimized through its AoT template generation. However, you can actually tune and refine Angular's router preloading options through some configuration options in your router. These options are most interesting when you are optimizing your web application for mobile contexts where your application's load performance has a very high impact on your application's user experience.

Getting ready

Let's make our posts module a lazy loading module so that our application will start more quickly. We'll pair that module loading behavior with Angular's module preloading capability so that our app will still launch quickly, but will also load the posts module in the background after the application has started up without waiting for the user to navigate to /posts.

How to do it...

1. To take advantage of route preloading, we first have to turn it on in our root router configuration. By default, the Angular router comes with one of two preloading strategies; preload everything with PreloadAllModules, or preload nothing with NoPreloading:

```
...
import {RouterModule, PreloadAllModules} from '@angular/router';

@NgModule({
  ...
  imports: [
    BrowserModule,
    FormsModule,
    HttpModule,
    RouterModule.forRoot(ROUTES, { preloadingStrategy:
PreloadAllModules })
  ],
  ...
})
export class AppModule { }
```

2. Now that we have enabled preloading on our root router configuration, we have to enable lazy loading modules. For our router configuration, we must provide our lazy loaded child module in a string format using the `loadChildren` property. We also must provide the name of the module class itself to be invoked by the preloading strategy:

```
. . .
const ROUTES = [{
    path: "posts"
    loadChildren: "posts/posts.module#postModule"
}];
. . .
```

3. With this configuration in place, the application will automatically start preloading this posts, lazy loading module after it initially bootstraps the Angular application.

How it works...

The point of lazy loading is that it delays the startup cost associated with loading a module until the application makes a specific call to load it. This lowers the overall start up cost of the application, but the potential downside is that the module will be a bit slower to get started when the user attempts to access it. By pairing this with a preloading strategy, we are actually having our cake and eating it too by asking Angular to preload the lazy loading module after startup, but before the user would potentially fetch the module.

Running tests in Angular-CLI

The component, directive, pipe, service, and guard generators in Angular-CLI also create a unique test file stub as well as their class' boilerplate files. These test files are very basic, but they are all differently pre-configured to test their unique type of content.

How to do it...

Let's see what sort of test results we get from these generated boilerplate tests by running them with the `test` command in Angular-CLI:

```
ng test
```

How it works...

When you run the `test` command, Angular will run through each of these generated test files and check whether they exist and initialize properly. These simple tests don't know enough about the functionality of your application to do much else, but they are helpful as a place to start writing your own tests. They also provide a small amount of coverage that all the individual parts of your application can properly initialize on its own. You should look at these automatically generated test stubs as a ready-made space for you to add your own tests for your application.

2
Enhancing Your User Interface

This chapter will provide recipes for common user interface enhancements in your single app web application using Angular. We will learn to use Sass to control the styling of our application as well as importing common user interface tools such as the Bootstrap & Font-Awesome to our application. We'll also cover the basics of internalizing our user interface in Angular-CLI with it's built-in i18n toolkit.

In this chapter, we will cover the following recipes :

- Configuring Sass for Angular
- Working with Angular component styles
- Using Sass variables for style reusability
- Using Sass nesting for better style specificity
- Importing Sass partials for style organization
- Working with Bootstrap in Sass
- Customizing Bootstrap for Angular
- Using Bootstrap Responsive layouts
- Working with Bootstrap components in Angular
- Working with Font-Awesome icons in Angular
- Internationalization with Angular i18n
- Setting your language with Angular i18n
- How to Localize dates in Angular

Introduction

Building a modern web application with Angular involves adding some sort of CSS framework to your application. CSS provides a robust and rich set of styling options to manage the look and feel of your web application. However, in many respects, vanilla CSS provides us with only the very basics to build modern, maintainable styles for our web applications. Luckily, similar to the advancements made in JavaScript compilation, there has been a revolution in CSS-based pre-compilers that add many useful enhancements and features to the CSS standard.

In this chapter we will cover common CSS configurations for Angular, including how to use the most popular CSS preprocessor, Sass. We will also take a look at a variety of ways we can use Sass that is unique to working within Angular-CLI that can streamline our frontend development productivity.

Configuring Sass in Angular

Angular-CLI supports all the major CSS preprocessors, including **Sass**, **Less**, and **Stylus**. Although each of these options has its own unique features and language syntax, Sass is, by far, the most popular CSS preprocessor used for web applications. For that reason it is what we will focus on in this book.

Sass works as as superset to CSS in a similar way that TypeScript acts as a superset of JavaScript in Angular. Our Sass styles will compile during our Angular-CLI build process, and output vanilla CSS for the browser. It will also allow us to use many useful features, such as defining variables, nesting for selectors for improved specificity, and better organizing our styles for reusable and composable styling.

Getting ready

There are two main flavors of Sass file extensions used in web applications today: `.sass` and `.scss`. While these formats have a different language syntax, they both have identical features and capabilities, so the choice largely comes down to the developer's personal preferences.

.sass files are a whitespace-sensitive version of Sass that omits the usual parenthetical nesting common to CSS. It is favored largely by developers familiar with whitespace-sensitive languages and tends to have a very clean, highly readable appearance:

```
@import reset
$font-stack:    Helvetica, sans-serif
$primary-color: #333

=text-style($color: $primary-color)
  font-family: $font-stack
  color: $color

.btn-blue
  +text-color(#0000B2)

section
  margin: 0
  padding: 0

  a
    +text-style
```

.scss files are simply Sass-extended CSS files that look functionally identical to CSS, except for the special Sass feature keywords and conventions that are layered on top of the language. It is the most common choice by developers because it allows CSS to be included directly, without any sort of conversion to make the whitespace uniform or remove the parentheses:

```
@import "reset";
$font-stack:    Helvetica, sans-serif;
$primary-color: #333;

@mixin text-style($color: $primary-color) {
  font-family: $font-stack;
  color: $color;
}

.btn-blue {
  @include text-style(#0000B2);
}

section {
  margin: 0;
  padding: 0;

  a {
    @include text-style;
```

```
      }
    }
```

By default, Angular-CLI has an internal dependency for sass-loader; a WebPack Sass loader that leverages the popular Sass compiler, **Node-sass**. Node-sass is a cross-platform implementation of Sass, which works in Windows, Mac OS, and Linux environments without requiring any other extra language frameworks, such as Ruby.

Angular-CLI supports both `.scss` and `.sass` formats. One of the main reasons to use the `.scss` Sass format is that many more developers are already familiar with working with vanilla CSS than with Sass. We can simply include any legacy or third-party CSS into a `.scss` file and it will continue working as vanilla CSS. For this reason, in all our examples moving forward in this book, we will focus on using the `.scss` Sass file extension.

How to do it...

Let's add Sass styles to our Angular project. We will configure our application to use Sass and automatically compile it to CSS and reload our application using live-reload:

1. With `sass-loader` already available and ready to be used in our Angular-CLI project, we just need to configure Angular to look for `.scss` files in our project's build, instead of normal CSS files. We can do this using Angular-CLI's `set` command:

   ```
   ng set defaults.styleExt scss
   ```

2. Next, we must update our Angular-CLI configuration to define that we want to use this new Sass file extension for our build, instead of our previous CSS file extension. To update your configuration to use Sass for your global styles file, you must edit your styles configuration in your `.angular-cli.json` file:

   ```
   {
     ...
     "apps": [
       {
         ...
         "styles": [
           "styles.scss"
         ],
         ...
   ```

3. By changing this value to `styles.scss`, sass-loader will automatically identify it as Sass to be precompiled and delivered as CSS in our application. We will also have to make a similar adjustment to any CSS style file definitions within our components. For example, our `app.component.ts` file has a CSS file reference that must be updated:

```
import { Component } from '@angular/core';

@Component({
  selector: 'app-root',
  templateUrl: './app.component.html',
  styleUrls: ['./app.component.scss']
})
export class AppComponent {
  title = 'Hello World!';
}
```

4. Here, we will update our `styleUrls` to `./app.component.scss` so that our Sass file will be loaded when we load this component. This pattern of only loading our styles when a component is invoked is known as **component styles**, and it offers some unique advantages in Angular over other web application frameworks that we will explore later in this chapter.

5. With our configurations updated, we will need to rename our style files to `.scss` extensions so that they can be found by the Angular-CLI build:

```
mv ./src/styles.css ./src/styles.scss
mv ./src/app/app.component.css ./src/app/app.component.scss
```

6. After changing any configuration in Angular-CLI, we must manually restart the built in web-server for configuration changes to be used in our application.

How it works...

With this change, we have told Angular-CLI to build `.scss` files instead of `.css` in our project. It will also automatically scaffold out new blueprints that have styles with `.scss` extensions instead. Changing this configuration initially does not alter anything in our existing Angular build, and any CSS style files we created before this configuration change will not be affected. We have to manually rename files and update style references in our Angular resources to use the `.scss` extension. In a freshly generated Angular-CLI application, we should only have two of these files: `/src/styles.css` and `/src/app/app.component.css`. In an existing application, you may have many more style files that would need to be renamed.

Renaming CSS files to Sass extensions without also updating your style configurations in your Angular project will result in a build error:

```
ERROR in multi ./src/styles.css
Module not found: Error: Can't resolve '/Users/nmcclay/my-projects/my-
angular4-project/src/styles.css' in '/Users/nmcclay/my-projects/my-
angular4-project'
@ multi ./src/styles.css
```

To fix this error, you must update the file path reference in your Angular project file to point to `.scss` file extensions instead of `.css`.

There's more...

In Angular-CLI's `new` command, there is an option to provide a style file extension type when you create a new project using the following command:

```
ng new my-angular-sass-project --style scss
```

When you choose this option, Angular-CLI will create a new Angular project, with ready-made Sass files at `/src/styles.scss` and `/src/app/app.component.scss`. It will also automatically set the default style file extension to `scss` in our `.angular-cli.json` file, requiring no further configuration.

Working with Angular component styles

Angular has a unique way of isolating styles on components in our application by scoping CSS selectors to dynamically generated component selectors. This approach gives us component-level style isolation that will prevent our component's styles from leaking across the rest of our application.

Let's add some component styles to our `/src/app/app.component.ts` and `/src/app/posts/posts.component.ts` components. We'll give our header some padding between it and the blog content below it. Adding negative space to our user interface like this will make our blog content easier to read. We will frame the blog content itself with a border and a silver background color.

How to do it...

Let's follow the steps to create a simple component style for our `PostsComponent`:

1. First, we will add a `<div>` element around our `router-outlet`, our `/src/app/app.component.html` template:

   ```
   <div>
     <router-outlet></router-outlet>
   </div>
   ```

2. This will wrap our `router-outlet` so that all subcomponents will be presented within this element. Next, we will add a simple style to `/src/app/app.component.scss` that will add a bit of padding to the top of our element:

   ```
   div {
       padding-top: 20px;
   }
   ```

3. In our `/src/app/posts/posts.component.scss`, we will style the `div` elements within it in a totally different way. We will add a silver background color with a gray border to all the `div` elements in our posts component template:

   ```
   div {
       background-color: silver;
       border: 1px solid gray;
   }
   ```

We have used the same selectors; however, since they are component styles, they do not cascade into each other and are effectively isolated from each other.

How it works...

Component styles work by isolating the generated selectors from their associated style files to a dynamic component ID that is appended to all its style selectors. For example, our app component's generated `div` selector will have an extra attribute, similar to `[_ngcontent-c0]`, added to it:

```
div[_ngcontent-c0] {
    padding-top: 20px;
}
```

These attribute component IDs are unique to each component in our application and prevent similar style selectors from cascading into each other:

```
div[_ngcontent-c1] {
    background-color: silver;
    border: 1px solid gray;
}
```

This is a powerful feature for preventing our styles from causing unintended cascading in our user interface. However, sometimes, we do want cascading styles in our application for easy style reuse. In that case, the styles should be elevated to our `/src/styles.scss` file, instead of the one that is shared globally with all components.

Using Sass variables for style reusability

A very handy advantage of using Sass is to define commonly used values in our styles as variables so that they can be easily reused in our project's styling.

Imagine that our Angular application has a very simple two-color theme for its background and text. For our navigation, we simply want to reverse the same two colors of theme for the background and text. With Sass, we can define these colors once and then apply them to the correct properties for the objects we want to style, without copying and pasting hexadecimal color definitions around.

How to do it...

We can define two-color variables by defining them in our `/src/styles.scss` stylesheet:

```
$background-color: #585858;
$text-color: #1E1E1E;

html, body {
  background-color: $background-color;
  color: $text-color;
}

nav {
  background-color: $text-color;
  color: $background-color;
}
```

A huge advantage with Sass variables over vanilla CSS is that we can always change the value of a variable we define later on to a different value, and it will update any property associated with it accordingly. If we suddenly decide that a different background color or text color is an improvement, we can make those changes in one place, and our styles will all be updated to work as expected.

How it works...

Sass is a CSS preprocessor that reads special keywords prefixed with the $ character as variables. Sass can apply the values of those variables to anywhere in a complied Sass file. The result is a vanilla CSS file, where the properties that referenced a variable are populated with the value of that variable.

There's more...

Sass also has a concept of placeholders, which can be used to dynamically assign selectors based on variable values. We can combine placeholders, and another Sass feature known as **loops,** together to save us from a lot of repetition in CSS. For example, we may want to define six different sizes of header elements, ranging from h1 through h6. We could manually define each of these values in our style sheet, but we could also use loops and placeholder variables to do the same thing with less boilerplate, as follows:

```
$title-font-size: 48px;

@for $i from 1 through 6 {
  h#{$i} {
    font-size: $title-font-size - ($i * 5);
  }
}
```

Here, we define our header selector with the h#{$i} placeholder. This may appear very strange at first, but it's simply a normal header element selector (h) appended to the placeholder helper (#{}). Similar to a templated property in Angular, any property that we provide to the placeholder will be resolved to its value. So, in this case, the local variable--$i--in our loop will always be a number in the sequence from *1* to *6*, so our selector will be resolved as h1 through h6.

The font-size part of this header styling relies on the ability to execute basic mathematical operations inside our Sass files. In this case, we are starting from a default title font-size of 48 px, and then reducing this number by a 5 px for every loop of our header loop (including the first one). This sort of dynamically generated styling is a big part of what makes Sass a very powerful toolkit for modern web application design.

Using Sass nesting for better style specificity

Another advantage of Sass is the ability to nest selectors to increase their styling specificity, as well as make relationships between content styles more manageable. Sass's ability to nest selectors helps enforce selector specificity through a clear visual relationship with its parent selectors. This makes creating style hierarchies in your application much more visually apparent in the stylesheet itself.

Getting ready

Imagine that we have two styles of links, one that is for our general content and another that is, specifically, for our navigation. We really want to be certain that these links are styled the same way, except for their coloring. We could write these as two different selectors, but that could duplicate a lot of styling CSS that would be easier to share as a common style:

```
a {
   font-size: 14px;
   text-decoration: underline;
   color: #666;
}

nav a {
   font-size: 14px;
   text-decoration: underline;
   color: #585858;
}
```

Alternatively, we could rely, instead, on CSS's cascading effect. This reduces duplication, but might be prone to specificity mistakes if we aren't mindful of all the other selectors in our application:

```
a {
    font-size: 14px;
    text-decoration: underline;
    color: #666;
}

nav a {
    color: #585858;
}
```

It can also be very easy to make selectors cascade too much, which causes unexpected styling leakage. Sass nesting gives us all the utility of CSS cascading while giving us more control over our style specificity.

How to do it...

With Sass nesting, we can actually "nest" the navigation link selector inside the nav element's own style declarations:

```
a {
    font-size: 14px;
    text-decoration: underline;
    color: $text-color;
}

nav {
    background-color: $text-color;

    a {
        color: $background-color;
    }
}
```

This results in a link element that has a different color than other links, but still inherits other properties, such font-size and underline. This works because Sass essentially compiles to three different CSS selectors for us.

```
a {
  font-size: 14px;
  text-decoration: underline;
  color: #585858;
}

nav {
  background-color: #585858;
}

nav a {
  color: #E8E8E8;
}
```

We can also use nesting for other things than just selector specificity; we can use it as a convenient way to qualify related selectors. For example, if we wanted to add a hover state to our links, we could use Sass's & parent selector to add a hover psuedo-selector to our links:

```
a {
  font-size: 14px;
  text-decoration: underline;
  color: $text-color;

  &:hover {
    color: $color-black;
  }
}

nav {
  background-color: $text-color;

  a {
    color: $background-color;

    &:hover {
      color: $background-color;
      opacity: 0.5;
    }
  }
}
```

The & selector in Sass is always equivalent to the current selector scope. This makes it easy to use nesting to encapsulate modifiers or variants of a given style into a related space, instead of breaking it out into a separate selector.

How it works...

The Sass preprocessor can parse closures within a selector to identify properties from other selectors. It uses this to track the hierarchy of a selector, and, when compiled, it builds a fully qualified vanilla CSS equivalent of it. The & parent selector is a special selector that always references the current selector scope and is also complied to its fully qualified equivalent selector in the output CSS.

There's more...

We can see that Sass nesting can go many levels deep, but just like many powerful features, it can be taken too far. Deeply nested selectors can cause problems, as they become difficult to read and potentially too specific for its context. Although many developers disagree on how many layers of nesting are too many, the general rule of thumb is using no more than 3-4 layers, depending on the application's styling complexity. Luckily, in Angular, we have other tools available to assist with limiting selector specificity besides Sass nesting, such as component styles.

When deciding whether to nest a selector in Sass or not, it may be worth checking the specificity needed to apply the selector. In cases where there isn't much difference in the specificity between two elements, it's likely that nesting isn't really required to get the desired outcome. However, in cases where there is a large difference in specificity, nesting can be a very useful tool to help close that gap in selector specificity.

You can visit the following link for more information:
`https://developer.mozilla.org/en-US/docs/Web/CSS/Specificity`

Using Sass partials for style organization

Sass has more features than just its advanced CSS syntax and language features. It also allows us to more easily modularize our styles into partials for easier reuse and configuration. The modularization aspect of Sass partials is one of the most powerful features for organizing and maintaining your app's styling.

Getting ready

Let's make the color definitions for our web application's Sass variables a separate configuration file from our other Sass files. This will make updating our branding or any other color configuration changes much easier to find and make in our application.

How to do it...

We will put our Sass color variables in a separate Sass file called _colors.scss in the same directory as /src/styles.scss:

```
$primary-color: #566FC6;
$secondary-color: #222c4f;
```

Sass's @import command acts very similarly to vanilla CSS3's @import command; however, since Sass is precompiled, it will not cause the extra unnecessary HTTP request:

```
@import "colors";

button {
    background-color: $primary-color;
}
```

We can use our imported color variables for setting the background color property of our button elements. If we change the primary color value in /src/_colors.scss, it will update our button's background color automatically.

How it works...

The "colors" portion of the import is a relative file path to the current Sass file, which Sass will resolve to ./_colors.scss. This extra underscore is a best practice when creating partials to denote that they are meant to be imported as partials in Sass. Files without underscores usually are meant to be root Sass files imported by Angular-CLI's build system. We also don't need to define the .scss file extension in the Sass import; the Sass compiler will automatically resolve that for us.

There's more...

When you are working with Sass partials, it's often useful to create a directory to organize the different layers of partials that make up your custom CSS. We can do this by simply creating a `styles` directory and moving our partials inside it. For example, if we moved our colors partial to `/src/styles/variables/_colors.scss`, we can import it into our `/src/styles.scss` root file just by updating our import path:

```
@import "styles/variables/colors";
```

With our styles now moved out of our root directory, we can continue to add more partials to organize any other variables or configuration that we might need. As long as we import them in our `styles.scss` file before we reference them, we can rely on them being available.

> **Sass-included paths in Angular**: Angular-CLI's build system allows you to provide Sass pre-included paths for use in any of your Sass files. This can be very useful to make styles globally available for import under their partial name. For example, if we want to make `/src/styles/variables/_colors.scss` available to any Sass file in our project, we will update the following configuration in `.angular-cli.json`:
>
> ```
> {
> ...
> "apps": [
> ...
> "styles": [
> "styles.scss"
> ],
> "stylePreprocessorOptions": {
> "includePaths": [
> "styles/variables"
> ]
> },
> ...
> ```
>
> This change will allow all our Sass files, including component Sass files, to import this color partially by just importing it by its partial name, `@import "colors"`. This is a very handy way to use shared Sass variables and partials with Component Styles in Angular.

Now that we know about how to work with Sass partials, we can apply these skills to leverage Sass-based CSS frameworks, such as Bootstrap 4.

Working with Bootstrap in Sass

In this section, we will discuss how to import CSS frameworks and utilities into our application to set up a basic, responsive layout in our Angular application using **Bootstrap**. Bootstrap is a very popular CSS framework developed by Twitter for responsive web design that works on a wide range of devices, from desktop computers to mobile phones. The latest version of Bootstrap 4 includes many improvements, including switching from Less to Sass for its source files, a new flex-box-based grid system, and many optimizations and performance tweaks to better support mobile devices.

How to do it...

Our Angular application may be modern on the inside, but its user interface is very retro looking, without a modern CSS framework to go with it. Let's install Bootstrap to give our application some nice default styling:

1. To get started with Bootstrap in our Angular project, we will first have to install it as a dependency:

   ```
   npm install bootstrap@4.0.0-alpha.6 --save
   ```

2. Once we have installed Bootstrap, we can import it in a similar manner to how we can import our own Sass modules. We simply add an import statement to the top of our /src/styles.scss file in our Angular project:

   ```
   @import '~bootstrap/scss/bootstrap';
   ```

This imports all of Bootstrap using a special loader mechanism provided by sass-loader. Our Angular application now has all of the Bootstrap 4 CSS framework available and ready to use.

How it works...

The ~bootstrap namespace is a helpful feature of sass-loader, which helps resolve Sass imports to our node_modules directory. If we look inside this folder in our Angular project, we will see that there is an scss directory that contains all the Sass files that Bootstrap uses. The node_modules/bootstrap/scss/bootstrap.scss file is a collection of imports that will load everything that Bootstrap uses for styling.

There's more...

When working with large Sass frameworks such as Bootstrap, it's easy to simply add them to the top of your /src/styles.scss file to get started. However, to get the best potential build performance, it's better to import your vendor styles through a separate vendor.scss file. This allows the Angular-CLI build to limit the regeneration of its stylesheets when you rebuild to only what has changed. This is because of a tree-shaking optimization built into Angular-CLI's WebPack build system that doesn't recompute unchanged branches of content. By separating your library styles such as Bootstrap from your own custom Sass styles, Angular-CLI will only recompile the part that has changed. Simply move all your bootstrap imports and variable customization over to this new vendor file and add it above styles.scss in your .angular-cli.json configuration:

```
"styles": [
  "vendor.scss",
  "styles.scss"
],
```

Customizing Bootstrap for Angular

Configuring Bootstrap will let you customize the parts of the Bootstrap framework you include in your application. Loading fewer parts of Bootstrap will reduce your file size, thus, increasing the performance of compiling your Sass stylesheets.

Getting ready

Loading all of Bootstrap is great, but what if we don't want or need all of the Bootstrap framework in our Angular application? Let's remove all the built-in JavaScript components used by Bootstrap so that we can implement our own Angular-based versions instead.

How to do it...

We can customize exactly which Bootstrap files are loaded in our application by copying the contents of `/node_modules/bootstrap/scss/bootstrap.scss` and customizing their import paths so that they use our advanced sass-loader mechanism instead:

```scss
// Core variables and mixins
@import "~bootstrap/scss/variables";
@import "~bootstrap/scss/mixins";
@import "~bootstrap/scss/custom";

// Reset and dependencies
@import "~bootstrap/scss/normalize";
@import "~bootstrap/scss/print";

// Core CSS
@import "~bootstrap/scss/reboot";
@import "~bootstrap/scss/type";
@import "~bootstrap/scss/images";
@import "~bootstrap/scss/code";
@import "~bootstrap/scss/grid";
@import "~bootstrap/scss/tables";
@import "~bootstrap/scss/forms";
@import "~bootstrap/scss/buttons";

// Components
@import "~bootstrap/scss/transitions";
@import "~bootstrap/scss/dropdown";
@import "~bootstrap/scss/button-group";
@import "~bootstrap/scss/input-group";
@import "~bootstrap/scss/custom-forms";
@import "~bootstrap/scss/nav";
@import "~bootstrap/scss/navbar";
@import "~bootstrap/scss/card";
@import "~bootstrap/scss/breadcrumb";
@import "~bootstrap/scss/pagination";
@import "~bootstrap/scss/badge";
@import "~bootstrap/scss/jumbotron";
@import "~bootstrap/scss/alert";
@import "~bootstrap/scss/progress";
@import "~bootstrap/scss/media";
@import "~bootstrap/scss/list-group";
@import "~bootstrap/scss/responsive-embed";
@import "~bootstrap/scss/close";

// Components w/ JavaScript
// @import "~bootstrap/scss/modal";
```

```
// @import "~bootstrap/scss/tooltip";
// @import "~bootstrap/scss/popover";
// @import "~bootstrap/scss/carousel";

// Utility classes
@import "~bootstrap/scss/utilities";
```

In our custom Bootstrap loader file, we can now comment out or remove modules we don't want in our application, such as these JavaScript-dependent components.

How it works...

With this approach, we can fully choose which components, features, and utilities will be compiled into the output CSS. It's worth noting that generally the files near the top of the list are more likely to be required by other Sass files in Bootstrap, in order to work as expected. If removing a file causes a compiler error, it's probably because it contained content that was required for a later imported component to work properly. Some trial and error may be necessary to figure out which files are dependent on each other, but, generally, components and utility classes are optional and can be safely removed from Bootstrap.

There's more...

Another type of Bootstrap customization you may want to try is to override some of the defaults Bootstrap uses for styling to make your application unique from the default theme. Bootstrap makes this easy to accomplish by overriding the values defined in _variables.scss. If we copied Bootstrap's Sass files into our application's style directory, we would accomplish this by just adding our variable declarations to the _custom.scss partial in Bootstrap's source. This file is empty by default, which might seem strange, but its intention is to be a place where you can safely override Bootstrap variables without conflicting with any of Bootstrap's Sass dependencies. In an Angular application, all we need to do is define our own custom variables at this same point in the process before any of the other Bootstrap partials are loaded:

```
// Core variables and mixins
@import "~bootstrap/scss/variables";
@import "~bootstrap/scss/mixins";

$body-bg:     $gray-dark;
$body-color:  $gray-light;
...
```

Sass variable defaults: These Bootstrap Sass overrides work due to a feature of Sass variables called variable defaults. We can make a default variable in Sass by providing the `!default` property after our variable's value:

`$variable: "Value" !default;`

Default variables in Sass are only set if the variable does not exist in Sass when it is declared. So, if we declare a Sass variable before it is set with a default flag, our custom value will continue on as the set value, with Sass ignoring this instruction to recreate an existing value. This is very useful for providing overrides to values in frameworks such as Bootstrap, but can also be used by Component styles in Angular or any custom Sass configurations in your application.

The Sass variables `$body-bg` and `$body-color` can be found in `/node_modules/bootstrap/scss/_variables.scss`. We are able to use colors declared earlier in Bootstrap's Sass to change the default style of our body background and text colors.

If we wanted to do a lot of customization, it would be cleaner to simply make our own Bootstrap reset partial, and simply import that instead:

```
// Core variables and mixins
@import "~bootstrap/scss/variables";
@import "~bootstrap/scss/mixins";

@import "styles/reset/bootstrap"
...
```

Using Bootstrap Responsive layouts

One of the best reasons to use a CSS framework such as Bootstrap is to more easily support responsive layouts in our web application. Using Bootstrap's layout classes and breakpoints, we can easily add responsive design to our Angular application.

Getting ready

Bootstrap 4 supports a modern flex-box-based responsive grid system. To use the grid system, we will need to declare a container that will contain the grid, rows for each line of elements we will lay out in the container, and columns for each item in the row:

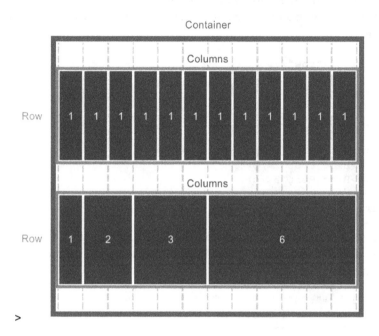

We can compose any combination of column widths together that we want as long as the total within the row adds up to 12 or fewer. Otherwise our column content will wrap to the next row and begin filling out the next row of 12 columns.

How to do it...

Now that we have Bootstrap loaded in our application, let's make the blog post page in our app responsively scale all the way down to mobile phone-sized devices:

1. Here is a simple example of a responsive application layout in our
   `/src/app/app.component.html` template:

```
<nav class="container-fluid">
  <a routerLink="/posts">Posts</a>
  <a routerLink="/authors">Authors</a>
```

```
    </nav>

    <div class="container">
      <router-outlet></router-outlet>
    </div>
```

2. Next, we will add rows and columns to our
    `/src/app/posts/posts.component.html` template to organize the content on
    our page:

```
    <div class="row">
      <div class="col-3">
        <p>Sidebar</p>
      </div>
      <div class="col-9">
        <h3>Blog Posts</h3>
        <p>Blog Post 1</p>
        <p>Blog Post 2</p>
        <p>Blog Post 3</p>
      </div>
    </div>
```

3. Finally, we will need to vary our column width, based on the resolution of the
    user's device. We can add this functionality by adding size modifiers to our
    column classes:

```
    <div class="row">
      <div class="col-3 col-sm-12">
        <p>Sidebar</p>
      </div>
      <div class="col-9 col-sm-12">
        <h3>Blog Posts</h3>
        <p>Blog Post 1</p>
        <p>Blog Post 2</p>
        <p>Blog Post 3</p>
      </div>
    </div>
```

Now, our blog page will dynamically scale the content at different resolutions and will
change layout on small screen resolutions, such as mobile devices.

How it works...

For our navigation, we are using the `container-fluid` class because we want it to cover the entire screen while still acting as a responsive container. This is a common design choice for navigation elements because they will be the same on every page. For our router-outlet content, we have surrounded it with the `container` class so that the content on the page will center at a maximum size on all the pages of our application, regardless of the content of our application. This approach is helpful because it will not only allow us to manage the rows and columns of a given route inside its own template, but it will also unify the overall page layout across our entire application.

We can see that the `row` class contains everything on our page. It is helpful to have this defined at the component level rather than at the application level, because we may have pages that would be easier to display in multiple rows. Inside our row, we have two columns, `col-3` and `col-9`. The first column sets up a sidebar element, which we can use for blog post categories or other blog utilities, such as search. The second column forms the main content of the blog, a list of blog posts. The `col-3` takes up approximately one-fourth of the container width, whereas the `col-9` makes up the remaining three-fourths of our 12 column grid.

When we apply the column size modifier classes, such as `col-sm-6`, we are referencing predefined pixel sizes in Bootstrap called **breakpoints**. Breakpoints in Bootstrap are available in a variety of sizes for different device resolutions:

Size	Breakpoint	Pixels
Extra-small	xs	<576px
Small	sm	≥576px
Medium	md	≥768px
Large	lg	≥992px
Extra-large	xl	≥1200px

Breakpoints can also be used for responsive design, without using any grid classes using **media queries**. Bootstrap provides us with a few handy tools to work with breakpoints in Sass, including a media query **mixin** called `media-breakpoint-up` that accepts breakpoint sizes and returns a conditional media query that will only apply the styles contained within, when the width of the device screen matches the breakpoint size or is higher than that:

```
@include media-breakpoint-up(xs) { ... }
@include media-breakpoint-up(sm) { ... }
@include media-breakpoint-up(md) { ... }
@include media-breakpoint-up(lg) { ... }
@include media-breakpoint-up(xl) { ... }
```

```
@include media-breakpoint-up(sm) {
  .my-class {
    display: block;
  }
}
```

This is very useful for creating styling that behaves responsively to different screen resolutions.

There's more...

When working with grids, it's important to remember how many columns your grid uses. With Bootstrap 4, there are 12 columns by default. It is possible to change this using Sass variables. Changing the `$grid-columns` variable has a big impact on how our column size classes work:

```
$grid-columns: 16;
```

For example, if we chose a 16-column grid for our application, our `.col-3` and `.col-9` columns together would only cover three-fourths of the width of our container, leaving four unused columns. Changing your column count after the beginning of a project can be a large effort depending on the complexity of your application. If you are uncertain about the layout needs of your application, its recommended that you leave your column count at the default value.

Working with Bootstrap components in Angular

Bootstrap 4 contains many different JavaScript-dependent components. Many of these components rely on jQuery for **Document Object Model** (**DOM**) manipulation and can adversely interact with Angular's own **View Encapsulation** based data-binding. We will solve this issue using the Angular-friendly versions of these components provided by the *ng-bootstrap* project.

Getting ready

Let's add an accordion component to our web application, so we can group blog posts by their author. When the user clicks on the author's name, they will see a list of blog posts they created.

In order to build this functionality, we will need to install and save the *ng-bootstrap* project as a dependency via NPM:

```
npm install --save @ng-bootstrap/ng-bootstrap
```

How to do it...

Let's follow the steps to add a Bootstrap accordion component to our application:

1. First, we will import ng-bootstrap as a module into /src/app/app.module.ts:

```
...
import {NgbModule} from '@ng-bootstrap/ng-bootstrap';

@NgModule({
  ...
  imports: [
    BrowserModule,
    BrowserAnimationsModule,
    FormsModule,
    HttpModule,
    RouterModule.forRoot(ROUTES),
    PostsModule,
    NgbModule.forRoot()
  ],
  ...
})
export class AppModule { }
```

2. When using submodules, such as our posts module, you will also need to import ng-bootstrap into it:

```
...
import {NgbModule} from '@ng-bootstrap/ng-bootstrap';

@NgModule({
  imports: [
    CommonModule,
    RouterModule.forChild(ROUTES),
    NgbModule
  ],
  ...
})
export class PostsModule { }
```

3. Now that the module is imported, we can use any of the components it provides to us. Let's add the accordion component to the side panel of our blog posts page:

```html
<ngb-accordion activeIds="ngb-panel-0">
  <ngb-panel title="Matt DeLucas">
    <ng-template ngbPanelContent>
      <ul class="list-unstyled">
        <li>Post 1</li>
        <li>Post 2</li>
        <li>Post 3</li>
      </ul>
    </ng-template>
  </ngb-panel>
  <ngb-panel title="Brandon Bittner">
    <ng-template ngbPanelContent>
      <ul class="list-unstyled">
        <li>Post 4</li>
        <li>Post 5</li>
        <li>Post 6</li>
      </ul>
    </ng-template>
  </ngb-panel>
  <ngb-panel title="Mallory Moore">
    <ng-template ngbPanelContent>
      <ul class="list-unstyled">
        <li>Post 7</li>
        <li>Post 8</li>
        <li>Post 9</li>
      </ul>
    </ng-template>
  </ngb-panel>
</ngb-accordion>
```

4. With that, our side panel now has a list of authors, and, when the user clicks on the author's name, the accordion will interactively reveal the template contained within it.

How it works...

ng-bootstrap is a project that provides ready-made Angular component wrappers for Bootstrap's components. It solves all the data binding and event-oriented aspects associated with using Bootstrap's vanilla jQuery components, while still looking and functioning identically. However, `ng-bootstrap` only provides the Angular component wrappers for generating Bootstrap components and does not import any Sass for styling components; we still have to do that ourselves.

The `ngb-accordion` and `ngb-panel` Angular components are adaptations of Bootstrap's collapsible group and collapsible card components, specifically tailored for Angular. The `activeIds` attribute on the component tells the `ngb-accordion` component which `ngb-panel` should be active by default. The `title` attribute provides the title that is displayed on the `ngb-panel`, while the `ngbPanelContent` directive on the template inside it contains the content that will be displayed when the panel is active. The `ngb-accordion` component automatically tracks and updates the state of these panels for us when we click on it.

There's more...

There are many customizations and enhancements that you can make to the `ngb-accordion` component, and many more different types of interactive components provided by `ng-bootstrap`. For example, there is another template directive available for `ngb-panel` to customize the title of the panel to allow for more styling control. For instance, if I wanted to display my titles in bold and add a preview of how many posts have been written beside it, I could use the `ngPanelTitle` directive to do that:

```
<ngb-panel>
  <ng-template ngbPanelTitle>
    <strong>Brandon Bittner</strong> <small>(3)</small>
  </ng-template>
  <ng-template ngbPanelContent>
    <ul class="list-unstyled">
      <li>Post 4</li>
      <li>Post 5</li>
      <li>Post 6</li>
    </ul>
  </ng-template>
</ngb-panel>
```

All of the components in `ng-bootstrap` are configurable and customizable for different styles, use cases, and behaviors. The best place to learn about all of your options for a given component is from the official `ng-bootstrap` project documentation--`https://ng-bootstrap.github.io`.

Working with Font-Awesome icons in Angular

Unlike the preceding version of Bootstrap, Bootstrap 4 does not come with a built-in icon set. You get to choose the icon set you'd like to include for your application.

The *Font-Awesome* project is a very popular font-based icon set with a robust collection of high-quality icons that cover a wide range of common application functionalities, all available for free as an open source resource.

Getting ready

Let's enhance our new Bootstrap accordion component by putting a user icon next to all our author's names and a newspaper icon next to their blog post titles. Before we can get started, we will need to install font-awesome as a dependency to our project. We will do this in the same way we did for Bootstrap using NPM:

```
npm install font-awesome --save
```

This will put the font-awesome package in our `node_modules` package so that we can reference it.

How to do it...

Let's follow the steps to add Font-Awesome icons to our Angular web application:

1. First, we will need to add Font-Awesome's font files and styles to our `/src/styles.scss` or another global Sass file in our project. Again, we use sass-loader's helpful lookup feature to reference both the font files inside `node_modules/font-awesome/fonts/` and then import its Sass styles from `node_modules/font-awesome/scss/`.

```
@import "~font-awesome/scss/font-awesome";
```

2. We will also need to tell font-awesome where it can find the font files required by its styles by providing it with a style path. We will define this before our Font-Awesome import so that this value will override the default variable value inside Font-Awesome's Sass.

```
$fa-font-path: "~font-awesome/fonts";
@import "~font-awesome/scss/font-awesome";
```

3. Now that we have font-awesome loaded, we can use its provided styles to start adding icons to our accordion component:

```
<ngb-accordion activeIds="ngb-panel-0">
  <ngb-panel >
    <template ngbPanelTitle>
      <strong><i class="fa fa-user"></i> Matt DeLucas</strong>
    </template>
    <template ngbPanelContent>
      <ul class="list-unstyled">
        <li><i class="fa fa-newspaper-o"></i> Post 1</li>
        <li><i class="fa fa-newspaper-o"></i> Post 2</li>
        <li><i class="fa fa-newspaper-o"></i> Post 3</li>
      </ul>
    </template>
  </ngb-panel>
  . . .
```

4. We now have a user icon next to our author's name and a newspaper icon next to every blog post under their name.

How it works...

Font-Awesome adds a collection of font files and Sass styles to our web application. You might be wondering how the font files inside `node_modules` are available as static files in your web application? Angular-CLI's sass-loader will resolve URL paths to assets, such as fonts, images, and svgs, and bundle them into our WebPack so that we don't have to do so. This is tremendously useful when working with libraries with style assets.

After we have added these files, we can invoke them by adding `<i>` tags to our template with the classes: `fa` and `fa-<name of icon>`.

You can find these associated icon names by consulting the Font-Awesome icon cheatsheet on its official website: http://fontawesome.io/cheatsheet/

There's more...

Another useful way to work with Font-Awesome in Angular is to use a directive, such as `angular2-fontawesome`, to make it easier to work with your icons in your templates. For example, you can provide a `size` property to the directive that will scale the icon to different sizes for you:

```
<ngb-panel>
  <ng-template ngbPanelTitle>
    <strong>
      <fa [name]="'user'" [size]=1></fa>
      Matt DeLucas
    </strong>
  </ng-template>
  <ng-template ngbPanelContent>
    <ul class="list-unstyled">
      <li><fa [name]="'newspaper-o'"></fa> Post 1</li>
      <li><fa [name]="'newspaper-o'"></fa> Post 2</li>
      <li><fa [name]="'newspaper-o'"></fa> Post 3</li>
    </ul>
  </ng-template>
</ngb-panel>
```

 There are also options for rotation, inverting colors, and much more that can be useful in getting more from your options; you can refer to these in the following link: https://github.com/travelist/angular2-fontawesome

Internationalization with Angular i18n

Modern web applications can often support millions of users distributed across the globe. Even if the audience for your application is limited, the advantages you gain from building an application supporting multiple languages or localized date and time formatting can be very important for any international customers who use it. Luckily, Angular has an advanced toolkit for managing translations and localizing content in our application.

To translate text files in Angular, we will use the i18n attribute that comes built-in with Angular core. We will use this tool to mark strings in our application for translation and run a utility in Angular-CLI to extract them. Once we've extracted the strings, we can hand them off as a static file to be translated, and we will be able to import this file to display a localized language version of our text.

Getting ready

Our blog is going international! While our blog content itself will not be translated, all our navigation items and labels can be, so it's a bit easier for international audiences to find the content that they are looking for.

How to do it...

We will start by localizing the Posts and Authors links in our main navigation:

1. We will start by localizing the Posts and Authors links in our main navigation. We'll also upgrade the styling of our header to use a more traditional bootstrap style navigation bar. Inside our navigation's nav-items we must mark the strings that we want to translate using the i18n attribute, as follows:

```
<nav class="navbar navbar-expand navbar-light bg-light">
  <a class="navbar-brand" href="#">MEAN Stack Blog</a>
  <ul class="navbar-nav">
    <li class="nav-item">
      <a class="nav-link" routerLink="/posts"
routerLinkActive="active" i18n>Posts</a>
    </li>
    <li class="nav-item">
      <a class="nav-link" routerLink="/authors"
routerLinkActive="active" i18n>Authors
      </a>
    </li>
  </ul>
</nav>
```

2. Here, I've attached two attributes, one to each of our main navigation links in our application. Translating strings without any context can be a bit tricky, so now is a good time to add some context to our string translations. We can add context in two ways with the `i18n` attribute, by adding meaning for our text and by adding a description:

```
...
<a class="nav-link" routerLink="/posts" routerLinkActive="active"
i18n="A collection of blog posts|Primary link to list of blog
posts">Posts</a>
...
<a class="nav-link" routerLink="/authors" routerLinkActive="active"
i18n="People who write blog posts|Primary link to list of blog
authors">Authors</a>
...
```

3. Now that the string is marked for extraction and its context is clear for translation, we can extract the strings using the xi18n command in Angular-CLI. Eventually, we are very likely to want multiple translations, so it's best to set this up as a directory in our project where all our translation files will live:

```
ng xi18n --output-path src/locale
```

4. Running the preceding command will generate a new file in your project called `/src/locale/messages.xlf`, as follows:

```
<?xml version="1.0" encoding="UTF-8" ?>
<xliff version="1.2" xmlns="urn:oasis:names:tc:xliff:document:1.2">
  <file source-language="en" datatype="plaintext"
original="ng2.template">
    <body>
      <trans-unit id="3e2ccc5737a76c65150a7cd6f3697bf0cf9b7015"
datatype="html">
        <source>Posts</source>
        <target/>
        <note priority="1" from="description">Primary link to list
of blog
         posts</note>
        <note priority="1" from="meaning">A collection of blog
posts</note>
      </trans-unit>
      <trans-unit id="c5a494f609f526f3ea569a490d7f7348b0da2f2f"
datatype="html">
        <source>Authors</source>
        <target/>
        <note priority="1" from="description">Primary link to list
```

```
of blog
         authors</note>
         <note priority="1" from="meaning">People who write blog
posts</note>
       </trans-unit>
    </body>
  </file>
</xliff>
```

5. This file contains extracted translation units for the text we marked with the i18n attribute. To provide a translation for these units, we must make a new copy of this file and rename it to /src/locale/messages.es.xlf. Inside our copied translation file, we will provide targeted translated text for the translation units inside the target tag, as follows:

```
. . .
<trans-unit id="3e2ccc5737a76c65150a7cd6f3697bf0cf9b7015"
datatype="html">
  <source>Posts</source>
  <target>Entradas</target>
</trans-unit>
<trans-unit id="c5a494f609f526f3ea569a490d7f7348b0da2f2f"
datatype="html">
  <source>Authors</source>
  <target>Autores</target>
</trans-unit>
. . .
```

6. We can also remove the note tags from this file to keep the file simple. Now that we have a new translation file ready to be used by our application, we will need to tell Angular to build our application using this new file. We will do that by providing a few extra flags for our Angular-CLI server to provide it with a locale, the i18n format, and the file itself to be complied into the application during its build:

```
ng serve --aot --locale es --i18n-format xlf --i18n-file
src/locale/messages.es.xlf
```

7. With these parameters, our application will build, and we will be able to see that our navigation now shows us Spanish translations for these items.

How it works...

The i18n attribute is a translation attribute provided by Angular's core library. It denotes a string as being available for extraction when running the Angular-CLI xi18n command. We can provide context to our exported attributes by adding meaning and description fields to the attribute:

```
i18n="<meaning>|<description>"
```

Both are optional values, with description being the default one if only one value is provided. The best way to think about the differences in these values is that meaning is the literal definition of what the translated word or phrase is attempting to communicate, whereas description relates to the context of what its function is in the application. An example would be whether it is a link in the main navigation, or a form element. Using both meaning and description is highly recommended, since they help translators provide the most accurate translations for your application.

The xi18n command in Angular-CLI leverages the @angular/compiler-cli and @angular/platform-server libraries to perform the actual extraction. If you are having trouble running this command, you should first check whether you have these two packages installed as dependencies in your package.json file. By default, this command will build your Angular application and search out references to the i18n attribute. It will track these translatable parts of your application as translation-units, and gives each unit a unique identifier. It is very important not to change these identifiers in the compiled output. These IDs are critical to Angular, mapping translated strings to the correct parts of your templates.

By default, the output translation file is a .xlf file, which is a common industry-standard translation file format using XML. If you want a different format of translation file, there are many options available for configuring xi18n to do what you want. The following is an example of few of the many options available:

```
ng xi18n <options...>
 Extracts i18n messages from source code.
  --i18n-format (String) (Default: xlf) Output format for the generated
file.
  aliases: -f <value>, -xmb (--i18n-format=xmb), -xlf (--i18n-format=xlf), -
-xliff (--i18n-format=xlf), --i18nFormat <value>
  --output-path (Path) (Default: null) Path where output will be placed.
  aliases: -op <value>, --outputPath <value>
  --verbose (Boolean) (Default: false) Adds more details to output logging.
  aliases: --verbose
  --progress (Boolean) (Default: true) Log progress to the console while
running.
```

```
aliases: --progress
--app (String) Specifies app name to use.
aliases: -a <value>, -app <value>
--locale (String) Specifies the source language of the application.
aliases: -l <value>, --locale <value>
--out-file (String) Name of the file to output.
aliases: -of <value>, --outFile <value>
```

We can tell Angular to use our translated file by providing flags to the Angular-CLI server to compile our application using them. This **ahead-of-time** (AOT) compilation means that there is a predetermined translation file that will be displayed to the user. This option is easy to implement, but not always desirable for all applications; so, in the next section, we will discuss how to make these translations display on the client side through the **just-in-time** (JIT) compilation.

There's more...

Sometimes, the labels in our application might change slightly based on the state of the application. Sometimes, we may wish to pluralize strings to show when there are multiple items, and singularize them when there is only one. For example, maybe we wanted Authors to be able to be displayed as Author if there is only one author for our blog. Luckily, there are options in Angular to pluralize strings with i18n.

```
<a class="nav-link" routerLink="/authors" i18n="People who write blog
posts|Primary link to list of blog authors">
   {authorCount, plural, =1 {Author} other {Authors}}
</a>
```

Once exported, our /src/locale/messages.xlf file will be structured with a source reference listed as <x id="ICU"/>. This is actually a reference to the ICU message format, which Google uses as an international standard for its pluralization format. You can define the values for these dynamic localizations in the target section of a given localization file, such as /src/locale/messages.es.xlf:

```
<trans-unit id="0cdd51e152e616c0bb63333fcb36dd00b99c939c" datatype="html">
   <source>
     <x id="ICU"/>
   </source>
   <target>
     {authorCount, plural, =1 {Autor} other {Autores}}
   </target>
</trans-unit>
```

For the target of this translation, we can provide a language-specific ICU pluralization keyword with a definition. There are actually quite a few of these pluralization keywords available, and they can be chained together to cover many different types of pluralization in your application's localization:

Pluralization keyword	Example definition
zero	No chickens
other	Chickens
one or =1	A chicken
two or =2	A pair of chickens
few	Some chickens
many	Lots of chickens

There are a lot of other ways to customize these messages as well, and you can learn more these about in the official ICU message format documentation and Angular's official i18n documentation, respectively:

```
http://userguide.icu-project.org/formatparse/messages
https://angular.io/docs/ts/latest/cookbook/i18n.html
```

Setting your language with Angular i18n

Although ahead-of-time (AOT) compilation of template strings can be useful, users may often wish to be able to manually decide the language that they would like to see, and have that served to them as a just-in-time (JIT) option. To support this, we will need to add providers to Angular to watch for a locale setting we can use to determine our user's language preference.

Let's configure our application to display whatever language the browser is defaulted to using. That way, content will automatically be displayed in any translation that matches the machine that they are using to access our application.

Getting ready

Before we can get started, to take advantage of just-in-time localization in Angular, we will have to eject our project from Angular-CLI:

```
ng eject
```

This is necessary to access the WebPack configuration file. After ejecting the project, you will have a new file in your project called `webpack.config.js`.

We will need to add a new module rule to this file to work with our `.xlf` files manually:

```
module.exports = {
  ...
  "module": {
    "rules": [
      ...
      {
        test: /\.xlf/,
        loader: 'raw-loader'
      },
      ...
```

How to do it...

Let's follow the steps to use browser language detection to drive our Angular `i18n` language localization settings:

1. First, we will set up a provider to look up our browser's locale property and use that to dynamically load our associated translation file, if it exists. We will create a new file for our provider at `/src/app/i18n-providers.ts`:

```
import { TRANSLATIONS, TRANSLATIONS_FORMAT, LOCALE_ID } from
'@angular/core';
export function getTranslationProviders(): Promise<Object[]> {
  const locale = document['locale'] as string;
  const noProviders: Object[] = [];
  if (!locale || locale === 'en-US') {
    return Promise.resolve(noProviders);
  }

  return getTranslationsWithES6Import(locale)
    .then((translations: string ) => [
      { provide: TRANSLATIONS, useValue: translations },
      { provide: TRANSLATIONS_FORMAT, useValue: 'xlf' },
      { provide: LOCALE_ID, useValue: locale }
    ])
    .catch(() => noProviders);
}

declare var System: any;
function getTranslationsWithES6Import(locale: string) {
  return System.import('../locale/messages.' + locale + '.xlf');
}
```

2. This provider may seem very complicated, but don't worry, we will dive deeper into working with data in Angular in the next Chapter. All we need to know for now is that this provider runs on startup and returns a promise that returns a locale string. Next, we will register our new provider with our `/src/main.ts` file to configure it to be loaded when our application is getting bootstrapped:

```
import { enableProdMode } from '@angular/core';
import { platformBrowserDynamic } from '@angular/platform-browser-
dynamic';
import { getTranslationProviders } from './app/i18n-providers';

import { AppModule } from './app/app.module';
import { environment } from './environments/environment';

if (environment.production) {
  enableProdMode();
}

getTranslationProviders().then(providers => {
  const options = { providers };
  platformBrowserDynamic().bootstrapModule(AppModule, options);
});
```

3. Finally, to test out this property and see whether its working as expected, we can update our `index.html` file to add our `document.locale` property to the browser's automatically provided `navigator.language`:

```
<html>
<head>
  <meta charset="utf-8">
  <title>MyAngular4Project</title>
  <base href="/">

  <meta name="viewport" content="width=device-width, initial-
scale=1">
  <link rel="icon" type="image/x-icon" href="favicon.ico">
  <script>
    document.locale = navigator.language;
  </script>
</head>
<body>
  <app-root>Loading...</app-root>
</body>
</html>
```

4. To test whether things are working in different languages, we can also try to manually set `document.locale` to different values. With these changes in place, we can restart our Angular-CLI project, and, after rebuilding it, we will see our Spanish translations.

```
document.locale = 'es';
```

How it works...

Currently, the only way to do JIT compilation for localization in Angular is to eject your project from Angular-CLI. This has some additional complexity and overhead to it, but it gives us the customization options we need in WebPack to enable this functionality. Future versions of Angular will support JIT language compilation as an add-on in Angular-CLI.

After ejecting, we configure WebPack to support loading language templates as raw modules in our build system. This lets us load the specific language file that we need when the client first loads Angular. We get those files into Angular through our custom i18n-provider. This provider may look complicated, but all it's doing is registering a promise with Angular's launch process that looks up and loads the correct language file for whatever document.locale is set to. If the value is empty, or a language doesn't exist, the provider simply resolves no changes for the application's configuration and will load as normal.

The document.locale property is our own custom value that we use to drive the language displayed to the user. By mapping this to `navigator.language`, we can get language options pre-populated for us by many browsers. There are many other ways we could modify this property as well, including saving and loading it from a cookie.

There's more...

Translation file maintenance is a natural part of upgrading your application over time. When you add new markup and components, your application Angular-CLI automatic ID generation for i18n translation units will naturally append new elements to your master translation file. However, when you make changes to the markup around existing translated strings, these IDs will end up changing significantly enough to generate a new automatic ID.

The best way to fix this problem is to check-in your translation files to source control, and rely on your source control tool to provide the change difference between your new version and earlier generated versions of your translation files. The process of updating these files to match your new IDs can be annoying, but, by making sure that you always use the newest IDs, you can minimize the scope and size of updates to a manageable level for each release of your application.

How to Localize dates in Angular

Many countries format dates and times in a different way. For example, between the US and UK, the order of months and days is often reversed in shortened dates. For example, *12/5/2017* is *December 5th, 2017 (MM/DD/YYYY)* in the US, while it would mean *May 12th, 2017 (DD/MM/YYYY)*. Unlocalized date format can be potentially very confusing to your users and is an easy localization option offered by Angular's built-in Pipes helper.

How to do it...

Let's follow the steps to add date localization to our blog posts so that they will display in the format our readers would expect:

1. We'll start by adding a simple date object to our `/src/app/posts/post/post.component.ts` component:

   ```
   postDate = new Date();
   ```

2. This will set the blog post date to the current time, which is good enough for this recipe. We can now use that date property in our template and pipe it into Angular's built-in date formatter:

   ```
   <small class="pull-left">Posted – {{ postDate | date:'shortDate'
   }}</small>
   ```

3. This will display the current date for us in a shortened format, such as *2/13/17*. Next, we will need to provide a `LOCALE_ID` for Angular to have available to localize content for us. Let's extend our `/src/i18n-providers.ts` file from the last section to add this capability:

   ```
   const locale = document['locale'] as string;

   export function getLocaleProvider(): String {
     return locale;
   ```

```
    }
```

4. This will return the locale setting from the document.locale property that we set in the preceding section. Finally, we will need to provide Angular with this value and map it to the LOCALE_ID property from Angular core in order for the Date formatter in Angular to use it:

```
import { NgModule, LOCALE_ID } from '@angular/core';
import { getLocaleProvider } from "./i18n-providers";

@NgModule({
  ...
 providers: [{ provide: LOCALE_ID, useFactory: getLocaleProvider
}],
  ...
})
export class AppModule {}
```

5. With this change, our application's shortened date will now display in a localized format, based on the locale value provided for it in the browser.

How it works...

Angular's Pipe helpers allows you to pass data through a formatter for easy content formatting in your Angular templates. The DatePipe helper is a built-in utility for formatting generic date objects into human-readable formats. The 'shortdate' property passed along tells Angular that we want to format the date into the shortdate format style, that is, *MM/DD/YYYY* for en-US locales.

There are many other formats available for date that you can find in the following official DatePipe documentation:

https://angular.io/docs/ts/latest/api/common/index/DatePipe-pipe.html

If Angular detects a LOCALE_ID different than en-US, it will transform the date format into a locale appropriate format for us. For example, for en-GB, it reorders the format to DD/MM/YYYY. We must provide this Locale property to our App module manually. This is because Angular does not share Bootstrap providers with the application context. In this case, this is easily done by simply looking up our document.locale property on the browser. By providing our custom LOCALE_ID to our App module providers, we will automatically get any DatePipe dates formatted for that locale in our application.

There's more...

Many browsers have differences in the way they return browser language configurations. For example, Safari returns the browser language locale as `en-us` instead of `en-US` like other browsers. Browsers such as IE 9 and 10 don't even provide `navigation.language` and instead rely on their own `navigation.browserLanguage` property. An easy fix to this problem is to normalize both options into your document.locale value in lowercase format, as follows:

```
document.locale = (navigator.language ||
navigator.browserLanguage).toLowerCase();
```

Angular will still recognize these as valid locale properties for our date localization.

You can learn more about how these language configurations are provided in the browser and their various compatibility quirks in the following Mozilla's official JavaScript documentation:
https://developer.mozilla.org/en-US/docs/Web/API/NavigatorLanguage/language

3
Working with Data

Working with data in Angular can be a common source of frustration and confusion. In this chapter, we will provide recipes for working with internal and external data in your Angular application and show you how to validate and handle errors caused by data.

In this chapter, we will cover the following recipes:

- Working with actions and events in Angular
- Working with form input and models in Angular
- Validating data with Angular form properties
- Creating services for data in Angular
- Using promises to create asynchronous services in Angular
- Retrieving API data using HTTP services in Angular
- Querying API sources using HTTP services in Angular
- Creating Concurrent API requests in Angular
- Handling API errors and invalid responses in Angular
- HTTP service optimization through client-side caching

Introduction

The primary role of a front-end web application is to provide an interface for the display and manipulation of data. This data handling aspect is provided in Angular through its use of **Observables** and **data-binding** between internal data model representations and the templated views of your application.

In this chapter we will explore the range of interactions with data that Angular supports, including user input, events, shared data services, and most importantly, loading content from external APIs. We will cover some of the most common types of data manipulation in Angular, as well as cover some more advanced topics such as error handling, concurrency and caching strategies for your data.

Working with actions and events in Angular

Your front-end application will allow user input of data for the rest of your application to use. Angular provides a robust set of data-binding input utilities for communicating state between what the user sees and Angular's internal data model.

A common type of user interaction is activating some state of the user interface when a user clicks a button. We can bind to events such as clicks directly on elements in Angular using **input events**. We can also pass parameters through input events to our components for configuring the response to the event in our application.

Getting ready

Let's add a **Create New Post** button on our blog application. We could accomplish this behavior by making the **Create New Post** button a router-link. However, the simplest approach would be to just keep within the current component context and use a modal to display an alternative state of the same template. We'll use input events to bind clicking on the button in the side panel to trigger a modal dialog from `ng-bootstrap` on the page. We will also configure events for closing the modal when we click on a **Cancel** button or click outside the modal dialog itself.

How to do it...

Let's perform the following steps to create an event to launch a bootstrap modal:

1. First, let's add the `ng-bootstrap` modal template to our `/src/app/posts/posts.component.html` template. We will bind this template to the local property--#modal--for easy retrieval later. If you included the `angular2-fontawesome` module from Chapter 2, *Enhancing Your User Interface*, we will use that for our close button. Otherwise, simply substitute your own close button. The modal component itself exposes a built-in action to close itself.

```
<ng-template #modal let-c="close">
  <div class="modal-header">
    <h4 class="modal-title">New Post</h4>
    <button type="button" class="close" aria-label="Close"
(click)="c()">
      <fa [name]="'close'"></fa>
    </button>
  </div>
  <div class="modal-body">
    <form>
      <div class="form-group">
        <label for="formGroupExampleInput">Title</label>
        <input type="text" class="form-control"
id="formGroupExampleInput"
          placeholder="New Blog Post Title">
      </div>
    </form>
  </div>
  <div class="modal-footer">
    <button type="button" class="btn btn-secondary"
      (click)="c()">Cancel</button>
    <button type="button" class="btn btn-primary">Submit</button>
  </div>
</ng-template>
```

2. Next, we must add an input event binding to our button in the side panel. This button will be bound to the `click` event and will activate the `open` method on our component when the event is fired. We must also pass the `modal` view reference defined in our template to this component method:

```
<div class="row">
  <div class="col-3">
    <button (click)="open(modal)" class="btn btn-block btn-primary">
      <fa [name]="'plus'" [fw]=true></fa>Create New Post
    </button>
    ...
  </div>
  <div class="col-9">
    <router-outlet></router-outlet>
  </div>
</div>
```

3. Finally, we will need to add our `open` method to `/src/app/posts/posts.component.ts` to receive the callback from the `click` event:

```
import { Component, OnInit } from '@angular/core';
import {NgbModal} from '@ng-bootstrap/ng-bootstrap';

@Component({
  selector: 'app-posts',
  templateUrl: './posts.component.html',
  styleUrls: ['./posts.component.scss']
})
export class PostsComponent implements OnInit {
  constructor(private modalService: NgbModal) {}

  open(content) {
    this.modalService.open(content);
  }
  ngOnInit() {}
}
```

4. Now, when we click on the **Create New Post** button in our side panel, we will see a **New Post** modal popup. Clicking on the **cancel** button, the **close** icon, or anywhere outside the modal will dismiss the modal and return us to the component's default state.

How it works...

The event binding syntax in Angular maps between DOM events on a particular element and an Angular component method, as well as any optional parameters that need to be passed along:

```
<element (event)="method([params])"></element>
```

 There are many different types of event available for *input event* binding; you can search for an official list in the following Mozilla's HTML5 events documentation:
`https://developer.mozilla.org/en-US/docs/Web/Events`

The `ng-bootstrap` modal defines a local alias to its own `close` method with the `let-c="close"` directive. This maps the `close` modal method in `NgbModal` to the local template property `c`, which can then be triggered like any other event. If you remove these local template input events, you will create a modal that can only be dismissed by clicking outside it. If you provide an optional backdrop parameter, you can define a modal that can only be closed by triggering the `close` event.

```
this.modalService.open(content, { backdrop: "static" });
```

Combining both of these customizations together would end up launching a modal you could never close, so be wary to leave at least one escape route available from the modal.

> You can learn more about modal customizations and events in `ng-bootstrap`'s official documentation: `https://ng-bootstrap.github.io/#/components/modal`

There's more...

Child components can also bubble up actions to parent components. For instance, let's convert our **Create New Post** button into a new `PostCreator` component. We can bubble our `click` action from the `PostCreator` to the parent `Posts` component:

```
<button (click)="launch($event)" class="btn btn-block btn-primary">
  <fa [name]="'plus'" [fw]=true></fa>Create New Post
</button>

import {Component, EventEmitter, Output} from '@angular/core';

@Component({
  selector: 'app-launcher',
  templateUrl: './launcher.component.html',
  styleUrls: ['./launcher.component.scss']
})
export class PostCreator {
  @Output() open = new EventEmitter();

  constructor() {}

  launch(event) {
    this.open.emit(event);
  }
}
```

The `@Output` decorator creates a new custom event on the component that we can bind to in our parent component. We simply invoke our new launcher component and attach its custom `open` event to call our own component's `open` method.

```
<app-post-creator (open)="open(modal)"></app-post-creator>
```

For routable child components, such as our `Posts` and `Post` components, there is no way to bubble events through the router-outlet because it is simply the placeholder for the router itself and doesn't function as a proxy for binding to it. The best way to pass events between routable components is through a shared service, which we will cover creating later on in this chapter.

Working with form input and models in Angular

Forms allow us to take multiple user inputs and submit them as a single transactional model of our applications state. We can bind input data to models in Angular using a two-way data binding with `ngModel`. Now that we understand the basics of actions with our modal, let's explore how to do more advanced form inputs data-binding with it.

Getting Ready

Let's use our new modal to input our title and blog content to create our first real blog post. We will consolidate all our **Create New Post** button functionalities into a new `CreatePostFormComponent` component. We'll configure the form inputs to bind to a new **BlogPost** model so that we can eventually save and reuse it to also display our blog posts to users.

Before we get started, we will need to scaffold out a new component called `CreatePostFormComponent`. Let's do that with Angular-CLI's `generate` command. While we're at it, we will also scaffold out a new `BlogPost` class to serve as our model for our blog posts:

```
ng generate component posts/create-post-form
ng generate class posts/blog-post
```

How to do it...

Let's follow the steps below to create a modal for creating a new blog post in Angular:

1. First, to use Forms in Angular, we will need to include the `FormsModule` from Angular in our `PostsModule`. If you don't yet have a `PostsModule` defined, make sure to check out the Chapter 1, *Working with Angular 4*, for instructions creating this module. We will also import our newly created `CreatePostFormComponent` into our module:

```
. . .
import { CreatePostFormComponent } from './create-post-form/create-post-form.component'
import { FormsModule } from "@angular/forms";

@NgModule({
  imports: [
    CommonModule,
    RouterModule.forChild(ROUTES),
    FormsModule,
    NgbModule,
    Angular2FontawesomeModule
  ],
  declarations: [
    PostsComponent,
    PostComponent,
    CreatePostFormComponent
  ]
})
export class PostsModule { }
```

2. Next, we'll include our newly added `CreatePostFormComponent` to our `/src/app/posts/posts.component.html` template:

```
<div class="row">
  <div class="col-3">
    <app-create-post-form></app-create-post-form>
    <hr>
    . . .
  </div>
  <div class="col-9">
    <router-outlet></router-outlet>
  </div>
</div>
```

3. Let's create a very simple model definition in our new `/src/app/posts/blog-post.ts` class. For now, our blog post will just be a `title` string and a `content` string:

```
export class BlogPost {
  constructor(
    public title: string = "",
    public content: string = ""
  ) {}
}
```

4. We will load our new blog post model into `/src/app/posts/create-post-form.component.ts` and create a new instance that we will call `model` in our component. We'll also set up a new event for logging the state of our blog post model to the browser's developer console when we click on the **submit** button.

```
import { Component } from '@angular/core';
import {NgbModal} from '@ng-bootstrap/ng-bootstrap';
import {BlogPost} from "../blog-post";

@Component({
  selector: 'app-create-post-form',
  templateUrl: './create-post-form.component.html',
  styleUrls: ['./create-post-form.component.scss']
})
export class CreatePostFormComponent {
  model: BlogPost;

  constructor(private modalService: NgbModal) {}

  open(content) {
    this.model = new BlogPost('New Post Title');
    this.modalService.open(content, {backdrop: 'static', size:
'lg'});
  }

  submit() {
    console.log(JSON.stringify(this.model));
  }
}
```

5. Finally, we can set up our new template `/src/app/posts/create-post-form.component.html` to include our **Create New Post** button, the modal for our form, and the form and its inputs.

```
<ng-template #modal let-c="close">
  <div class="modal-header">
    <h4 class="modal-title">New Post</h4>
    <button type="button" class="close" aria-label="Close"
(click)="c()">
      <fa [name]="'close'"></fa>
    </button>
  </div>
  <div class="modal-body">
    <form #postForm="ngForm" (ngSubmit)="submit()">
      <div class="form-group">
        <label for="formTitleInput">Title</label>
        <input type="text" class="form-control" id="formTitleInput"
          placeholder="New Blog Post Title" name="title"
          [(ngModel)]=model.title>
      </div>
      <div class="form-group">
        <label for="formBodyInput">Content</label>
        <textarea type="text" class="form-control"
id="formBodyInput"
          rows="6"
          placeholder="New Blog Content" name="content"
          [(ngModel)]=model.content>
        </textarea>
      </div>
    </form>
  </div>
  <div class="modal-footer">
    <button type="button" class="btn btn-secondary"
      (click)="c()">Cancel</button>
    <button type="button" class="btn btn-primary"
      (click)="submit()">Submit</button>
  </div>
</ng-template>

<button (click)="open(modal)" class="btn btn-block btn-primary">
  <fa [name]="'plus'" [fw]=true></fa>Create New Post
</button>
```

6. Now, we can click on the **Create New Post** button to reveal our new Post modal with two input fields that default to empty. When we type values into these inputs and click on **Submit**, we can see that our input data now drives our modal property's state.

How it works...

Angular's `FormsModule` allows us to do a two-way data binding between component properties and our form input values. We must first include `FormsModule` into the imports declaration of our module in order to use this functionality. We must also declare to Angular the form element that will contain our data-bound inputs.

```
<form #formID="ngForm">...</form>
```

Behind the scenes, Angular will transform this form element into an `ngForm` directive, which will facilitate the input data binding for us. The data binding on the input is configured using the `ngModel` directive to bind the value of input to the declared property in the scope of our component. We must also provide a `name` value for the input for `ngForm`.

```
<input name="label" [(ngModel)]="property"></input>
```

Our model itself is a simple class with two optional constructor options for the default title and body content. We can actually see the inverse data-binding direction at play by configuring our model with a different default title.

```
this.model = new BlogPost("My First Blog Post!");
```

When the modal launches now, it will be pre-populated with this title instead. Another interesting byproduct of this component is that the model state is reset everytime we open the component. That means that if you close the modal and reopen it, the title and content would reset to this default value.

```
model: BlogPost;

open(content) {
   this.model = new BlogPost("New Post Title");
   this.modalService.open(content, {backdrop: "static", size: "lg"});
}
```

There's more...

This type of form construction is what is known as **template forms** in Angular and is a very common way to bind user inputs to component properties. However, there is another way of building forms in Angular called **reactive forms**.

Reactive forms aren't inherently better or worse than template forms. They are just a different paradigm to approach form data manipulation using **reactive programming** techniques. Reactive forms may be a good idea for you if you are interested in having tighter control over the data-flow between your component model and your form input's data-binding. Using reactive forms involves creating a low level FormControl that handles changes in value and validity states of an input in a synchronous manner. We will discuss form validation in the next section, but suffice to say that asynchronous changes in the state of inputs can sometimes result in timing issues in your user interface that may be better managed with reactive forms.

 To use reactive forms, you will need to import the ReactiveFormsModule from Angular. You can learn about this module and reactive forms through the following Angular official documentation: https://angular.io/docs/ts/latest/guide/reactive-forms.html

Validating data with Angular form properties

Allowing users to input data into forms also allows users to input mistakes into the data. Validation is the process of checking whether any input data meets our application's expectations. In Angular, we use ngModel and its relationship to our input data-binding to inspect the state of our data and tell us whether it is valid.

Getting Ready

Let's add a title length validation to our blog post's title field. We don't want to allow any title shorter than 5 characters, or longer than 140 (we have to keep it tweet-able). We will also surface this error to our users when the title field is invalid and show them a warning with an explanation of what is wrong.

How to do it...

Let's follow the steps below to to add validations to the input fields of our blog post modal:

1. First, we will need to provide a local property for our ngModel reference on our input. We can also add required, minlength, and maxlength properties to our input for validation:

```
<div class="form-group">
  <label for="formTitleInput" class="form-control-
```

```
label">Title</label>
  <input type="text" class="form-control" id="formTitleInput"
    placeholder="New Blog Post Title" name="title"
    [(ngModel)]="model.title" #title="ngModel" required
    minlength="5" maxlength="140">
</div>
```

2. Having validation errors without any sort of user feedback isn't very helpful, so we'll add some conditional error classes to our input using the `ngClass` directive on our form-group and form-control classes:

```
<div class="form-group" [ngClass]="{'has-danger': title.invalid}">
  <label for="formTitleInput" class="form-control-
label">Title</label>
  <input type="text" class="form-control"
    [ngClass]="{'form-control-danger': title.invalid}"
id="formTitleInput"
    placeholder="New Blog Post Title" name="title"
    [(ngModel)]="model.title" #title="ngModel" required
    minlength="5" maxlength="140">
</div>
```

3. Finally, we should add some instructions for the user, first as a subtle instruction and then as a more severe warning when the title field is invalid. We'll put both of these as new elements underneath our input:

```
<div class="form-group" [ngClass]="{'has-danger': title.invalid}">
  <label for="formTitleInput" class="form-control-
label">Title</label>
  <input type="text" class="form-control"
    [ngClass]="{'form-control-danger': title.invalid}"
id="formTitleInput"
    placeholder="New Blog Post Title" name="title"
    [(ngModel)]="model.title" #title="ngModel" required
    minlength="5" maxlength="140">
  <div [hidden]="title.valid" class="form-control-feedback">
    Sorry, name is required & has a minimum of 5 characters
  </div>
  <small class="form-text text-muted">
    Title must be between 5 & 140 characters
  </small>
</div>
```

4. Now, when the user views the modal, they will see the basic instructions for how to title their blog post. If they attempt to input a value shorter than five characters, they will see an additional error display, and the entire field will be highlighted. If they attempt to input a value longer than 140 characters, the title field will simply not allow any more characters.

How it works...

When we invoked `ngModel` as the means to bind data between our input and our component properties. We also get an additional layer of functionality to look into the state of that data. Angular gives us the following three different input states we can check for:

State	Class if true	Class if false
The input has been touched	ng-touched	ng-untouched
The input has changed	ng-dirty	ng-pristine
The input is valid	ng-valid	ng-invalid

We can directly inspect these states of our input data by getting a local reference to it in our template.

```
#title="ngModel"
```

This local reference maintains a relationship with our `ngModel` form, and we can use it to inspect for validations states to use in other directives. For example, the `hidden` directive, which hides itself when the value it is given is true.

```
[hidden]="title.valid"
```

The `valid` property is managed by `ngModel`, based on the validations added to the input field. There are five of these default validations: `required`, `minlength`, `maxlength`, `pattern`, and `email`. The pattern validator accepts a regular expression that must be matched in order to be considered valid. For example, to make an input that requires a 10-digit phone number might look like this:

```
<input type="tel" class="form-control" name="telephone"
[(ngModel)]="model.body"
        #telephone="ngModel" required maxlength="10" minlength="10"
        pattern="[0-9]{10}">
```

The email validator is new in Angular 4, and simply provides a ready-made pattern validator preconfigured for email addresses.

There's more...

If you carefully inspect the model data, you will note that the model is still updating with an invalid data even if the ngModel's state is invalid. This would cause quite an issue if a user attempted to submit the form, knowing that there were errors on it. Luckily, Angular's ngForm context is also aware of the state of all ngModel instances within it. We can inspect this state in a similar manner to our ngModel states.

```
<div class="modal-body">
  <form #postForm="ngForm" (ngSubmit)="submit()">
    ...
  </form>
</div>
<div class="modal-footer">
  ...
  <button type="button" class="btn btn-primary"
    (click)="submit()" [disabled]="!postForm.form.valid">Submit
  </button>
</div>
```

By looking for the valid property of our form, we can help prevent the user from being able to submit our form before all the inputs within it are valid.

Validating user inputs for content length and required values is one thing, but sometimes, it's important to have validations that can only be checked by submission of the form to a backend server. We will revisit this type of validation in Chapter 5,*REST APIs and Authentication* later in this book.

Creating services for data in Angular

Sharing data across different layers of the application can be a common way to manage application state. In Angular, we can share data state through a provider known as a **service**. Services are often used as **singleton** classes in Angular, but they can also be scoped to specific modules or components of your application, if necessary. You should be using a service whenever you have a shared state of data in your application that is used by more than one part of your application.

The most common way to use a service is to set up a shared data source at the AppModule level of your application. This will ensure that the service is available downstream to all other components and modules in your application.

Getting ready

Let's create a current user service to manage the current user in our application. To start with, we can use this service to do basic things for us, such as giving us the full name of the user when they create new blog posts. Going forward, we could expand this service to also handle user authentication as well, so only authorized users will be able to create blog posts in our application.

Before we get started, we will generate a new current user service using Angular-CLI. We will also need a new class that will act as our user model, so we will generate that as well:

```
ng generate service current-user
ng generate class user
```

How to do it...

Let's perform the following steps to create a new current user service:

1. First, we'll set up our /src/app/users.ts model as a very simple model, with an extra method that will construct a full name for us from the first and last name properties:

```
export class User {
  constructor(
    public firstName: string = "",
    public lastName: string = "",
    public email: string = ""
  ) {}

  getName() {
    return this.firstName + ' ' + this.lastName;
  }
}
```

2. Next, we will set up our current user service at /src/app/current-user.service.ts. It is a very simple service that simply reads and returns our user model:

```
import { Injectable } from '@angular/core';
import {User} from "./user";

@Injectable()
export class CurrentUserService {
  user: User;
```

```
      getUser() {
        return this.user;
      }

      setUser(newUser:User) {
        return this.user = newUser;
      }
    }
```

3. Angular-CLI doesn't automatically provide us with new services we generate, so we will need to manually add our new service to the provider list in `/src/app/app.module.ts`, as follows:

```
...
import { CurrentUserService } from "./current-user.service";
...

@NgModule({
  ...
  providers: [
    { provide: LOCALE_ID, useFactory: getLocaleProvider },
    CurrentUserService
  ],
  ...
})
export class AppModule {
  constructor(private currentUserService: CurrentUserService) { }
}
```

4. Since our current user service doesn't self-initialize itself with a user, we will need to create one in our `AppModule` constructor:

```
...
import { CurrentUserService } from "./current-user.service";
import { User } from "./user";
...
export class AppModule {
  constructor(private currentUserService: CurrentUserService) {
    let user = new
User('George', 'Washington', 'gwashington@history.gov');
    currentUserService.setUser(user);
  }
}
```

5. To check whether our current user service is indeed available in the rest of our application, let's add our current user's name to our `/src/app/posts/create-post-form/create-post-form.component.ts` modal:

```
import {Component, OnInit} from '@angular/core';
import {NgbModal} from '@ng-bootstrap/ng-bootstrap';
import {BlogPost} from "../blog-post";
import {CurrentUserService} from "../../current-user.service";
import {User} from "../../user";
...
export class CreatePostFormComponent implements OnInit {
  model: BlogPost;
  user: User;
  constructor(private modalService: NgbModal, private
currentUserService:
    CurrentUserService) {}
  ...
  ngOnInit() {
    this.user = this.currentUserService.getUser();
  }
}
```

6. Finally, we'll add the current user's full name to our modal's title header. So, now when we launch our modal, we will see **New Post - by George Washington**:

```
<ng-template #modal let-c="close">
  <div class="modal-header">
    <h4 class="modal-title">
      New Post
      <small>- by {{user.getName()}}</small>
    </h4>
    <button type="button" class="close" aria-label="Close"
(click)="c()">
      <fa [name]="'close'"></fa>
    </button>
  </div>
  ...
</ng-template>
```

How it works...

Services are registered as providers at the module level of your application. When we register a service with Angular, it's automatically injected into our module via dependency injection when the service is marked with the @Injectable decorator. After injection, any component or module of our application has access to our shared service through its constructor.

```
constructor(private injectedService: ServiceName) {}
```

By setting a value of the service in our AppModule, we can retrieve the same value from the service in our CreatePostFormComponent. This is because the service is effectively a *singleton* class that is dependency injected into the different parts of our application. This provides a great method of sharing state across the application.

You can also set a service as a provider for a specific component or module. For instance, if I include CurrentUserService in the list of providers for my CreatePostFormComponent, I will actually create a new, totally separate CurrentUserService instance:

```
...
@Component({
  selector: 'app-create-post-form',
  templateUrl: './create-post-form.component.html',
  styleUrls: ['./create-post-form.component.scss'],
  providers: [CurrentUserService]
})
export class CreatePostFormComponent implements OnInit {
  model: BlogPost;
  user: User;
  constructor(private modalService: NgbModal, private currentUserService:
  CurrentUserService) {
    let user = new User('John', 'Adams', 'jadams@history.gov');
    this.currentUserService.setUser(user);
  }
  ...
  ngOnInit() {
    this.user = this.currentUserService.getUser();
  }
}
```

Sometimes, this behavior may be desired for an instance service, such as setting up a web-sockets connection for a component. Usually, this isn't how services are used; make sure that you do not declare your service dependencies more than once if you want to avoid duplicate service instances.

There's more...

Practically speaking, having a user service that just creates an arbitrary user isn't very useful in a real application. Sharing application state across many different parts has a variety of uses, but without a real authentication service, our current user service has a limited prototyping use at this time.

However, we could expand our service to work with an authentication strategy, such as **JSON web token (JWT)**, to be set by an authentication service, such as **angular2-jwt**. Setting up authentication requires a backend service to provide and enforce the authorization layer. We will dive into this subject in depth in Chapter 5, *REST APIs and Authentication*, when we will discuss how to use Expressfor our backend APIs.

Using promises to create asynchronous services in Angular

In the preceding section, our current user data was essentially synchronous, so there wasn't an opportunity to observe any asynchronous behavior between the service and component. Services can be very useful for resolving asynchronous dependencies in Angular through the use of **promises**.

Getting ready

Let's create a `BlogPostsService` to retrieve our blog posts. We will set this service up as an asynchronous promise that will resolve when it has loaded our posts. We will mock the blog post results for now, but will set it up so that we can eventually swap out with the internals to use an API request instead.

Before we get started, we'll once again scaffold out our content using Angular-CLI's generate command. We will need a new `BlogPostsService`, as well as as a new `PostListComponent` to display all our blog posts to the user:

```
ng generate service posts/blog-posts
ng generate component posts/post-list
```

How to do it...

Let's carry out the following steps to create an asynchronous blog post service:

1. First, we will import our new service into our `PostsModule` so that it can be injected into any components in the module that need to use the service. We should also add our routes for our new `PostListComponent` so that it is the default child component in the router-outlet when navigating to `/posts`:

```
...
import { BlogPostsService } from "./blog-posts.service";
import { PostListComponent } from './post-list/post-list.component';

const ROUTES = [{
  path: "posts",
  component: PostsComponent,
  children: [
    {
      path: "",
      component: PostListComponent
    },
    {
      path: ":id",
      component: PostComponent
    }
  ]
}];

@NgModule({
  imports: [
    ...
    RouterModule.forChild(ROUTES)
  ],
  declarations: [
    ...
    PostListComponent
  ],
  providers: [BlogPostsService]
})
export class PostsModule {}
```

2. Let's set up our `BlogPostsService` with a set of mock blog posts. Eventually, this is the data-set that we will retrieve from an external API instead. We will return a promise instead of a static data set since we are expecting this to become asynchronous in the near future:

```
import { Injectable } from '@angular/core';
import {BlogPost} from "./blog-post";

export const POSTS: BlogPost[] = [
  new BlogPost('How data-binding works', "coming soon..."),
  new BlogPost('What\'s the deal with directives?', "coming
soon..."),
  new BlogPost('Cha-cha-ng-ges...', "coming soon..."),
  new BlogPost('Components & services', "coming soon..."),
  new BlogPost('Express.js in a nutshell', "coming soon..."),
  new BlogPost('Hu-MONGO-ous DB', "coming soon..."),
  new BlogPost('Component Style Secrets', "coming soon..."),
  new BlogPost('Angular Deployment', "coming soon..."),
  new BlogPost('Internationalization Tips', "coming soon..."),
];

@Injectable()
export class BlogPostsService {
  getPosts(): Promise<BlogPost[]> {
    return Promise.resolve(POSTS);
  }
}
```

3. Next, we will need to upgrade our `/src/app/posts/blog-post.ts` model to include some more details for us about the author of the post and its published date. We'll use our new `User` model to make authors a reference to a specific user:

```
import {User} from "../user";
export class BlogPost {
  constructor(
    public title: string = "",
    public content: string = "",
    public published: Date = new Date(),
    public author: User = new User("Nicholas", "McClay",
      "nmcclay@nickmcclay.com")
  ) {}
}
```

4. Our new `/src/app/posts/post-list.component.ts` component will use our `BlogPostsService` to display the list of blog posts. Since `getPosts` returns an asynchronous promise, we will need to use the promise chain method to set up an asynchronous callback to get the array of blog posts:

```
import { Component, OnInit } from '@angular/core';
import {BlogPostsService} from "../blog-posts.service";
import {BlogPost} from "../blog-post";

@Component({
  selector: 'app-post-list',
  templateUrl: './post-list.component.html',
  styleUrls: ['./post-list.component.scss']
})
export class PostListComponent implements OnInit {
  posts: BlogPost[];

  constructor(private blogPostsService: BlogPostsService) { }

  ngOnInit() {
    this.blogPostsService.getPosts().then(posts => this.posts =
posts);
  }
}
```

5. Finally, we can create a view that will display all of our posts as a list of items to our users. We can use `ngFor` to loop through our posts and alias the post to the local variable, `post`:

```
<section class="row" *ngFor="let post of posts;">
  <div class="col col-sm-12">
    <div class="card">
      <div class="card-header">
        <small class="pull-left">
          Posted - {{ post.published | date:'shortDate' }}
        </small>
        <small class="pull-right">
          {{post.author.getName()}}
        </small>
      </div>
      <div class="card-block">
        <h4 class="card-title">{{post.title}}</h4>
        <p class="card-text">{{post.content}}</p>
      </div>
    </div>
  </div>
</section>
```

6. We now have a list of blog posts, including default author information and published dates.

How it works...

Promises are simply an abstraction for handling callback functions in asynchronous code, that are easier to read. We declare the result of our service call `getPosts` as a promise to return BlogPost's array . By calling `Promise.resolve`, we are returning the `Promise` object in its asynchronously incomplete state:

```
getPromiseObject(): Promise<Model[]> {
    return Promise.resolve(ASYNC_MODEL_SOURCE);
}
```

When the source of this promise's data is resolved, we will receive a callback through the `then` method in our component:

```
this.service.getPromiseObject().then(object => {/* use object */});
```

The **ES6 arrow function** (or *fat-arrow*), wraps the scope of our promise result so that we can act on it in the same scope of our component that we originally invoked the promise in.

With the `post` variable, we can access the title, content published, and even author name through the included user model reference of the `BlogPost`. The strength of Angular's TypeScript type-system is really on show when you are able to relate models easily to each other with tight type-checking.

There's more...

Promises are an ES2015 standard that exists today largely as a poly-fill within popular frameworks such as Angular. The standard itself has evolved over time, as its adoption and popularity have increased. However, these days, the details of working with promises is fairly stabilized, and up-to-date documentation is available in a number of places that covers how to use promises, agnostic of any specific framework.

You can learn more about the promise standard and how to use it for asynchronous applications from the following official Mozilla JavaScript documentation:
https://developer.mozilla.org/en-US/docs/Web/JavaScript/Referenc e/Global_Objects/Promise

Retrieving API data using HTTP services in Angular

Single page applications such as Angular are often a component in **service-oriented architecture** (**SOA**) that relies on external web services as the data sources for our web application. Introducing networked services into our application also brings with it a lot of asynchronous behaviors that we have to resolve both technically, and in our user interface.

The most common form of interaction between these services and a frontend application is via an HTTP request to a RESTful API. In this section, we will cover how to connect to a RESTful API in Angular and work with that data in our application.

Getting ready

Let's wire our `BlogPostsService` to an actual external API source. We could mock our blog API using Angular's `InMemoryDataService` to create a more realistic prototype data source. However, considering that would only be a marginal improvement on the last section, let's instead use a publicly available blog post API for this section.

First, we'll need to acquire a Blogger API key from *Google's API developer console*. You can acquire a key for free by navigating to `https://console.developers.google.com/apis/api/blogger.googleapis.com/overview` and selecting **Create Project**. You will have to name your new project and accept Google's Terms of Service for using their APIs.

You can visit the following link for more information:

```
https://console.developers.google.com/projectcreate
```

Once you've created your Angular blog project, you can generate a new API key for your project in the **Credentials** section:

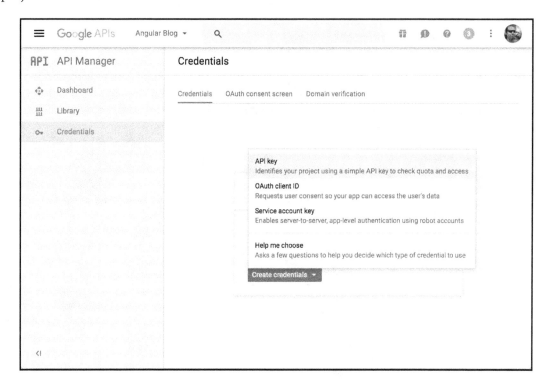

Finally, in the search bar, type and select **Blogger API v3** as the API you want to enable. Click on the **Enable** button, and your Google API key will now be able to request blog data from any public blogger web app. To verify that everything works as expected, try getting the blog posts from the official Angular blog:

```
https://www.googleapis.com/blogger/v3/blogs/7159470537406093899/posts?key={API
KEY}
```

How to do it...

Let's perform the following steps to load real API data into our blog service:

1. First, we will need to provide our Blogger API key to our application's `/src/environments/environment.ts` configuration:

```
export const environment = {
  production: false,
  bloggerAPIKey: 'YOUR UNIQUE API KEY'
};
```

2. Next, we will overhaul our `/src/app/posts/blog-posts.service.ts` service to load our blog post data from an external URL and resolve the response into a promise of BlogPost model result:

```
import { Injectable } from '@angular/core';
import {BlogPost} from './blog-post';
import {Http} from '@angular/http';
import { environment } from '../../environments/environment';
import 'rxjs/add/operator/toPromise';

@Injectable()
export class BlogPostsService {
  private apiHostUrl = 'https://www.googleapis.com';
  private blogUrl = this.apiHostUrl +
    '/blogger/v3/blogs/7159470537406093899';
  private postsUrl = this.blogUrl + '/posts?key=' +
    environment.bloggerAPIKey;
  constructor(private http: Http) {}

  getPosts(): Promise<BlogPost[]> {
    return this.http.get(this.postsUrl)
      .toPromise()
      .then((response) => {
        let posts = response.json().items;
        console.log(posts);
        return posts as BlogPost[]
      })
  }
}
```

3. Finally, we'll update our `/src/app/posts/post-list.component.html` template to use the `displayName` user property instead of our previous custom function. We'll also inline the HTML content of the blog post using the `innerHTML` directive, as follows:

```html
<section class="row" *ngFor="let post of posts; let i = index;">
  <div class="col col-sm-12">
    <div class="card">
      <div class="card-header">
        <small class="pull-left">
          Posted - {{ post.published | date:'shortDate' }}
        </small>
        <small class="pull-right">
          {{post.author.displayName}}
        </small>
      </div>
      <div class="card-block">
        <h4 class="card-title">{{post.title}}</h4>
        <p class="card-text" [innerHTML]=post.content></p>
      </div>
    </div>
  </div>
</section>
```

4. Now, we can visit our `/posts` page and see that our blog posts are full of content from the official Angular blog.

How it works...

The blogger platform provides a set of public APIs available for getting blog post data from any public blog. Each blog has a unique ID that you will need in order to make requests to it, such as 7159470537406093899 for the official Angular Blog. Once you provide this ID, a valid API key, and the appropriate API endpoint, we can receive all the data we need for our BlogPost model.

We have been already providing an asynchronous service to return our `BlogPost` models, so our main change here is the usage of the HTTP library from Angular to make a GET request to our defined Blogger API endpoint. The HTTP library handles any type of HTTP requests our Angular application makes and was imported for us in our `/src/app.module.ts` module.

```
...
import { HttpModule } from '@angular/http';
...
```

```
@NgModule({
  ...
  imports: [
    ...
    HttpModule
  ],
  ...
})
...
```

The ability to convert an HTTP response object into a promise is not a default feature of the HTTP library in Angular. This feature is provided by the **RxJS** `toPromise` operator. We can import this operator because it is packaged as a dependency in our `package.json` file. RxJS is technically an officially endorsed third-party library that Angular uses to create robust asynchronous observers. Angular's HTTP library relies heavily on RxJS for asynchronous network handling, so it's not considered an optional dependency if you are using the HTTP library in Angular.

There's more...

The best practice for API keys like this is to keep them as secret as possible. It's worth noting that any value that is loaded into Angular is discoverable via a careful inspection of the front-end application's source code. Most importantly, **you should never commit any API keys into your project** if it's uploaded to a public repository, such as GitHub. There are many automated bots and scanning tools that automatically look for and exploit accidentally published API keys in a variety of nefarious ways. It is a good practice to keep these keys secret so that they can't be easily abused and blocked for mis-use.

In this recipe, we stored our API key values in Angular application's environment configuration. This can be a convenient way to store these values so that if you needed to point to different hostnames for different environments, you could configure them differently as needed. Just make sure that you tell your source control solution to ignore any changes to these files, so you don't accidentally commit them to source control if you intend to share your source code online. You can do this with `git` using the following command:

```
git update-index --assume-unchanged /src/environments/environment.ts
```

Querying API sources using HTTP services in Angular

Hardcoding parameters into HTTP requests is a valid approach to making simple calls to an API resource, but often we compose requests based on the state of our application. One of the nice things about a large web application framework, such as Angular, is that it has tools such as `URLSearchParams` that make querying APIs with configurable parameters very easy to wire into our application's logic.

Getting ready

Our blog is loading a paginated data-source for its content. This is efficient from an API performance point of view, but our users will not be able to read more than the first page of blog posts. We will need to pass along a `pageToken` parameter to the Blogger API so that we can request the next page of blog posts. Let's add a **More Posts** button to the bottom of our blog post list page that will request the next page of posts, as well as every sequential page after that the user wants to view.

How to do it...

Let's perform the following recipe to add pagination to our blog:

1. First, we will need to refactor our `/src/app/posts/blog-posts.service.ts` service to set query parameters for our HTTP request using the `URLSearchParams` class:

```
import { Injectable } from '@angular/core';
import {BlogPost} from "./blog-post";
import {Http, URLSearchParams} from "@angular/http";
import { environment } from '../../environments/environment';
import 'rxjs/add/operator/toPromise';

@Injectable()
export class BlogPostsService {
  private apiHostUrl = 'https://www.googleapis.com';
  private blogUrl = this.apiHostUrl +
'/blogger/v3/blogs/7159470537406093899';
  private postsUrl = this.blogUrl + '/posts';

  constructor(private http: Http) {}
```

```
getPosts(): Promise<BlogPost[]> {
  let params:URLSearchParams = new URLSearchParams();
  params.set('key', environment.bloggerAPIKey);
  return this.http.get(this.postsUrl, {params: params})
    .toPromise()
    .then((response) => {
      return response.json().items as BlogPost[]
    })
    .catch(this.handleError);
  }
}
```

2. Next, we will upgrade our BlogPostService's `getPosts` method to accept an optional parameter for a `pageToken`. We will also save this token from each sequential request as a property so that we can use it for a new `getNextPage` method, as follows:

```
...
@Injectable()
export class BlogPostsService {
  ...
  private nextPageToken: string;

  constructor(private http: Http) {}

  getNextPage(): Promise<BlogPost[]> {
    return this.getPosts(this.nextPageToken);
  }

  getPosts(pageToken?: string): Promise<BlogPost[]> {
    let params:URLSearchParams = new URLSearchParams();
    params.set('key', environment.bloggerAPIKey);
    if (pageToken) params.set('pageToken', pageToken);

    return this.http.get(this.postsUrl, {params: params})
      .toPromise()
      .then((response) => {
        let postJSON = response.json();
        this.nextPageToken = postJSON.nextPageToken;
        return postJSON.items as BlogPost[]
      })
  }
}
```

3. Now, we will add a new `loadMorePosts` method to `/src/app/posts/post-list.component.ts` component. This method will call our new `getNextPage` method in our `BlogPostsService` and merge our new posts with our preceding set of posts:

```
export class PostListComponent implements OnInit {
    ...
    loadMorePosts() {
        this.blogPostsService.getNextPage().then(posts => {
            this.posts = this.posts.concat(posts);
        });
    }
}
```

4. Finally, we will add a new button to the bottom of our `/src/app/posts/post-list.component.html` template that is wired with a click event to our new `loadMorePosts` method:

```
<button class="btn btn-block btn-outline-primary"
    (click)="loadMorePosts()">More Posts</button>
```

5. When we load our app to our /posts route, we will see the first page of most recent blog posts, with our **More Posts** button at the bottom of it. Clicking on **More Posts** will automatically request the next page of blog posts, appending them to the bottom of our current list of posts. Clicking on **More Posts** again will continue to load the next blog post page in a reverse chronological order until we reach the first blog post.

How it works...

Angular HTTP library has separate methods for each of the main HTTP verbs used for communicating with an API. All of these methods return an `Observable Response` object, and all of them can accept `RequestOptionsArgs`. Request is a special method that allows you to provide a `Request` object instead of a URL string, so it can be any HTTP verb:

Angular HTTP Method	HTTP Verb
`this.http.get(url: string, [RequestOptionsArgs])`	GET
`this.http.post(url: string, [RequestOptionsArgs])`	POST
`this.http.put(url: string, [RequestOptionsArgs])`	PUT
`this.http.delete(url: string, [RequestOptionsArgs])`	DELETE

`this.http.patch(url: string, [RequestOptionsArgs])`	PATCH
`this.http.head(url: string, [RequestOptionsArgs])`	HEAD
`this.http.options(url: string, [RequestOptionsArgs])`	OPTIONS
`this.http.request(url: string|Request, [RequestOptionsArgs])`	any

The `ResponseOptionsArgs` interface provides a common set of options that can be provided to any of the HTTP library's methods. These options can be customized in a number of ways and are merged with the default options for each HTTP method, as follows:

Option	Type	Description
`url`	`url|string`	The URL for the HTTP request
`method`	`string|RequestMethod`	The HTTP method must be a valid verb from the preceding list
`params`	`string|URLSearchParams`	URL parameters appended to the URL
`headers`	`Headers`	Additional HTTP Headers passed along in the HTTP request
`body`	`any`	The HTTP body property passed along in the HTTP request
`withCredentials`	`boolean`	Allows *XMLHttpRequest* cross-site *Access-Control*-based cookies or authorization headers
`responseType`	`ResponseContentType`	Sets the acceptable response types allowed based on the `fetch responseType standard`

There's more...

Adding asynchronous network behaviors to our application can also create unexpected side-effects in our application's behavior. One of the most common issues is dealing with concurrency, or what happens when multiple events are happening simultaneously.

One unexpected behavior of our BlogPosts Service's `getNextPage` method is that it could be clicked many times by a user before the first click finally resolves its HTTP request. These duplicate requests are a waste of network resources and would actually cause a bug, whereby duplicates of blog posts could be appended to our posts list.

A simple solution to this problem is to prevent multiple calls to our service by having our `loadMorePosts` event manage its own asynchronous state:

```
private loadingPosts: boolean = false;
loadMorePosts() {
  if (!this.loadingPosts) {
    this.loadingPosts = true;
    this.blogPostsService.getNextPage().then(posts => {
      this.posts = this.posts.concat(posts);
      this.loadingPosts = false;
    });
  }
}
```

Then, in our template, we simply use the disabled directive to make the button disabled when the `loadingPosts` flag is true:

```
<button class="btn btn-block btn-outline-primary" [disabled]="loadingPosts"
  (click)="loadMorePosts()">More Posts</button>
```

Creating Concurrent API requests in Angular

What if a component in our application requires multiple asynchronous HTTP requests to properly display the correct information? For example, what if we also needed to load the blog's metadata to fetch the total number of blog posts? We can do this using the Promise standard's `all` callback to run all our asynchronous requests simultaneously while still returning a single result when they complete.

Getting ready

Let's add a new API request to our blog service for getting the total count of Angular blog posts. We'll show this count and its link to the official Angular blog in the header of our `PostsList` component template. We can fetch this metadata from the default blog API endpoint:

```
https://www.googleapis.com/blogger/v3/blogs/7159470537406093899?key={API KEY}
```

How to do it...

Let's perform the following steps to add caching to our blog posts:

1. First, let's add a new method to our `/src/app/posts/blog-posts.service.ts` service to request the blog's metadata.

```
...
getBlogMetadata(): Promise<number> {
  let params: URLSearchParams = new URLSearchParams();
  params.set('key', environment.bloggerAPIKey);
  return this.http.get(this.blogUrl, {params: params})
    .toPromise()
    .then((response) => {
      return response.json();
    })
}
...
```

2. Next, let's modify our `/src/app/posts/post-list.component.ts` component to fetch the Angular blog's metadata and the post data that we have been already requesting:

```
...
private metadata: Object;
ngOnInit() {
  let promises:Promise<any>[] = [];
  promises.push(this.blogPostsService.getPosts());
  promises.push(this.blogPostsService.getBlogMetadata());
  Promise.all(promises).then(
    (data) => {
      this.posts = data[0];
      this.metadata = data[1];
    }
  );
}
...
```

3. Finally, let's add a place for these `metadata` values to be displayed in our `/src/app/posts/post-list.component.html` template:

```
<span *ngIf="metadata">
  <h1>
    <a href="{{metadata.url}}">Angular Blog Posts</a>
    <small>({{metadata.posts.totalItems}})</small>
  </h1>
```

```
    <hr>
  </span>
  . . .
```

4. Now, when we load the page, it will fetch the blog's metadata at the same time as
   it requests the blog posts. After both are loaded, it will display our new header
   element at the top of the page with a link that navigates to the official Angular
   blog, and a count of the total number of blog posts.

How it works...

We construct an array of promises, and then push into that array both our `getPosts`
method and our new `getBlogMetadata` method, both of which return promise HTTP
requests to our API. We then register a callback--known as `all`--on this promise array,
which will fire after all the promises in our array have completed. When the promises are
completed, our data will be returned as an array of results, with each index matching the
index of the original promise array. In this case, the first array value will be our blog posts
data, and our second value will be our blog metadata.

This sort of concurrent request management can come in handy if you have multiple pieces
of data that all need to be retrieved before updating your application's state. However,
linking requests together like this can also cause your application's loading performance to
suffer by making your total callback time equal to your longest running API request. It's
important to be aware of these performance trade-offs when deciding whether to handle
multiple requests as one concurrent request or multiple asynchronous ones.

Handling API errors and invalid responses in Angular

An unfortunate side effect of relying on external data sources for an application is that they
can sometimes let us down. Service outages, API changes, and even network latency can all
result in errors in API requests that have to be dealt with in our application. Luckily,
promises have a built-in support for error handling that we can leverage to handle these
situations.

Getting ready

Let's make our blog post metadata request fail by failing to pass its API key. Google's Blogger API requires a valid API key for any request to it. By removing it, we can simulate an error for when our request doesn't go as expected.

How to do it...

Let's perform the following steps to add error handling to our blog post service API:

1. First, let's create an error handler in our `/src/app/posts/blog-post.service.ts` service. Since our error handler is for our promise-based HTTP requests, we will also make this handler return a promise object. This error handler will also parse out an error object from the API that we can inspect for details about our API failure:

```
. . .
private handleError(error: any): Promise<any> {
  let errorJSON = JSON.parse(error._body).error;
  console.error('An error occurred', errorJSON);
  return Promise.reject(errorJSON || error);
}
. . .
```

2. Next, let's add our new error handler function to our `getBlogMetadata` method. We'll also want to set our parameters option in our request to null so that it will not pass our API key through the request to simulate a forbidden error response from the API.

```
. . .
getBlogMetadata(): Promise<number> {
  let params: URLSearchParams = new URLSearchParams();
  params.set('key', environment.bloggerAPIKey);
  return this.http.get(this.blogUrl, {params: null})
    .toPromise()
    .then((response) => {
      return response.json();
    })
    .catch(this.handleError);
}
. . .
```

3. Now, when errors happen in our API requests, we will get an error callback in our promise that we can use the `catch` callback of the promise standard to respond to. We can simply add a new `postLoadError` property to our component to hold any error results we get back. We will also be able to use this object as a flag to tell our template to display an error to the user.

```
. . .
private postLoadError: Object;
ngOnInit() {
  let promises:Promise<any>[] = [];
  promises.push(this.blogPostsService.getPosts());
  promises.push(this.blogPostsService.getBlogMetadata());
  Promise.all(promises).then(
    (data) => {
      this.posts = data[0];
      this.metadata = data[1]
    }
  ).catch(error => { this.postLoadError = error });
}
. . .
```

4. Finally, let's add an error message to our `/src/app/posts/post-list.component.html` template. To make sure that this error is only shown to users when an error occurs, we will put it behind a `ngIf` directive and make sure that the **More Posts** button is only accessible when there is no error.

```
<span *ngIf="postLoadError; else loadMoreBlock">
  <div class="alert alert-warning" role="alert">
    <strong>{{postLoadError.code}} -</strong>
{{postLoadError.message}}
  </div>
</span>
<ng-template #loadMoreBlock>
  <button class="btn btn-block btn-outline-primary"
[disabled]="loadingPosts" (click)="loadMorePosts()">More
Posts</button>
</ng-template>
```

5. Now, when we view the `/posts` page, we will see an error displayed:

403 - *Daily Limit for Unauthenticated Use Exceeded. Continued use requires signup.*

HTTP service optimization through client-side caching

Making lots of API requests in a modern web application is normal, but being more careful about limiting when, and if, we make additional requests can make a big difference in the performance of our application. Caching is a common solution that can be employed to prevent making requests for content we already have loaded in our application.

Getting Ready

Let's provide a caching strategy for our BlogPosts service. We'll build a cache of blog post results when we load them for the first time. After that, if we request the same data, it will simply load from a cache instead of making another HTTP request for the same data.

Before getting started, we will need to make a new class for our cached blog post pages. We'll create a new model for our pages called `PostPage`, using Angular-CLI generate:

```
ng generate class posts/post-page
```

How to do it...

Let's follow the steps below to add client-side caching to our blog post service:

1. First, we'll set up our newly generated `/src/app/posts/post-page.ts` class to match the schema of the blog post results we get from the Blogger API:

```
import {BlogPost} from "./blog-post";

export class PostPage {
  constructor(
    public kind: string,
    public nextPageToken: string,
    public items: BlogPost[],
    public etag: string
  ) {}
}
```

2. Next, we'll add a `pageCache` property to our `/src/app/posts/blog-posts.service.ts` service that will work as our service's local cache of blog pages that we've loaded. We will also need `writePageToCache` and `readPageFromCache` methods to store `PostPage` data inside our cache and get it back out:

```
...
import {PostPage} from "./post-page";

@Injectable()
export class BlogPostsService {
  ...
  private pageCache: { [token: string]: PostPage } = {};

  private writePageToCache(token: string, page: PostPage) {
    this.pageCache[token] = page as PostPage;
  }

  private readPageFromCache(token: string): PostPage {
    if (this.pageCache[token]) {
      return this.pageCache[token];
    }
  }
  ...
}
```

3. Now, we will need to refactor our BlogPosts service to know when it should load content from the API and when to load it from our local cache. We will use the `pageToken` parameter as a key to check whether we have a locally cached version of the page. If we have a cached version of the page, we will resolve the promise with that result instead of making an HTTP request. Otherwise, everything will work as it had before:

```
private requestPosts(params: URLSearchParams = new
URLSearchParams()): Promise<any> {
  params.set('key', environment.bloggerAPIKey);
  return this.http.get(this.postsUrl, {params: params})
    .toPromise()
    .then((response) => {
      return response.json();
    })
}

getPosts(pageToken: string = 'first-page'): Promise<BlogPost[]> {
  let cachedPage = this.readPageFromCache(pageToken);
  if (cachedPage) {
```

```
        this.nextPageToken = cachedPage.nextPageToken;
        return Promise.resolve(cachedPage.items);
    } else {
        let params: URLSearchParams = new URLSearchParams();
        if (pageToken !== 'first-page') params.set('pageToken',
pageToken);
        return this.requestPosts(params).then((JSON) => {
            let posts = JSON.items;
            this.nextPageToken = JSON.nextPageToken;
            this.writePageToCache(pageToken, JSON);
            return posts as BlogPost[]
        }).catch(this.handleError);
    }
}
```

4. When we visit the /posts route of our application the first time, it will request the post data through the API. However, every time after that, it will simply return the post data from the cache without making an unneeded HTTP request.

How it works...

Our page caching strategy relies on us having a reliable key with which we can look up pages before bothering to set up an external HTTP request. To do this for our first page, we changed our optional pageToken parameter to be automatically defined as the first page if there is no value provided. This means that, when the first page result is loaded, it will be automatically added to our cache under this key value. Then, the next time we load this component without providing a key, it will default to the first page and find and reload the cached value instead of making an HTTP request. We can reuse this solution for the same requests that provide defined pageToken parameters, so we get great flexibility from this caching solution.

It's worth noting that the first page value for this pageToken is explicitly not used for the actual HTTP request we make to the blogger API. It's an internal tracking ID that we made up for our own purposes, and passing it to the blogger API would only cause a *404* error for that pageToken.

4
Using Express Web Server

Even if a web application is a **single-page application** (**SPA**), we will very likely need a backend web server to serve the SPA files and secure API services for our SPA. In this chapter, we will examine recipes to set up an **Express.js** web server as the backend for our MEAN stack web application. We will cover how to add routing for our server and serve our Angular application and other common backend needs, such as logging and handling cookies.

In this chapter, we will cover the following recipes:

- Creating a new Express project with express-generator
- Working with routes in Express
- Serving an Angular web application with Express
- Working with headers in Express
- Working with cookies in Express
- Creating Express middleware for routes
- Logging traffic and activity with Morgan
- Running your Express web server with Forever
- Securing your Express web server

Introduction

JavaScript's history in backend web server development can be traced all the way back to NetScape's (now Mozilla's) Rhino engine as early as 1997 as the first attempt to create a robust JavaScript-based web server implementation.

The potential of using the same programming language on both the server and client of an application has fueled many explorations into creating different **isomorphic** programming frameworks, but resulted in only limited success.

Now, 2 decades later, Node.js has brought forth a new wave of JavaScript-based backend frameworks. Finally, we have realized the one-language paradigm for web development with an all JavaScript application stack known as the **MEAN Stack**.

One Node.js framework called Connect introduced a modular, compositional style of web server development inspired by Ruby's Sinatra framework. This framework quickly gained popularity in the emerging Node community and served as a middleware layer to many other Node.js micro-frameworks to form a modern, lightweight, and modular JavaScript web server framework, known as **Express**.

Express stands out from many other popular web server frameworks in that it is very minimal in what it provides as a web server by default. This choice, to behave more like a small, powerful toolkit of web server functionality instead of an opinionated, robust framework, means that Express brings only what a developer needs for their application. This minimizes any wasted overhead of other functions, abstractions, or complexity that may not be needed in your web application.

This also means, however, that Express doesn't provide any extra bells-and-whistles out of the box that aren't explicitly defined by a developer. So, let's explore the Express framework together and configure a web server for our MEAN stack web application that covers some of the most common types of web server needs.

Creating a new Express project with express-generator

Very similar to Angular-CLI, there is a command line tool to quickly create a new Expressproject called `express-generator`. We will use express-generator to create a new Express web server project to serve as the back-end of our blog application. We will eventually integrate this back-end web server with our front-end Angular project to create a full-stack JavaScript web application.

Getting ready

First, we will need to install both Express and `express-generator` with NPM. If you haven't already, you will also need to install the latest version of Node.js and NPM package manager:

```
npm install -g express express-generator
```

How to do it...

Let's perform the following steps to create a new Express web server:

1. First, let's create a new Express project using express-generator's `express` command:

   ```
   express my-express-project
   ```

2. A new Express project will be scaffolded out in the `/my-express-project` directory. After installation, we will need to install our project's dependencies defined in the generated `package.json` file:

   ```
   cd my-express-project
   npm install
   ```

3. Finally, we can start our Express project the same way we started our Angular project using the NPM script's `start` command, as follows:

   ```
   npm start
   ```

4. When you navigate to `http://localhost:3000/` in your web browser, you will see a **Welcome to Express** page displayed.

How it works...

Express as a web server framework relies on a collection of Node.js modules that serve as middleware layers for our web application's backend. Middleware is simply a pattern for defining an asynchronous operation for a given request type. We will explore how to use and create our own middleware in the *Creating Express middleware for routes* section of this chapter.

For now, suffice to say that middleware are simply layers of operations on requests within your application, and Express provides a logical way to set the context and order of those layers in concert with the rest of your application. This compositional web server control is what makes Express such a powerful tool, despite its small size and simplicity.

By default, Express only has a single configuration file called /app.js. At only 53 lines long, this file defines everything Express needs to know to start a web server and provide the basic middleware needed to serve content:

```
var express = require('express');
var path = require('path');
var favicon = require('serve-favicon');
var logger = require('morgan');
var cookieParser = require('cookie-parser');
var bodyParser = require('body-parser');
var sassMiddleware = require('node-sass-middleware');

var index = require('./routes/index');
var users = require('./routes/users');

var app = express();

// view engine setup
app.set('views', path.join(__dirname, 'views'));
app.set('view engine', 'hbs');

// uncomment after placing your favicon in /public
//app.use(favicon(path.join(__dirname, 'public', 'favicon.ico')));
app.use(logger('dev'));
app.use(bodyParser.json());
app.use(bodyParser.urlencoded({ extended: false }));
app.use(cookieParser());
app.use(sassMiddleware({
  src: path.join(__dirname, 'public'),
  dest: path.join(__dirname, 'public'),
  indentedSyntax: true, // true = .sass and false = .scss
  sourceMap: true
}));
app.use(express.static(path.join(__dirname, 'public')));

app.use('/', index);
app.use('/users', users);

// catch 404 and forward to error handler
app.use(function(req, res, next) {
  var err = new Error('Not Found');
  err.status = 404;
```

```
    next(err);
});

// error handler
app.use(function(err, req, res, next) {
    // set locals, only providing error in development
    res.locals.message = err.message;
    res.locals.error = req.app.get('env') === 'development' ? err : {};

    // render the error page
    res.status(err.status || 500);
    res.render('error');
});

module.exports = app;
```

This is a stark contrast when compared to the complicated relationships of components, modules, services, and assorted class constructs of our Angular application. This configuration file is, remarkably, a vanilla Node.js JavaScript file, with no classes, typing, or unnecessary abstractions. It's this minimalistic aspect that makes Express very popular with both beginner and expert developers alike.

You may note that there are two files called `/routes/index.js` and `/routes/users.js` also included in this configuration. These are default routes that are configured to handle the `/index` and `/users` routes of our web server. We will not use either of these routes for our web server configuration and will instead explore how to create our own routes in the next recipe: *Working with routes in Express*.

There's more...

Express can also generate projects that are preconfigured to use different view and style frameworks. We will do virtually all our front-end development inside our Angular application, but it isn't uncommon for certain pages in web applications to be served using traditional server-side page rendering.

If you want to configure your Express application to use the same handlebars, view templates, and Sass styles that we use in our Angular project, simply provide these options as flags to `express-generator`:

```
express my-express-project --css sass --view hbs
```

This will make any frontend template work you do in Express very similar to the work we have done in Angular. It's also worth noting that this configuration defaults to using the `.sass` extension flavor of Sass. If you want to use `.scss`, such as in your Angular recipes, you will need to tweak your `/app.js` file's `sassMiddleware` configuration, as follows:

```
app.use(sassMiddleware({
  src: path.join(__dirname, 'public'),
  dest: path.join(__dirname, 'public'),
  indentedSyntax: false, // true = .sass and false = .scss
  sourceMap: true
}));
```

Working with routes in Express

Building routes for our backend application in Express is key to separating the static content that will be served for our Angular application from our API endpoints, which will respond with JSON data. Routes in Express are actually just layers of middleware defined to work on specific routes of our web server.

Getting ready

Let's create a simple status page for our future API to check whether it's working. We will make two different endpoints; one that simply returns the **API is running** text, and one that will return a JSON representation of our route parameters merged with any query parameters.

How to do it...

Let's perform the following steps to create an API status endpoint for our Express application:

1. First, let's create a new route for all our API requests. Create a new file called `/routes/api.js`; inside this file, we will define two new routes:

```
var express = require('express');
var router = express.Router();

router.get('/', function(req, res, next) {
 res.send('API is running');
});
```

```
router.get('/:param', function(req, res, next) {
  var params = req.params;
  var query = req.query;
  Object.assign(params, query);
  res.json(params);
});

module.exports = router;
```

2. Next, we will update our /app.js configuration to import this new route, and provide it to Express as middleware using the use command:

```
...
var api = require('./routes/api');
var app = express();

...
app.use(express.static(path.join(__dirname, 'public')));
app.use('/api', api);
...
```

3. Finally, we must restart our Express server. Now, when we visit localhost:3000/api, we will see the API is running text; if we visit localhost:3000/api/foobar?search=barfoo, we will see a JSON response:

```
{
  "param":"foobar",
  "search":"barfoo"
}
```

 It's important to note that unlike Angular-CLI, Express doesn't automatically reload changes to its configuration. You will need to manually restart the server every time you make a change to its configuration. In Chapter 9, *Build Systems and Optimizations*, we will cover how to add automatic live-reload to our Express web server.

How it works...

The /routes/api.js file is a simple vanilla Node.js module that we import into our main Express /app.js file using the require command. This file's contents could have been put into the same place as the rest of our server's configuration. However, it's best practice in Express to separate middleware and routing layers from top-level application configuration, for the purpose of better modularization.

Keeping these layers separate in this way also makes it easier to make changes to your web server's routing at the top level, if needed. For instance, we defined all our API routes as relative routes in our `/routes/api.js` file, but **namespaced** them to `/api` in our `app.js` file. If we suddenly had a reason to change this namespace, for instance, due to a conflict with another API in our web application, we could simply change this mapping in the `/app.js` file, and it would update all our relative API routes for us:

```
app.use('/blog/api/', api);
```

This example would now resolve our test page at `localhost:3000/blog/api`. By layering these routing abstractions, you can create a very orderly and clean routing configuration that is still quite flexible.

Our routes are defined as a `GET` request method on a `router` object provided by Express. This `router` object is an interface for a route definition that Express knows how to use as middleware, when it's included. There are many request methods available for use by Express, but they all follow the same basic structure:

```
router.METHOD('/path', function(req, res, next) { /*callback*/ });
```

These HTTP methods are identical to the methods supported by Angular's HTTP library, but also includes a few special options unique to Express. These are the basic HTTP methods that are supported by Express:

• checkout	• mkcol	• put
• copy	• move	• report
• delete	• m-search	• search
• get	• notify	• subscribe
• head	• options	• trace
• lock	• patch	• unlock
• merge	• post	• unsubscribe
• mkactivity	• purge	

There are also a few special non-HTTP method request types that use **wildcard** matching, or route scoping capabilities, to create far-reaching route control capabilities.

Non-HTTP Method Request Types	Description
`router.all`	Matches any request that uses a default HTTP method
`router.use`	Includes middleware on any route defined within this route configuration; its functionality is identical to `app.use`
`router.params`	Matches any request that uses a specific route parameter
`router.route`	Matches a route path and creates a relative scope for defining any other HTTP methods within that path

The callback within the route configuration provides three parameters by default.

```
router.METHOD('/path', function(req, res, next) { /*callback*/ });
```

The first is the `request` object, which can be inspected for information about the incoming request. We use this object to read the route parameters and URL query parameters from the route in our recipe:

```
var params = req.params;
var query = req.query;
```

The second parameter is the `response` object, which handles anything we want to return from this request back to the client. In this recipe we used the `send` and `json` options to return content back to the browser, but Express provides a variety of different response types, depending on the type of response we want to provide:

Response Type	Description
`res.download()`	Prompts a file to be downloaded
`res.end()`	Ends the response process
`res.json()`	Sends a JSON response
`res.jsonp()`	Sends a JSON response with JSONP support
`res.redirect()`	Redirects a request
`res.render()`	Renders a view template
`res.send()`	Sends a response of various types
`res.sendFile()`	Sends a file as an octet stream
`res.sendStatus()`	Sets the response status code and send its string representation as the response body

Finally, the third parameter in our route configuration callback is the `next` method. This method is simply a callback to invoke the next step of our asynchronous middleware for this route. If a piece of middleware is the last step of the process, calling `next()` will simply end the request. We will discuss more on how middleware is used in the *Creating Express middleware for routes* recipe later in this chapter. For now, the most important thing to know is that if a callback returns a response, there is usually no reason for the `next` call, because we are done with processing the request. Calling `next` is usually only necessary when working with middleware that transforms or configures data before returning a response.

There's more...

Some requests provide more than simple URL paths and query parameters to a web server. They might provide a whole request **body** that contains rich content. By default, Express comes preconfigured with a middleware library called **body-parser** that will read both `JSON` and `URL-encoded` form content. The values of this body content will be available on the `request` object as a `body` property:

```
route.post('/post', function (req, res) {
  if (!req.body) return res.sendStatus(400)
  res.send('New Post, ' + req.body.title)
})
```

There are many complexities to consider when working with a large body content in HTTP requests. To learn more about body-parser and how to use it for reading body content in Express, check out the official documentation on GitHub at `https://github.com/expressjs/body-parser`.

Serving an Angular web application with Express

Single-page-applications (SPAs) are generally built into a collection of static assets that can be served through any web server without any need for an application state or routing behind it. However, in production environments, we often will need to provide routing configuration to compose SPA content with application services from our application's backend. Luckily, Express offers excellent built-in support for working with static assets and configuring them within our web server.

Getting ready

Let's set up our Express web server to serve our Angular application's files. We want our Angular app to be served on the same domain as our web server's API, while still being able to access our API endpoints for when we eventually have services for our Angular application to use.

How to do it...

This section covers how to implement static file serving in Express.

1. First, let's build our Angular application by running the Angular-CLI `build` command in our project directory:

   ng build

2. Next, let's create a new `/routes/angular.js` route in our Express project, to configure serving our Angular application. We will need to define a relative route from this project to our Angular project using Node.js's core `path` module:

   ```
   var path = require('path');
   var express = require('express');
   var router = express.Router();
   var angularBuildPath = path.resolve(__dirname,
     '../../my-angular-project/dist');

   router.use(express.static(angularBuildPath));

   router.get('*', (req, res, next) => {
    if (req.url.startsWith('/api')) return next();
    res.sendFile(path.join(angularBuildPath,
     'index.html'));
   });

   module.exports = router;
   ```

3. We will have to update our `/app.js` Express configuration to load our new route configuration. Since it will serve most of the content for our application, we will place it before our API configuration. We'll also remove the `index` and `user` routes that were generated when we originally created the project with express-generator:

   ```
   ...
   var api = require('./routes/api');
   ```

```
      var angular = require('./routes/angular');
      ...
      app.use('/', angular);
      app.use('/api', api);
      ...
```

4. Finally, we no longer need to render views from our Express app, so we should update our error handler in /app.js so that it will instead serve JSON error messages to us when there is an unresolved request:

```
      ...
      app.use('/', angular);
      app.use('/api', api);
      app.use(function(req, res) {
        var error = new Error('Not Found');
        res.status(404).json({
          status: 404,
          message: error.message,
          name: error.name
        });
      });

      module.exports = app;
```

5. Restart your Express server and navigate to localhost:3000/. You will see your Angular application load. Navigating to localhost:3000/api/ will still serve the API status page.

How it works...

Express's concept of middleware allows you to control the order of operations performed on requests. Each piece of middleware is loaded into Express using the app.use command. When requests are received by Express, they are evaluated in a sequential order by the middleware. By defining our Angular route configuration before our API route configuration, we are setting up Express to handle those routes first.

In our /app.js we mounted our Angular route configuration to use the root route of our Express web server, which is simply denoted as '/':

```
      app.use('/', angular);
```

This means that the root/ route will attempt to resolve static file paths on the root to the provided directory. It doesn't matter that the resources in question are in a different directory--as long as our Node.js process can reach them, they will be served through Express.

From within the Angular route configuration, we provide another layer of middleware that defines our static file resources for Angular:

```
router.use(express.static(angularBuildPath));
```

The next route configuration after our static file resource route is a bit more interesting:

```
router.get('*', (req, res, next) => {
 if (req.url.startsWith('/api')) return next();
 res.sendFile(path.join(angularBuildPath, 'index.html'));
});
```

It essentially acts as a wildcard catch-all for all routes that weren't served by our static middleware. The logic behind this is that if a user lands on /posts, we want it to serve the Angular application and have it load to the /posts page. From our Express web server's perspective, that just means to respond to all traffic that isn't a static resource with the Angular application's index.html file. Angular will take care of the /posts routing itself within its own router configuration.

However, we also have an API that we will want to be able to reach, so we have to provide a way to allow API requests through this wildcard route configuration.

Since we only have one API endpoint, the easiest way to allow this is to simply check the URL of the request object and check whether it's a /api request. By checking the URL string with startsWith, we can detect whether a request is indeed an API request. To pass through this request to the next step of middleware, we will return the next() callback. This stops the execution of the current middleware before it returns the index.html file. If you attempt to send a response back multiple times in Express, you will see an exception. You should always be sure to only respond in one place in Express, either returning the next() callback before sending a response or not using the next() callback at all and fulfilling the request response.

The final change here is updating the 404 error handling logic to return a JSON response. It's worth noting that if you generate an error object in Express and pass it along to the next piece of middleware, it will be handled using the default error handler.

Note that the default error handler can get triggered if you call `next()` with an error in your code more than once, even if custom error handling middleware is in place:
`https://expressjs.com/en/guide/error-handling.html`

A simple way to resolve this default configuration is to simply handle the response in the same place you instantiate the error. In this case, we will simply respond with a serialized version of our error object. We must provide a status code for our response as well, or we will render our JSON response with a status code of *200* by default.

There's more...

Being able to serve our Angular content under the same domain as our web server is very useful in a production environment, but if you are doing local development, the cycle of rebuilding and redeploying the web server can be a tedious process.

Luckily, Angular-CLI offers tools to proxy services on other ports in your local environment so that you can continue to work in Angular-CLI while still connecting to an API as though it were served on the same domain. To do this, you must create a proxy configuration in the root of your Angular-CLI project called `/proxy.conf.json`.

```
{
  "/api": {
    "target": "http://localhost:3000",
    "secure": false
  }
}
```

Now, when you start Angular-CLI, simply provide that path with the `proxy-config` option:

```
ng serve --proxy-config proxy.conf.json
```

This configuration will tell Angular-CLI's WebPack build to pass this configuration object to `webpack-dev-server`, the WebPack plugin that provides Angular-CLI's default web server. You can learn more about proxying API services with WebPack by checking out the following official plugin documentation:

`https://webpack.github.io/docs/webpack-dev-server.html#proxy`

Working with headers in Express

HTTP headers are a common way for web servers to share information about their content with other servers and web applications. Reading and writing headers can be necessary for a variety of web server needs, including **cross-origin resource sharing** (**CORS**).

Getting ready

Let's use HTTP headers to enhance our Express route configurations. For our API routes, we will add headers to enable CORS via pre-flight OPTIONS requests. This will come in handy if we ever need to run our API on a different domain than our Angular web application.

For our Angular routes, we will read the incoming Accept-Language header and parse it into a locale property that we can inject into our index.html file's locale definition. This will leverage the existing internationalization work we have for our Angular app and allow us to set the displayed language in our frontend from our backend web server using headers.

To do the parsing and injection of the script tag for our index.html file, we will use a lightweight DOM manipulation library called **Cheerio**. You will need to install Cheerio to your package.json file in order to import it:

```
npm install cheerio --save
```

How to do it...

Let's walk through reading and writing headers in Express to implement CORS headers and language locale preferences using the Accept-Languages header:

1. First, in our /routes/api.js route configuration, we will add a new route for any incoming options requests. We will want to add this route before any other API routes in this configuration file so that it is handled first:

```
...
router.options('*', function (req, res, next) {
  res.header('Access-Control-Allow-Origin', '*');
  res.header('Access-Control-Allow-Methods',
    'GET,PUT,POST,DELETE,PATCH,OPTIONS');
  res.header('Access-Control-Allow-Headers', 'Content-
    Type, Authorization, Content-Length, X-Requested-
```

```
    With');
  res.send(200);
});
...
```

2. Now, when API requests make pre-flight requests to our API, their client will allow them to make normal requests even if the API is on a different domain than the client.

3. Next, we will enhance our `/routes/angular.js` route configuration to load our Angular application's `index.html` file into memory when the web server starts. We will then preparse the contents in *cheerio* so that they are ready for us to use in our wildcard route:

```
var path = require('path');
var fs = require('fs');

var express = require('express');
var router = express.Router();

var cheerio = require('cheerio');
var angularBuildPath = path.resolve(__dirname,
  '../../my-angular-project/dist');
var angularIndexFile = cheerio.load(
  fs.readFileSync(
    path.join(angularBuildPath, 'index.html'),
    {encoding: "utf8"}
  )
);
...
```

4. Now, we will update our wildcard route to parse out the locale property from the incoming `Accept-Language` header and insert it into our `document.locale` script tag in the header of our `index.html`:

```
...
router.use(express.static(angularBuildPath));

router.get('*', (req, res, next) => {
  if (req.url.startsWith('/api')) return next();
  var locale = req.get('Accept-Language').split(',')[0];
  angularIndexFile('head script').html('document.locale = "' +
locale + '"');
  res.contentType('text/html; charset=UTF-8');
  res.send(angularIndexFile.html());
});
```

```
module.exports = router;
```

5. Now, when our Angular app loads, it will automatically inject the locale code from the incoming `Accept-Language` header into the `index.html` page. Angular will pick up this configuration and load the localization file for the locale.

How it works...

Reading headers in Express is done using the `get` or `header` method on a request object. You can also use `req.headers` to find a dictionary of all the headers passed along in the request:

```
req.get('user-agent');
req.header('user-agent');
req.headers['user-agent'];
```

Sending headers in Express is done by providing a header name and value to the `set` or `header` method of a response object. You can also set multiple headers at once by providing a dictionary. Some common response headers, such as `Content-Type`, also have aliases available on the response object:

```
res.set('Content-Type', 'text/html');
res.set({
  'Content-Type': 'text/html',
  'X-Frame-Options': 'SAMEORIGIN'
});
res.header('Content-Type', 'text/html');
res.contentType('text/html');
```

It's important to note that headers can only be set on a response object before it is sent back to the client. Attempting to set headers on a request object after it is returned will result in an exception in your application.

There's more...

In our `/routes/angular.js` route configuration, we will use the `path` and `fs` core libraries of Node.js, as follows:

```
fs.readFileSync(
  path.join(angularBuildPath, 'index.html'),
  {encoding: "utf8"}
)
```

The `fs` module is Node.js's file system library that allows us to read and write from the operating system's file system. Here, we are using it to synchronously read the `index.html` file from our Angular project. We could have just as easily used the asynchronous version of the `fs.readFile` method; however, seeing as it is a one-time operation on server startup, the simplicity of just making this call synchronous works fine.

The `path` module is Node.js's core library for working with file system paths. Windows and Unix operating systems suffer from incompatible file path standards, so this library deals with normalizing operations for consistently building file paths. When you are writing paths to load files, you should always use the path library so that your file paths will work on all node-compatible environments.

You can learn more about the `fs` and `path` modules and their capabilities in the official Node.js documentations:

```
https://nodejs.org/api/fs.html
https://nodejs.org/api/path.html
```

Working with cookies in Express

Cookies are a standard method of storing and retrieving persistent properties and values between a web server and a web application. Express contains tools out of the box to read and write cookies and sign cookies to make sure that they are genuine.

Getting ready

Let's create a user session so that we can track user behaviors as individuals. We'll also make a special route, which when hit will set our session as a special administrator role.

By default, Express installs the `cookie-parser` module, and we will need that for this recipe, but, in case you don't have it installed, you can do so with NPM:

```
npm install cookie-parser --save
```

How to do it...

Let's follow the steps below to create a user session cookie in Express:

1. First, let's create a new route configuration called `routes/session.js`. This will contain all the logic needed to read and write our user session using cookies:

```
var express = require('express');
var router = express.Router();

router.all('*', function(req, res, next) {
  var hasSession = req.cookies.session;

  if (hasSession) {
    req.session = hasSession;
  } else {
    var newSession = Math.floor(Math.random() *
      1000000000);
    res.cookie('session', newSession);
    req.session = newSession;
  }

  console.log('Current Session: ', req.session);
  next();
});

module.exports = router;
```

2. Next, let's add our new session route to our /`app.js` Express configuration. We will want the session to be handled for every route in our application, so let's put it before the Angular and API configurations. We will also add a cookie *secret key* so that we can sign and read secure cookies from Express:

```
...
var cookieParser = require('cookie-parser');

var api = require('./routes/api');
var angular = require('./routes/angular');
var session = require('./routes/session');

...
app.use(cookieParser('my-cookie-secret'));
app.use(session);
app.use('/', angular);
app.use('/api', api);
...
```

3. To ensure that our cookies are genuine, we will update our
   `/routes/session.js` middleware to only use signed cookies, as follows:

```
...
router.all('*', function(req, res, next) {
  var hasSession = req.signedCookies.session;

  if (hasSession) {
    req.session = hasSession;
  } else {
    var newSession = Math.floor(Math.random() * 1000000000);
    res.cookie('session', newSession, { signed:
      true });
    req.session = newSession;
  }

  next();
});
...
```

4. Finally, we can add a secret route to our session middleware that will set our user
   session up as a secret admin role. After setting the admin role, we will redirect it
   to the Angular application:

```
...
router.get('/admin', function(req, res, next) {
  var adminId = 'super_secret_session';
  res.cookie('session', adminId, {signed: true});
  req.session = adminId;
  res.redirect('/');
});

module.exports = router;
```

5. Now, when we visit any route of our application, we will be assigned a session
   cookie. When we visit `localhost:3000/` admin, our session is set to our special
   admin role, and we are redirected to the Angular application.

How it works...

Our Express app can read and write cookies using the cookie-parser middleware. This
module adds new cookie features to both the response and request objects in our Express
routes. By reading from these values, we can determine behaviors of our web server, such
as writing a new session if it doesn't exist yet.

By signing our cookies, we use the secret key we configured in our /app.js cookie-parser configuration. Needless to say, this key should be considered secret and **should not be checked into the source control** for the purpose of keeping your application's cookies protected from forgery. Ultimately, session-based security, such as this secret key, is only as good as your own vigilance and encryption strength. A much safer way to handle this key is to use Node's built-in environment variables:

```
app.use(cookieParser(process.env.cookieSecret));
```

Alternatively, you can look into using an environment configuration file, such as dotenv. For more information, you can go to https://github.com/motdotla/dotenv.

Signed cookies are a simple hash of the cookie's content and your secret key. If either of the value of the cookie or appended hash is changed, Express will consider the cookie invalid and resolve it with the false value.

Enabling signing on cookies is actually only one of many optional parameters that can be provided when writing a cookie:

Property	Type	Description
domain	String	Domain name for the cookie that defaults to the domain name of the app
encode	Function	A synchronous function used for cookie value encoding that defaults to encodeURIComponent
expires	Date	The expiry date of the cookie in GMT; if not specified or set to 0, creates a session cookie
httpOnly	Boolean	Flags the cookie to be accessible only by the web server
maxAge	Number	Convenient option for setting the expiry time relative to the current time in milliseconds
path	String	Path for the cookie; defaults to "/"
secure	Boolean	Marks the cookie to be used with HTTPS only
signed	Boolean	Indicates whether the cookie should be signed
sameSite	Boolean or String	Value of the SameSite Set-Cookie attribute

There's more...

This user session that we've created isn't a real unique identifier; it's a simplified example for the purpose of demonstrating how cookies work in Express. To get a better user session, we should use the popular middleware `express-session` instead of our custom implementation:

```
npm install express-session --save
```

`express-session` provides a lot of additional functionalities to manage user sessions, including using unique identifiers and support for writing user sessions to database stores. It's very easy to convert to using `express-session`, simply replace our custom session import with the `express-session` module instead, and then configure it to use the following secret and configuration options:

```
...
var session = require('express-session');
...
app.use(cookieParser(process.env.cookieSecret));
app.use(session({
  secret: process.env.cookieSecret,
  resave: false,
  saveUninitialized: true
}));
...
```

Creating Express middleware for routes

Middleware can be used for both generic Express route configurations and in very specific use cases. The general pattern of middleware transformations in Express is always consistent, so your main concern is the scope and order of when middleware should be used. Let's explore how to create custom Express middleware that we will use only on specific route contexts.

Getting ready

Let's create a new middleware layer that uses our application's session property to check whether a user is authorized to use a specific API. This middleware will be included on all the secured API routes of our application and will check whether the user session is an admin role, before allowing the request through. This sort of user role middleware is useful to protect sensitive parts of your application from unauthorized users.

How to do it...

Perform the following steps to create custom Express middleware for authentication:

1. First, let's create a new middleware file called /middleware/auth.js. Separating routes from middleware can be useful if you want to import middleware into specific routes configuration. In our middleware, we will define a single function, setRole, to set a role property on our user.session object and save it:

```
module.exports = {
  setRole: function (role) {
    return function (req, res, next) {
      req.session.role = role;
      req.session.save(function (err) {
        next();
      });
    }
  }
};
```

2. Next, we will include our middleware in our Express /app.js configuration. We will make a new route called /admin that we will use to set the role admin. Our middleware should be included after our express-session middleware, but before our Angular or API routes:

```
...
var auth = require('./middleware/auth');
...
app.use(session({
  secret: process.env.cookieSecret,
  resave: false,
  saveUninitialized: true
}));
app.use('/admin', auth.setRole('admin'));
app.use('/', angular);
app.use('/api', api);
...
```

3. Next, we'll enhance our /middleware/auth.js middleware by adding another method to check whether a certain role exists. If it does not exist, then we will serve a *403* forbidden message instead:

```
module.exports = {
  ...
  requireRole: function (role) {
```

```
        return function (req, res, next) {
          if (req.session.role && req.session.role === role) {
            next();
          } else {
            var error = new Error("Requires Admin");
            res.status(403).json({
              status: 403,
              message: error.message,
              name: error.name
            });
          }
        }
      }
    };
```

4. Finally, we will use our new `requireRole` middleware in our API route configuration. We will pass this method in with the value admin after the `/api` route mapping, but before our `api` route configuration:

```
...
var auth = require('./middleware/auth');
...
app.use(session({
  secret: process.env.cookieSecret,
  resave: false,
  saveUninitialized: true
}));
app.use('/admin', auth.setRole('admin'));
app.use('/', angular);
app.use('/api', auth.requireRole('admin'), api);
...
```

5. Attempting to visit `localhost:3000/api` or any API route will now show us a *403* error. However, after we visit `localhost:3000/admin`, we will be able to view the API. If we restart our Express web server, this role will reset to being undefined.

How it works...

Middleware and route configurations are very similar in Express. Route configurations are a specialized type of middleware based around Express' router object. Unlike Express route configurations, custom middleware can take any properties we want. Custom middleware acts as a **closure** that associates your custom parameters with Express's callback to handle the request:

```
middleware: function (params) {
  return function (req, res, next) {
    // this call back use both params & Express objects
  }
}
```

By placing our middleware in Express's `app.use` method, we are wiring our middleware to a route in the same manner as our Express route configurations. We can also take this a step farther by nesting our middleware in an existing `app.use` configuration:

```
app.use('/', first, second, third, function(req, res, next) { /* fourth */
});
```

This scopes our middleware to the same path as the route configuration, and all middleware are processed in a sequential order. Express's `next()` callback will invoke the next middleware's callback as it is defined for a given route. This is an incredibly powerful way to deterministically transform and work with request data in our routes, but it is can also be easy to make mistakes with. Failing to call `next()` or calling `next()` too early can result in routes failing to return values or returning invalid ones. It's important to consider what asynchronous operations your middleware is handling and place your callback to proceed in the proper place.

Our session object provided by express-session has some predefined methods for persisting data on the session object. The `save` function is an asynchronous callback that will write the current state of the session object to a data store for us:

```
req.session.save(function (err) {
  next();
});
```

By default, this store is a simple in-memory data store, but there are easy ways to make this store persistent.

There's more...

Persisting your user sessions makes sure that session-related behaviors, such as user authentication, don't need to be unnecessarily repeated by the user every time your web server restarts. Adding a store is done by importing the store adapter, configuring it for your application, and providing it to express-session using the `store` property:

```
var MyExpressSessionStore = require('my-express-session-
store')(storeConfig);

app.use(session({
```

```
    secret: process.env.cookieSecret,
    resave: false,
    saveUninitialized: true,
    store: MyExpressSessionStore
}));
```

 There are dozens of available express-session-compatible store adapters available on npm. You can see a comprehensive list of available options, including MySQL, PostgreSQL, Redis, CouchDB, and MongoDB at `https://github.com/expressjs/session#compatible-session-stores`.

Logging traffic and activity with Morgan

A real web server can have a multitude of requests and events happening over a given day. Logging your traffic and activity on your web server can be very important for diagnosing unexpected behaviors after they happen. Express comes ready with a logging module called **Morgan** that provides all that you will need to record events in your application and even save those events to a log file.

Getting Ready

Let's enhance our logging for our normal HTTP traffic. We'll use a predefined logging format provided by Morgan to record visits to our Angular application and our API usage. We'll also create a custom event log to track admin authorized requests so that we know which admin sessions are responsible for certain requests. We can write these events to a log file as well, so we can check the history of events even between server restarts.

How to do it...

Let's follow the steps below to add custom Morgan logging to our Express web server:

1. First, we'll simply change our default Morgan logger configuration to use the `short` predefined logging style. We do that by simply changing the string value provided to our `logger` instance:

    ```
    ...
    var logger = require('morgan');
    ...
    app.use(logger('short'));
    ```

. . .

2. After restarting our server, we will note that our log messages now have a new format in our console when we visit pages of our application.

3. Next, let's add some custom logging to our `/middleware/auth.js` middleware. We will create a new logger method, in that it will configure a custom log token and return a custom log format. This logger will record the admin's role and session ID as well as the HTTP method, status, and URL:

```
module.exports = {

  logger: function(morgan) {
    morgan.token('role', function (req, res) {
      return req.session.role;
    });
    morgan.token('session', function (req, res) {
      return req.session.id;
    });

    return morgan(':role :session - :method :status :url');
  },
  . . .
```

4. To use our custom `auth.logger`, we will update our `/app.js` Express configuration to include it on our `/api` routes. We will provide our custom logger method with the already imported Morgan `logger` instance:

```
. . .
var auth = require('./middleware/auth');
. . .
app.use('/api', auth.requireRole('admin'), auth.logger(logger),
api);
. . .
```

5. Finally, let's update our custom logger to write out our logs to a log file, instead of just reporting them in our console. We will import Node's `fs` and `path` core libraries to help us create a new file path, and write any logged messages as a stream to our new `/admin.log` file:

```
var fs = require('fs');
var path = require('path');

module.exports = {

  logger: function(morgan, filename) {
    if (!filename) filename = 'admin.log';
```

```
    var adminLogFilePath = path.resolve(__dirname, "../",
filename);
    var adminLogStream = fs.createWriteStream(adminLogFilePath,
{flags: 'a'});

    morgan.token('role', function (req, res) {
      return req.session.role;
    });
    morgan.token('session', function (req, res) {
      return req.session.id;
    });

    return morgan(':role :session - :method :status :url', {stream:
adminLogStream});
  },
```

6. After restarting our Express web server, we will not see any messages logged to
   our console when we visit the authenticated /api routes. However, if we inspect
   the newly created /admin.log file in our project, we will see that all these events
   are instead being written to this log file. Even if we restart the web server, this log
   will persist and continue to have new log entries appended to it.

How it works...

Morgan provides the default logging capability for our Express server. By simply providing
the already included Morgan logger instance a predefined format string, we will update the
logging format of all our incoming web server requests. There are quite a few different
predefined logging formats, each with different content and information density based on
your logging needs.

Format	Structure and example
combined	:remote-addr - :remote-user [:date[clf]] ":method :url HTTP/:http-version" :status :res[content-length] ":referrer" ":user-agent" ::1 - - [20/May/2017:00:40:20 +0000] "GET /posts HTTP/1.1" 200 - "-" "Mozilla/5.0 (Macintosh; Intel Mac OS X 10_12_4) AppleWebKit/537.36 (KHTML, like Gecko) Chrome/58.0.3029.110 Safari/537.36"
common	:remote-addr - :remote-user [:date[clf]] ":method :url HTTP/:http-version" :status :res[content-length] ::1 - - [20/May/2017:00:41:09 +0000] "GET /posts HTTP/1.1" 200 -

dev	:method :url :status :response-time ms - :res[content-length] `GET /posts 200 7.802 ms - 665`
short	:remote-addr :remote-user :method :url HTTP/:http-version :status :res[content-length] - :response-time ms `::1 - GET /posts HTTP/1.1 200 - - 19.831 ms`
tiny	:method :url :status :res[content-length] - :response-time ms `GET /posts 200 - - 1.708 ms`

Morgan can also be used to create custom log messages using log tokens. There are many default log tokens provided by Morgan that can be used to compose a custom log message.

Token	Description
:url	The HTTP request URL
:date[format]	The current date and time in UTC; it can be formatted in several ways: • web (default) - `Tue, 10 Oct 2000 13:55:36 GMT` • clf - `"10/Oct/2000:13:55:36 +0000"` • iso - `2000-10-10T13:55:36.000Z`
:http-version	The HTTP version of the request
:method	The HTTP method/verb of the request
:status	The HTTP status code of the request
:referrer	The Referrer HTTP header of the request
:remote-addr	The remote ip/connection address of the HTTP request
:remote-user	The HTTP request providing basic authentication credentials
:req[header]	The value for the specified HTTP header for the request
:res[header]	The value for the specified HTTP header in the response
:response-time[digits]	The time in milliseconds it takes Express to respond to the request; you may optionally provide the number of digits of precision
:user-agent	The contents of the User-Agent header of the request

These tokens can be composed along with custom token definitions in Morgan to create a custom log entry:

```
morgan(':role :session - :method :status :url');
```

Our `/middleware/auth.js` middleware logger method generates log file messages that look like this:

```
admin UcW2vmdJUmdZRxDTTHxJgznDbo0DbDGT - GET 304 /api
admin UcW2vmdJUmdZRxDTTHxJgznDbo0DbDGT - GET 200 /api/foobar
admin UcW2vmdJUmdZRxDTTHxJgznDbo0DbDGT - GET 200 /api/barfoo
admin UcW2vmdJUmdZRxDTTHxJgznDbo0DbDGT - GET 200 /api/testing
admin UcW2vmdJUmdZRxDTTHxJgznDbo0DbDGT - GET 404 /api/testing/invalid
admin wykpBVhRUAaVfgmZ84uHcowL8c8hNff9 - GET 304 /api
admin wykpBVhRUAaVfgmZ84uHcowL8c8hNff9 - GET 304 /api/foobar
```

You can see that by putting the URL token last, we can get very readable and clean log messages that can show us exactly what individual admin sessions are doing and what pages of our application they are visiting. This sort of log file can later be mined for useful insights concerning application debugging, security, and user usage and behavior.

There's more...

The official Express web server documentation explains why using `console.log` or `console.error` isn't recommended for real-production web applications.

> *In general, there are two reasons for logging from your app--for debugging and for logging app activity (essentially, everything else). Using* `console.log()` *or* `console.error()` *to print log messages to the terminal is a common practice in development. However, these functions are synchronous when the destination is a terminal or a file, so they are not suitable for production, unless you pipe the output to another program. For more information, visit the following link:*
> `https://expressjs.com/en/advanced/best-practice-performance.html`

Running your Express web server with Forever

Web servers, like any application, can crash unexpectedly. When developing an application, these failures are easily fixed with a quick restart. However, when running a production web application, you will need the server to quickly and easily restart itself so that your application stays functioning for as many users as possible. One common solution to this problem is using a process manager to watch your application's process and restart it if it stops.

There are many different process managers available for Express, but we will use **Forever**, a simple but very popular process manager.

Getting ready

Let's set up the Forever process manager to watch our Express server. We'll create a simple kill route to test a failure case of our web server. We will have Forever automatically restart our web server if it stops running, and log any errors to a log file so that we can inspect them, if needed.

To use Forever, you will need to install the node module first. Depending on the permissions of your environment, you may need to install forever with `sudo` for it to be able to restart processes on your behalf:

```
npm install forever -g
sudo npm install forever -g
```

How to do it...

Let's follow these steps to implement Forever as a process manager for our Express application:

1. First, let's make a test route that will cause an artificial crash in our application:

```
app.get('/crash', function(req, res) {
  this.does.not.exist;
  process.exit(1);
});
```

2. To run our application with Forever, we will stop our web server and restart it using Forever instead. We will also provide configuration details for how and where error logs should be saved:

```
FOREVER_ROOT=~/my-express-project forever start -e error.log
./bin/www
```

3. Now, when we visit the /crash route of our web application, our process will be terminated, but Forever will automatically restart it for us. We can test this by visiting /posts afterward to verify that the server has been restarted for us automatically.

4. When we want to stop our Forever process, we can use stopall to kill all watched processes:

```
forever stopall
```

How it works...

By default, simple exceptions in requests won't cause Express's session to crash, but it is still possible for a process to be killed unexpectedly by the operating system itself, application configuration issues, or other unrecoverable exceptions. Forever provides a fault tolerant **daemon** to watch for disruptions to your application's process.

Forever is most likely to be used in a production environment that is responsible for keeping your application running all the time. To configure Forever to run on different operating system environments, you should consult the specific installation guide for your OS. For more information, you can visit the following link:

```
ttps://github.com/foreverjs/forever/wiki/Detailed-installation
```

There's more...

The process module is an Node.js core library for managing processes that is always implicitly loaded in a Node.js application because the application is itself a process. This global process contains many useful properties and methods, such as process.env for accessing environment variables, process.argv for accessing process arguments for the Node application, and process.exit() for closing the current Node.js application process.

There are many more useful things you can do with the process module; you can learn more about its capabilities in the following official Node.js documentation:

```
https://nodejs.org/api/process.html
```

Securing your Express web server

Deploying a web application to the internet also exposes your application to threats of hacking. Whether an attacker is attempting to access private user information, abusing your service, or otherwise exploiting a vulnerability for personal gain, it's important that you know how to protect yourself from the most common types of threats to minimize your application's risk.

Getting ready

The most important thing that you can do to help secure your Express web application for users is to encrypt content between your user's browser and your web server. Generating an SSL certificate to enable secure HTTPS communications between your Express web server and frontend application can be easy, but the nature generating and utilizing SSL certificates can be quite complicated.

For the sake of simplicity, we will generate a simple, unprotected, generic SSL certificate using `openssl` to help explain how to configure a SSL certificate in Express:

```
openssl req -x509 -newkey rsa:4096 -keyout key.pem -out cert.pem -nodes
```

When you have correctly run the `openssl` certificate generator, you will have `/key.pem` and `/cert.pem` files in the root of your `my-express-project`.

These will work for learning purposes, but for a production website, you will need to acquire a certificate that is verifiable with a **certificate authority,** or else your browser will show the certificate as invalid to your users. SSL certificates can be purchased from many certificate authorities online for very little money, and are sometimes bundled with web hosting packages from various web hosting providers.

To further secure our application, we will also install an npm module called **Helmet**:

```
npm install --save helmet
```

Helmet is a collection of Express middleware designed to prevent abuse of various HTTP header configurations to exploit an Express application.

How to do it...

Let's follow these steps to secure our Express application:

1. First, we will create a custom Express launch script configured to use HTTPS. You can duplicate the /bin/www launch script and make the following adjustments to it:

```
#!/usr/bin/env node

var https = require('https');
var fs = require('fs');
var app = require('../app');
var debug = require('debug')('my-express-project:server');

var port = normalizePort(process.env.PORT || '3000');
app.set('port', port);

var options = {
  key  : fs.readFileSync('key.pem'),
  cert : fs.readFileSync('cert.pem')
};

var server = https.createServer(options, app);
server.listen(port);
server.on('error', onError);
server.on('listening', onListening);

function normalizePort(val) {
  var port = parseInt(val, 10);

  if (isNaN(port)) {
    // named pipe
    return val;
  }

  if (port >= 0) {
    // port number
    return port;
  }

  return false;
}

function onError(error) {
  if (error.syscall !== 'listen') {
    throw error;
```

```
    }

    var bind = typeof port === 'string'
      ? 'Pipe ' + port
      : 'Port ' + port;

    // handle specific listen errors with friendly messages
    switch (error.code) {
      case 'EACCES':
        console.error(bind + ' requires elevated privileges');
        process.exit(1);
        break;
      case 'EADDRINUSE':
        console.error(bind + ' is already in use');
        process.exit(1);
        break;
      default:
        throw error;
    }
  }

  function onListening() {
    var addr = server.address();
    var bind = typeof addr === 'string'
      ? 'pipe ' + addr
      : 'port ' + addr.port;
    debug('Listening on ' + bind);
  }
```

2. The easiest way to use this new Express launch script is to create a new npm script alias in our /package.json file:

```
{
  "name": "my-express-project",
  "version": "0.0.0",
  "private": true,
  "scripts": {
    "start": "node ./bin/www",
    "start:https": "node ./bin/https"
  },
  ...
```

3. Now, we can launch an HTTPS secured version of our web server by running npm run start:https. To view our web server, we will need to visit https://localhost:3000. You will see an error from your browser if you are using your self-generated certificate. You can bypass this error by choosing to proceed past the error notification in your browser.

4. Next, we should include `helmet` into our `/app.js` Express configuration as middleware:

```
...
var helmet = require('helmet');
...
app.use(helmet());
...
...
```

5. Finally, we will need to update our express-session configuration to further secure our cookies. We can do this by adding a non-default name property to our session, as well as a cookie configuration object:

```
app.use(session({
  secret: process.env.cookieSecret,
  resave: false,
  saveUninitialized: true,
  name: 'project-session',
  cookie: {
    secure: true,
    httpOnly: true,
    domain: 'localhost',
    expires: new Date(Date.now() + 60 * 60 * 1000)
  }
}));
```

6. Now, when we run our application, if our cookies aren't sent via an encrypted HTTPS request, or they come from a domain other than the localhost, they will be considered invalid.

How it works...

Express's HTTP server capability is built on top of the Node.js HTTP core library. This library provides the bare-bones HTTP server capability, but is generally considered too low-level for your average developer's web-server needs. Node also provides an HTTPS core library that does the same for HTTPS web servers. The main difference is the need to provide an SSL key and certificate to the HTTPS web server. We can load these items as a configuration object in our Express launcher script in `/bin/www`.

This client-to-server encryption paired with the header protection provided by Helmet and the session security layer by express-session have greatly improved our web application's security. However, security is much more a developer mentality than a single set of solutions. You will need to consider the security implications of the enhancements you make to your application as you expand the capabilities and interfaces to your web application.

5
REST APIs and Authentication

This chapter focuses on connecting our Angular front-end with our back-end Express API. We will explore how to create and configure **RESTful APIs** and provide **JSON API-**compliant services within an Express web server. We will also explore how to secure those APIs with user authentication using **JSON Web Tokens (JWT)**.

- Building REST APIs with Express
- Configuring JSON API in Express
- Creating a user authentication API in Express
- Building a login page with Angular
- Using JWT authentication with Express and Angular

Introduction

The rapid pace of change in the JavaScript ecosystem has fueled the evolution of backend services to embrace **service-oriented architecture (SOA)** as the means of providing resources for client web applications. These backend services commonly rely on **Representational State Transfer (REST)** APIs as the primary means of communication with a front-end application.

The use of JSON to communicate via REST APIs is one that also unlocks a new layer of compatibility for a full stack JavaScript web application, such as the MEAN stack. Without a need to serialize and deserialize between different object representations, manipulating and working with API requests and responses can be done using pure JavaScript. Express, in its minimalist spirit, doesn't offer us a default approach for how to implement a REST API. However, it has all the parts we will need to easily build our own, using HTTP methods, middleware and JSON. In this chapter, we will discuss how to harness these fundamental building blocks in Express to build our own modern REST API implementation.

Implementing a service, such as a REST API, is often accompanied by the need to control access to the resource, usually by enforcing user ownership or permissions in some way. This authentication and authorization aspect is one of the most important roles for a web server to provide, because ultimately the front-end application can easily be compromised in terms of its data security. Only through our back-end services can we verify and validate user requests in a secure manner. Up until now, we've only worked on the periphery of the web server authorization lifecycle. In this chapter, we will finally close the loop on implementing a full user authentication and authorization system, including user login and session management.

By the end of this chapter, we will finally have all the parts needed to provide secure, robust REST API endpoints in your MEAN Stack web application.

Building REST APIs with Express

Let's create a simple REST API to replace our `/posts` route for our blog. The API will be able perform the **create, read, update,** and **delete** (CRUD) actions for blog posts for our web application. Express middleware can serve as a helpful, reusable layer for configuring our RESTful API to make sure that any future APIs we want to implement can be done in a consistent way.

Getting ready

When working on developing REST APIs, it can be very useful to have a client other than your application handy for hitting API endpoints and checking the format of the response data. You can use anything from a simple `curl` command to a wide variety of REST API client applications to do this. For those unfamiliar with such tools, I recommend that you download the free REST API client, **Postman**. It is available for virtually every operating system and provides a simple and robust toolkit for testing your REST APIs.

You can download the Postman API client from its official website:

```
https://www.getpostman.com/
```

We will also need to install the `resource-router-middleware` and `enforce-content-type` modules with NPM into our project's `package.json` file:

```
npm install --save resource-router-middleware enforce-content-type
```

These modules will help us make an easy job of mapping our resources to RESTful JSON standards in Express. For the purpose of locally testing our REST APIs, you may also want to temporarily remove our `auth middleware` from your `/app.js` API route configuration:

```
...
app.use('/api', api);
...
```

If you visit the `localhost:3000/api` API endpoint, get a status code of *200*, and the response text `API is running`, then you should have an easy time moving forward with this recipe.

How to do it...

Perform the following steps to implement a REST API to create, read, update, and delete blog posts for our web application:

1. First, we will create a new `/middleware/rest.js` middleware to serve as a factory class of sorts to consistently format our REST API resources. Our middleware will take a resource ID and a store object, which will contain our content. We'll then define a helper function called find, which we will use to look up content in our store using an ID. Our `resource-router-middleware` configuration will contain all the callbacks for our REST API HTTP methods:

```
var resource = require('resource-router-middleware');

module.exports = function(resourceId, store) {

  var find = function(id, callback) {
    var itemPosition = store.map(function(item) {
      return item.id;
    }).indexOf(id);
    var item = store[itemPosition];
    if (item) {
      callback(item, itemPosition);
```

```
      } else {
        callback(false);
      }
    };

    return resource({
      id : resourceId,

      load : function(req, id, callback) {
        find(id, function(item) {
          if (!item) {
            callback('Not found');
          } else {
            callback(null, item);
          }
        });
      }
    });
  };
```

2. Let's start by defining our `read` routes. The list callback will trigger for all GET requests, whereas our read callback will trigger on requests with specified IDs. The read callback loads its item from the request object, which, in turn, gets it from our `load` callback:

```
...
module.exports = function(resourceId, store) {
  ...
  return resource({
    ...
    list: function(req, res) {
      res.json(store);
    },

    read: function(req, res) {
      res.json(req[resourceId]);
    }
  });
}
```

3. The `create` route callback will activate on POST requests with JSON body values. It will read its content from the request body, which should be parsed into a JSON object, thanks to the `body-parser` module. We then just generate a simple ID before pushing it back into the store and sending it back to the client:

```
...
module.exports = function(resourceId, store) {
```

```
...
return resource({
  ...
  create : function(req, res) {
    var item = req.body;
    item.id = store.length.toString(36);
    store.push(item);
    res.json(item);
  }
});
}
```

4. For PUT requests, we will use the `update` callback to find the item in the store and merge its state with the JSON body that is passed along to us. If we fail to find any item with this ID, we will send a *404* error instead:

```
...
module.exports = function(resourceId, store) {
  ...
  return resource({
    ...
    update : function(req, res) {
      var id = req.params[resourceId];
      find(id, function(item, i) {
        if (item) {
          Object.assign(store[i], req.body);
          store[i].id = id;
          return res.status(204).send('Accepted');
        } else {
          res.status(404).send('Not found');
        }
      });
    }
  });
}
```

5. For our `delete` requests, we have the `delete` callback. This method is very similar to our `update` callback, but it will extract an item from our store instead:

```
...
module.exports = function(resourceId, store) {
  ...
  return resource({
    ...
    delete : function(req, res) {
      var id = req.params[resourceId];
      var itemPosition = find(id, function(item, i) {
```

```
        if (item) {
          store.splice(i, 1);
          return res.status(200).send('Deleted');
        } else {
          res.status(404).send('Not found');
        }
      });
    }
  });
}
```

6. Now that we have our middleware set up, we can set up a route to use it. Let's create a new `/routes/api/posts.js` route configuration to use our new REST API middleware for blog posts. We'll provide it with the resource ID posts and a mock store of a single default post:

```
var restFactory = require('../../middleware/rest');

var posts = [{
  id: "123",
  title: string = "My First Blog Post",
  content: string = "... brevity is the soul of wit...",
  published: new Date(),
  author: {
    firstName: "Nicholas",
    lastName: "McClay",
    email: "nmcclay@nickmcclay.com"
  }
}];

module.exports = restFactory('posts', posts);
```

7. We now need to add our new post's route configuration to our `/routes/api.js` route configuration. We'll simply include it as a new sub-route configuration under the namespace `/posts`:

```
...
var posts = require('./api/posts');
...
router.get('/', function (req, res, next) {
  res.send('API is running');
});
router.use('/posts', posts);
...
```

8. Finally, we want to make sure that our `req.body` properties are indeed valid JSON requests, so let's add the enforce-content-type middleware to our `/routes/api.js` route configuration to enforce `application/json` Content-Type headers for all incoming API requests. Otherwise, these requests will receive a **415 unsupported media** type error.

```
...
var enforceContentType = require('enforce-content-type');

router.use(enforceContentType({
  type: 'application/json'
}));
...
```

9. We can now restart our express server, and we will have a fully functional REST API in our Express application that can create, read, update, and delete blog posts.

How it works...

Express provides default HTTP methods that we can listen to for specific routes. When implementing a full REST API, we want to start thinking about our API endpoints as **resources** that we perform operations upon using specific HTTP methods. The most common operations are to **create**, **read**, **update**, and **delete** (CRUD) resources. These operations are associated with the POST, GET, PUT, and DELETE HTTP methods in a RESTful API. Besides the HTTP method, there is also a significance in whether the resource is specifically identified or generic. For instance, GET /api/posts will return all blog posts, whereas GET /api/posts/123 will only return a blog post with the ID *123*.

The following is a table that lists all the routes in our application, their associated HTTP methods, and what they actually do:

Route	HTTP method/verb	Description
/api/posts	GET	Get all blog posts
/api/posts	POST	Create a new blog post
/api/posts/:post_id	GET	Get a specific blog post using its ID
/api/posts/:post_id	PUT	Update a specific blog post using its ID
/api/posts/:post_id	DELETE	Delete a specific blog post using its ID

Strictly speaking, there is no reason we couldn't have a DELETE /api/posts route that would delete all posts, or a /api/posts/:post_id that creates a new post with the specified ID. However, conventionally, these operations would be too powerful or have undesired complications or ambiguities about their behavior.

Our implementation of the /middleware/rest.js middleware is a factory of sorts to provide a consistent implementation for our REST APIs. Our factory has several mappings provided by resource-router-middleware that automatically trigger certain methods based on the incoming HTTP method and resource identifiers.

Method	Description
load	A callback to load a given resource by an ID of this type from the store
list	A callback to read the list of all resources of this type
read	A callback to read a specific resource of this type
create	A callback to create a new resource of this type and save it to the store
update	A callback to update a specific resource of this type and save it to the store
delete	A callback to delete a specific resource of this type and remove it from the store

Ultimately, our /middleware/rest.js middleware serves as an abstraction between the route configuration, which provides the resource configuration and store, and the API structure, which should be the same for all our REST APIs. It's potentially possible that we may eventually want more granular control over our routes. For example, what if the DELETE route was only allowed if the current user was the author of the blog post? However, as we will see in practice in later sections in this chapter, it's possible to accommodate these customizations without losing the value of having a factory that sets up consistent default behavior for us.

This abstraction between the route configuration and REST API implementation isn't the only way to build a REST API in Express. However, as we will see in Chapter 8,*Relationships*, it provides a logical foundation for which future enhancements--such as JSON API serialization and, eventually, database persistence with MongoDB--is much easier and more consistent to implement.

 If you are getting unexpected **415** errors on a given route, you should check whether you are sending the correct Content-Type header. The enforce-content-type middleware will only allow application/json through the API, as it is defined in this recipe. If you are having trouble with that, try explicitly defining your request's headers in your REST API utility.

There's more...

There is one more HTTP method supported by `resource-router-middleware`, that is, the PATCH method. There is quite a lot of confusion about when to use PATCH versus when to use PUT in your REST API. Let's review the official *RFC 5789* specification for PATCH and PUT to better understand the difference:

> *The difference between the* PUT *and* PATCH *requests is reflected in the way the server processes the enclosed entity to modify the resource identified by the Request-URI. In a* PUT *request, the enclosed entity is considered to be a modified version of the resource stored on the origin server, and the client is requesting that the stored version be replaced. With* PATCH, *however, the enclosed entity contains a set of instructions describing how a resource currently residing on the origin server should be modified to produce a new version. For more information, you can visit the following link:*
> `https://tools.ietf.org/html/rfc5789`

In short, PUT is considered a *replacement* for a resource, whereas PATCH is considered a *modification* to an existing resource. Technically speaking, our REST API is not in compliance with this definition. This is a surprisingly common situation for web application APIs; PUT as an update operation is often treated as PATCH, although they are technically very different ways to change the state of a resource. To correct this, we will need to introduce a new modify method to our middleware and change our update method:

```
...
update : function(req, res) {
  var id = req.params[resourceId];
  find(id, function(item, i) {
    if (item) {
      store.splice(i, 1);
      item.id = id;
      store.push(item);
      return res.status(204).send('Replaced');
    } else {
      res.status(404).send('Not found');
    }
  });
},

modify : function(req, res) {
  var id = req.params[resourceId];
  find(id, function(item, i) {
    if (item) {
      Object.assign(store[i], req.body);
      return res.status(204).send('Accepted');
    } else {
```

```
            res.status(404).send('Not found');
      }
    });
  },
  ...
```

This change allows our `PUT` update calls to completely rewrite an object, except for its ID, whereas `PATCH` will only modify an existing resource, including being able to update the ID. Ultimately, we end up with a slightly more flexible REST API, but the choice of how you implement your API's logic is up to you.

 You can learn more about resource-router-middleware, including some nice ES6 friendly options, from the official GitHub repository: `https://github.com/developit/resource-router-middleware`

Configuring JSON API in Express

Although JSON's compact size and object-friendly nature make it very easy to use as a data representation, it's lack of a standard model schema can prompt some developers to invent different ways for representing complex model relationships in their data. As the complexities of JSON modeling between front-end applications and back-end web servers has increased, so has the advantages of standardizing JSON model representations in web applications. The JSON API standard is a popular way of standardizing how applications interact with REST API response models of API resources. The JSON API format is simply a schema for structuring your model so that its relationships with other data can be represented in a consistent, normalized manner.

Consider our blog post model schema. We have an array of blog posts items, each with an ID as well as a number of attributes, including a nested relationship for the author of the blog post, which has its own ID and attributes:

```
[{
    id: "123",
    title: "My First Blog Post",
    content: "... brevity is the soul of wit...",
    published "2017-05-28T03:08:25.837Z"
    author: {
      id: "1",
      firstName: "Nicholas",
      lastName: "McClay",
      email: "nmcclay@nickmcclay.com"
    }
```

```
}];
```

This format is very simple, but what if we had many blog posts and only a few authors? How do we know whether an author is its own model or whether it's simply a nested property of a blog post? How can we distinguish between the ID for blog and the ID for author? These are all problems that JSON API is well suited to handle for us. Let's take a look at how the same model schema would be represented in JSON API:

```
{
    "data": [{
        "type": "posts",
        "id": "123",
        "attributes": {
            "title": "My First Blog Post",
            "content": "... brevity is the soul of wit...",
            "published": "2017-05-28T03:08:25.837Z"
        },
        "relationships": {
            "author": {
                "data": {
                    "type": "authors",
                    "id": "1"
                }
            }
        }
    }],
    "included": [
        {
            "type": "authors",
            "id": "1",
            "attributes": {
                "first-name": "Nicholas",
                "last-name": "McClay",
                "email": "nmcclay@nickmcclay.com"
            }
        }
    ]
}
```

Clearly, JSON API is a much larger representation of the same REST API response, but it does provide some very powerful advantages in return. One of the first advantages is the clear distinction between identifiers of models and the attributes. The `type` and `id` properties inside the `data` property of our request are used to identify exactly what this model is, independently from its attributes. Conversely, the `attributes` property only contains the attribute properties for our primary model.

Perhaps the most obvious change is that there is a reference for relationships in our data now. Our author model is now mapped to an `included` property in the root of our request. This means that, if there were multiple posts in our response that all referenced the same author, we would see only this single model definition for that author. This is very useful for shared services in Angular because it means that we can now cache models independently by type. With a simple model lookup by type and ID, we could easily make a service that could join together data relationships on the front-end without the need to request the entire state of an object and its descendent relationships every time. This can result in improvements to application performance when using cached data and better project maintainability through model normalization.

One final advantage is that data now has a consistent schema when it is transmitted by the REST API. This standard means that we can rely on our data being formatted consistently across our application, which can pay dividends for code reuse and simplicity in our project. All of these advantages combined show the value of standardizing to using JSON API for our REST API.

Let's spend some time digging into how to convert our REST API over to using JSON API.

Getting ready

To use the JSON API in our Express application, we will need to install a dependency for a JSON API serialization library called `jsonapi-serializer`:

```
npm install jsonapi-serializer --save
```

We will use this library for both serialization and deserialization of our data into and out of the JSON API format.

How to do it...

Let's perform the following recipe to upgrade our `/middleware/rest.js` middleware to support JSON API serialization and deserialization:

1. First, we will define serialization and deserialization configurations for `jsonapi-serializer` in our `/routes/api/posts.js` route configuration. We will provide these configuration options as new optional properties for our `/middleware/rest.js` middleware:

   ```
   var restFactory = require('../../middleware/rest');
   ```

```
var posts = [{
  id: "123",
  title: string = "My First Blog Post",
  content: string = "... brevity is the soul of wit...",
  published: new Date(),
  author: {
    id: "1",
    firstName: "Nicholas",
    lastName: "McClay",
    email: "nmcclay@nickmcclay.com"
  }
}];

var serialize = {
  attributes: ['title', 'content', 'published', 'author'],
  author: {
    ref: function (user, author) {
      return author.id;
    },
    attributes: ['firstName', 'lastName', 'email']
  }
};

var deserialize = {
  keyForAttribute: 'dash-case'
};

module.exports = restFactory('posts', posts, serialize,
deserialize);
```

2. In our /middleware/rest.js middleware, we will import the Serializer and
   Deserializer classes from jsonapi-serializer and create their new
   instances using our new configuration options:

```
var resource = require('resource-router-middleware');
var JSONAPISerializer = require('jsonapi-serializer').Serializer;
var JSONAPIDeserializer = require('jsonapi-
serializer').Deserializer;

module.exports = function(resourceId, store, serialize,
deserialize) {
  var serializer = new JSONAPISerializer(resourceId, serialize);
  var deserializer = new JSONAPIDeserializer(deserialize);
  ...
}
```

3. Now, we can upgrade our individual REST API routes to use the `serializer` and `deserializer` instances. We'll start with the `list` and `read` methods, which will now serialize our result data before sending it as a JSON response:

```
...
module.exports = function(resourceId, store, serialize,
deserialize) {
  ...
  return resource({
    ...
    list : function(req, res) {
      res.json(serializer.serialize(store));
    },

    read : function(req, res) {
      res.json(serializer.serialize(req[resourceId]));
    },
    ...
  });
};
```

4. Next, we will update our create method to use the deserialize option to transform the JSON API POST request body into our normal store model representation. Note the `then` callback. This is because deserialization is asynchronously handled as a promise:

```
...
module.exports = function(resourceId, store, serialize,
deserialize) {
  ...
  return resource({
    ...
    create : function(req, res) {
      deserializer.deserialize(req.body).then(function(item) {
        item.id = store.length.toString(36);
        store.push(item);
        res.json(item);
      });
    },
    ...
  });
};
```

5. Finally, we'll upgrade our `update` and `modify` methods to use the same asynchronous promise callback for deserialization:

```
...
module.exports = function(resourceId, store, serialize,
deserialize) {
  ...
  return resource({
    ...
    update : function(req, res) {
      var id = req.params[resourceId];
      find(id, function(item, i) {
        if(item) {
          deserializer.deserialize(req.body).then(function(itemReplace) {
            store.splice(i, 1);
            itemReplace.id = id;
            store.push(itemReplace);
            return res.status(204).send('Replaced');
          });
        } else {
          res.status(404).send('Not found');
        }
      });
    },

    modify: function(req, res) {
      var id = req.params[resourceId];
      find(id, function(item, i) {
        if(item) {
          deserializer.deserialize(req.body).then(function(itemUpdates) {
            Object.assign(store[i], itemUpdates);
            return res.status(204).send('Accepted');
          });
        } else {
          res.status(404).send('Not found');
        }
      });
    },
    ...
  });
};
```

6. Now, our REST API will read and write JSON API. We don't need to update the delete method because it never needed to parse any model data to function correctly.

How it works...

Our upgrades to our `/middleware/rest.js` middleware include providing configuration options to serialize our JSON API responses. There are many options available in the JSON API specification, including ways to provide metadata and links to resources and related data. There are also several configuration options to format purposes, such as how attributes should serialized. These properties can be applied to any level of hierarchy in the model, including relationships:

Serializer property	Description
id	The identifier for the resource; defaults to `id`
attributes	The array of attributes for the resource
included	Checks whether relationships are included as a compound document; defaults to `true`
ref	Defines object as a relationship; values can be string for the field that will contain the relationship identifier or a function that returns the value
topLevelLinks	Describes a JSON API `link` property for the top-level of the resource; its values can be a string or a function
relationshipLinks	Describes a JSON API `link` property for a relationship of a resource; its values can be a string or a function
dataLinks	Describes a JSON API `link` property for the current level of the resource; its values can be a string or function
dataMeta	Describes a JSON API `meta` property for a resource; its values can be any value or a function
relationshipMeta	Describes a JSON API `meta` property for a relationship of a resource; its values can be any value or a function
ignoreRelationshipData	Flag to not include the `data` key inside the relationship; it defaults to `false`
keyForAttribute	Defines how to format attribute properties on serialization; its valid values are `dash-case`(default), `lisp-case`, `spinal-case`, `kebab-case`, `underscore_case`, `snake_case`, `camelCase`, `CamelCase`, or a custom function
nullIfMissing	Defines whether attributes should be displayed as `null` if they are missing; it defaults to `false`

pluralizeType	Flag to define whether the type must be pluralized or not; it defaults to `true`
typeForAttribute	A callback to define the resource type before serialization. If it does not return a value, it will be ignored and the default type will be used. The `pluralizeType` flag is ignored if this is used
meta	Describes any other nonstandard JSON API properties to be provided on the serialized response; it can be any value or a function
transform	A callback to transform a resource before serialization

Deserialization has its own configuration for how JSON API requests should be translated back into a resource's model. The only option we are using in this recipe is `keyForAttribute` to demonstrate how it is used to configure deserialization options.

Deserialization property	Description
keyForAttribute	Defines how to format attribute properties upon deserialization; its valid values are `dash-case`(default), `lisp-case`, `spinal-case`, `kebab-case`, `underscore_case`, `snake_case`, `camelCase`, `CamelCase`, or a custom function
valueForRelationship	A callback to define how to format a resource's relationship on deserialization. This callback can return a promise to be resolved using the deserializer's built-in promise handler
transform	A callback to transform a resource after deserialization

If you are seeing any odd behavior in your POST or PUT routes, you may want to check the format of the data property you are sending. JSON API supports both individual and multiple datasets, based on whether they are provided as a JSON object or an array. Providing the data property as an object will result in the individual item being returned from the deserializer, as follows:

```
{
  "data": {
    "type": "posts",
    "id": "123",
    ...
  }
}
```

Providing an array of items to the data property, even if there is only a single item in it, will result in an array being returned from the deserializer, as follows:

```
{
  "data": [{
    "type": "posts",
    "id": "123",
    ...
  }]
}
```

For our REST APIs, we are only creating and updating individual items, so we should make sure that we only send our API data in this individual format.

There's more...

Another useful feature built into `jsonapi-serializer` is providing JSON API-formatted error responses. We can update our `/middleware/rest.js` middleware to provide *404* error responses in our REST API that are formatted consistently to align with the JSON API specification.

```
...
var JSONAPIError = require('jsonapi-serializer').Error;

module.exports = function(resourceId, store, serialize, deserialize) {
  var serializer = new JSONAPISerializer(resourceId, serialize);
  var deserializer = new JSONAPIDeserializer(deserialize);

  var error = function(status, title, description) {
    return new JSONAPIError({
      status: status,
      title: title,
      detail: description
    });
  };

  var fileNotFound = function() {
    return error(404, 'Not found', 'Resource does not exist.');
  };
  ...
  return resource({
    id : resourceId,

    load : function(req, id, callback) {
      find(id, function(item) {
        if (!item) {
```

```
            callback(fileNotFound());
        } else {
            callback(null, item);
        }
    });
},
...
```

Now, when our API can't find a resource, it will return the JSON API error response:

```
{
  "errors": [{
    "status": 404,
    "title": "Not found",
    "detail": "Resource does not exist."
  }]
}
```

There are many ways to customize these error responses, including providing error status codes, source pointers to identify request body format issues, and much more.

You can learn more about error handling in JSON API specification and jsonapi-serializer by checking out their official documentations, respectively:
http://jsonapi.org/
https://github.com/SeyZ/jsonapi-serializer

Creating a user authentication API in Express

Handling authentication through username and password is the most common way of securing a back-end API. This requires a front-end form to input and submit user credentials and a back-end API to validate and authorize a user session. Let's explore how to implement the back-end part of this relationship first, in Express.

Getting ready

We will continue to use Postman or another API client other than our web browser for this recipe. If you haven't set up an API client from our previous recipes, you will need one that can POST a JSON body with a content-type of `application/json` to our API. Any other content-type header will result in a **415 unsupported media** response.

How to do it...

Let's create a `/api/login` route to authenticate a user using a username and password:

1. First, we will need to create a new `/routes/api/login.js` route configuration to manage our API authentication. This route configuration will be similar to our `/routes/api/posts.js` route configuration that contains both a `users` store of user records and a JSON API serializer configuration:

```
var express = require('express');
var router = express.Router();
var JSONAPISerializer = require('jsonapi-serializer').Serializer;

var users = [{
  id: "1",
  firstName: "Nicholas",
  lastName: "McClay",
  email: "nmcclay@nickmcclay.com",
  password: 'Secret',
  role: 'admin'
}];

var serializer = new JSONAPISerializer('users', {
  attributes: ['firstName', 'lastName', 'email'],
});

module.exports = router;
```

2. We will create a login middleware that will check a username and password provided in a request body against the available user records in our `users` store. We will also create a POST route to pass in our middleware and write an authenticated user to our Express request `session`:

```
...
var login = function(req, res, next) {
  var username = req.body.username;
  var password = req.body.password;
```

```
      if (username && password) {
        var match = users.find(function(user) {
          return user.email === username && user.password === password;
        });
        if (match) {
          req.session.user = match;
          next();
        }
      }
    };

    router.post('/', login, function(req, res, next) {
      req.session.save(function (err) {
        var user = req.session.user;
        res.json(serializer.serialize(user));
      });
    });
    ...
```

3. We will also need to add error handling to our login middleware. We will return JSON API error objects if we don't receive the correct parameters or receive invalid credentials:

```
    var express = require('express');
    var router = express.Router();
    var JSONAPISerializer = require('jsonapi-serializer').Serializer;
    var JSONAPIError = require('jsonapi-serializer').Error;
    ...
    var authError = function(message) {
      return new JSONAPIError({
        status: 401,
        title: 'Invalid Authorization Parameters',
        detail: message
      });
    };

    var login = function(req, res, next) {
      var username = req.body.username;
      var password = req.body.password;

      if (username && password) {
        var match = users.find(function(user) {
          return user.email === username && user.password === password;
        });
        if (match) {
          req.session.user = match;
          next();
        } else {
```

```
        res.status(401).json(authError('Invalid username or password
for user authentication.'));
    }
  } else {
    res.status(401).json(authError('Must provide username or
password for user authentication.'));
  }
};
...
```

4. Next, we will need to update our /middleware/auth.js middleware's requireRole method to use our new session.user property. We will inspect the user session for a valid role property and either allow or reject the request accordingly:

```
...
var JSONAPIError = require('jsonapi-serializer').Error;

module.exports = {
  ..
  requireRole: function (role) {
    return function (req, res, next) {
      var user = req.session.user;
      if (user && user.role && user.role === role) {
        next();
      } else {
        res.status(403).json(new JSONAPIError({
          status: 403,
          title: 'Requires ' + role + ' Role',
          detail: 'You do not have the correct authorization to
access this resource.'
        }));
      }
    }
  }
};
```

5. Finally, let's include our new login route configuration into our /routes/api.js route configuration. To test it, we can also experiment by requiring a user to be authorized as an admin to visit our /posts route:

```
...
var auth = require('../middleware/auth');
var login = require('./api/login');
...
router.get('/', function (req, res, next) {
  res.send('API is running');
```

```
    });

    router.use('/login', login);
    router.use('/posts', auth.requireRole('admin'), posts);
    ...
```

6. Now, when we attempt to visit /api/posts with our API client, we will get an **403 unauthorized** error. After sending a POST request with the body:

```
{"username": "nmcclay@nickmcclay.com", "password": "Secret"}
```

to our /api/login API end-point, we will get back our serialized user record. After this we will be able to successfully access /api/posts until we restart our web server, which will invalidate all our sessions again.

How it works...

Our /routes/api/login.js route configuration is a stand-alone route configuration and middleware for handling authentication in our Express application. Usually, middleware that is reusable would be put in our /middleware directory for easy access. However, in this case, our login middleware is only used by this same route configuration, so it is simpler to just include it in the same place as the route configuration.

Our user store is a simple JSON array of user objects that contain all the fields that define a user, including a password and role field. It's worth noting that storing a password as plain text such as this is not a good idea in a production environment. In a real application, we would want to hash this password using a library, such as crypto, to make sure that we were not storing plain text passwords in our store. However, for the simplicity of this recipe we have omitted that part of the process.

We use the JSON API serializer to serve as a filter between our back-end representation of our user record and our front-end representation. Details such as password and role are not relevant to the front-end application, so we simply omit them from the serializer attribute definition, and they are not included in the data sent back to the front-end. This sort of conservative object attribute serialization is a good idea to prevent unintentional leaking of secure information to the front-end of our application.

There's more...

One of the trickiest parts of working with authentication is debugging it. Luckily, we can update our custom Morgan logging middleware to log details about authenticated user behaviors.

By adding custom tokens for `email` and `role`, we can automatically log these properties on authenticated requests. We can also provide the callback `skip` to Morgan to tell it to only log requests that have an authorized user session on them already:

```
var fs = require('fs');
var path = require('path');
var JSONAPIError = require('jsonapi-serializer').Error;

module.exports = {
  logger: function(morgan, filename) {
    if (!filename) filename = 'admin.log';
    var adminLogFilePath = path.resolve(__dirname, "../",
filename);
    var adminLogStream = fs.createWriteStream(adminLogFilePath,
{flags: 'a'});

    morgan.token('role', function (req, res) {
      return req.session.user.role;
    });

    morgan.token('email', function (req, res) {
      return req.session.user.email;
    });

    return morgan(':email :role - :method :status :url', {
      skip: function (req, res) {
        return !req.session.user
      },
      stream: adminLogStream
    });
  },
  ...
};
```

Then, we can add this custom logger after our normal application logger in our `/app.js` Express configuration:

```
app.use(logger('short'));
app.use(auth.logger(logger));
```

Now, our user's behavior in our application will be logged to an `/admin.log` file in our application and will include their username and role for each request.

Building a login page with Angular

The login page represents the other half of our user authentication feature. We have an authentication API; now, we need the form to input our username and password. We will build this user interface in Angular using `ngForm`, our current user service, and Observables for data-binding.

Getting ready

Before we can get started building our login page, we will need to generate a new login component to handle our login user experience. We will create that using Angular CLI's `generate` command:

```
ng generate component login
```

We will also need to remove any previous usage of the `CurrentUserService` service from our application. The main place we had used it previously was the `/src/app/app.module.ts` module. Ensure that the main module class export does not do anything with the `CurrentUserService` provider by removing its reference from the module.

We will also need to make sure that our `LoginComponent` component and `Angular2FontawesomeModule` are loaded in our application module properly.

Finally, we will need to make sure that our login route is accessible via the routing configuration under `/login`:

```
...
import { Angular2FontawesomeModule } from 'angular2-
fontawesome/angular2-fontawesome';
import { LoginComponent } from './login/login.component';

const ROUTES = [
  {
    path: "",
    redirectTo: "/posts",
    pathMatch: 'full'
  },
  {
```

```
      path: "login",
      component: LoginComponent,
    },
    {
      path: 'authors',
      component: AuthorsComponent,
    },
    {
      path: "**",
      component: PageNotFoundComponent
    }
];

...
@NgModule({
 declarations: [
 AppComponent,
 AuthorsComponent,
 PageNotFoundComponent,
 AuthorComponent,
 LoginComponent
 ],
 imports: [
 BrowserModule,
 BrowserAnimationsModule,
 FormsModule,
 HttpModule,
 RouterModule.forRoot(ROUTES),
 PostsModule,
 NgbModule.forRoot(),
 Angular2FontawesomeModule
 ],
 providers: [{ provide: LOCALE_ID, useFactory: getLocaleProvider },
CurrentUserService],
 bootstrap: [AppComponent]
})
export class AppModule {}
```

With these changes, we should be good to get started with implementing our login user interface.

How to do it...

In this recipe, we will build a login user interface for authenticating with our back-end and create an Observable for monitoring the user authentication:

1. First, we will need to update our `/src/app/current-user.service.ts`
   service to connect to our back-end API. We will do this by adding two new
   methods for `login` and `logout` . We will send an HTTP Post request to our API's
   `/api/login` route using Angular's HTTP module. We will also change our
   relationship with our user object to be managed through an Observable provided
   by our `getUser` method. This will allow different parts of our app to listen to
   data-binding changes on our user object in real time:

```typescript
import { Injectable } from '@angular/core';
import {User} from "./user";
import {Http, Headers, Response, RequestOptions} from
'@angular/http';
import {Observable, BehaviorSubject} from "rxjs";
import 'rxjs/add/operator/toPromise';

@Injectable()
export class CurrentUserService {
  private user = new BehaviorSubject<User>(new User());

  constructor(private http: Http) {}

  getUser(): Observable<User> {
    return this.user.asObservable();
  }

  setUser(newUser:User) {
    this.user.next(newUser);
  }

  login(username: string, password: string): Promise<User> {
    let headers = new Headers({ 'Content-Type': 'application/json'
});
    let options = new RequestOptions({ headers: headers });
    return this.http.post('/api/login', JSON.stringify({ username:
username, password: password }), options)
      .toPromise()
      .then((response) => {
        let userJSON = response.json().data.attributes;
        let user = new User(userJSON.firstName, userJSON.lastName,
userJSON.email);
        this.setUser(user);
        return user
      }).catch((error) => {
        let errorJSON = JSON.parse(error._body).errors[0];
        return Promise.reject(errorJSON);
      })
  }
```

```
logout(): void {
  this.setUser(new User());
}
```

2. Next, we will need to build out our `/src/app/login/login.component.ts` component to call our new login method. The method resolves a promise as either successful or not. If it fails, it will parse the failure to present an error message to the user instead. We will also use the asynchronous state of our login operation to show a loading spinner to the user while the request is pending:

```typescript
import { Component, OnInit } from '@angular/core';
import { Router } from '@angular/router';
import { CurrentUserService } from "../current-user.service";

@Component({
  selector: 'app-login',
  templateUrl: './login.component.html',
  styleUrls: ['./login.component.scss']
})
export class LoginComponent implements OnInit {
  model:any = {};
  loading:boolean = false;
  error:string = '';

  constructor(private router: Router,
              private currentUser: CurrentUserService) {
  }

  ngOnInit() {
    this.currentUser.logout();
  }

  login() {
    this.loading = true;
    this.currentUser.login(this.model.username,
this.model.password)
      .then((user) => {
        this.router.navigate(['/']);
      }).catch((error) => {
        this.error = error.detail;
        this.loading = false;
      });
  }
}
```

3. Finally, we will need to build out the actual login form in `/src/app/login/login.component.html`. This form will submit our login's username and password to our `login.component.ts` component's `login` method using ngForm's `ngSubmit` directive. We'll also include conditional logic for showing warning messages for empty fields and showing our loading spinner and error messages if they exist in our component:

```html
<div class="row justify-content-md-center">
  <div class="col col-md-6 ">
    <div class="card">
      <div class="card-body">
        <h2 class="card-title">Login</h2>
        <div *ngIf="error" class="alert alert-danger">{{error}}</div>
        <form name="form" (ngSubmit)="f.form.valid && login()"
        #f="ngForm" novalidate>
        <div class="form-group" [ngClass]="{ 'has-danger':
        f.submitted && !username.valid }">
            <label for="username">Username</label>
            <input type="text" class="form-control" name="username"
            [(ngModel)]="model.username" #username="ngModel"
            required />
            <div *ngIf="f.submitted && !username.valid" class="form-
            control-feedback">Username is required</div>
        </div>
        <div class="form-group" [ngClass]="{ 'has-danger':
         f.submitted && !password.valid }">
          <label for="password">Password</label>
          <input type="password" class="form-control"
           name="password" [(ngModel)]="model.password"
           #password="ngModel" required />
        <div *ngIf="f.submitted && !password.valid" class="form-
         control-feedback">Password is required</div>
        </div>
        <hr>
        <div class="form-group">
          <button [disabled]="loading" class="btn btn-primary btn-
          block">Login</button>
          <fa *ngIf="loading" [name]="'spinner'"
[spin]=true></fa>
        </div>
      </form>
    </div>
  </div>
</div>
```

```
        </div>
```

4. Now, we can successfully log in to our application by visiting `/login` and entering our credential's username--`nmcclay@nickmcclay.com`--and password--`Secret`. Upon successful login, we will be redirected to our `/posts` home page; upon failure, we will see an error displayed in the login form.

How it works...

Our `CurrentUserService` tracks the current user's status through a special type of Observable provided by RXJS called a `BehaviorSubject`. `BehaviorSubject` has the special property of always having a subject associated with it that changes over time. When our current user status changes, any other part of our application that gets its value from our `getUser` method as an Observable will be updated via data binding. By default, we set this object to an empty `User` instance, but, upon login we pass in a new value using the `next` method of `BehaviorSubject`. Using observables for these sorts of long-running dynamic values can be useful for getting the asynchronous state of an object whenever it changes.

Our login method uses Angular's HTTP module to make a *POST* request to our backend authentication API. One key detail of this API is that it manually sets the `Content-Type` header to `application/json` using `RequestOptions`. Failing to do this would result in a **415 Unsupported Media** response from our API. The request itself is fulfilled as a promise, with which we provide a `catch` callback, which will be called if the request fails for any reason. Failures in our `CurrentUserService` will bubble up to the catch defined within our login component. It's important to define failure cases in our web application when depending on external APIs to ensure a good user experience even if data isn't in the expected format.

The login form itself is very similar to other `ngForms` that we covered in `Chapter 3`,*Working with Data*. Its main difference is the need to disable the form itself, when data is processing, to prevent multiple authentication requests from running at the same time. To do this, we will need to bind disabled state and the revealing of our spinner to a simple `loading` flag that will enable itself when our login request begins and remove itself after a result is returned. For the spinner, we will simply use our font-awesome directive from `angular2Fontawsome` and provide it the `[spin]=true` property so that it applies a simple CSS spinning animation to itself.

There's more...

Having a login screen is useful, but most web applications allow users to see their authenticated status and logout as well. Let's explore how we can leverage our new current user Observable to dynamically hide and show a login button in our main application's navigation.

First, we will need a way to check whether a user is authenticated or not. For the sake of simplicity, let's just add a new method to our `/src/app/user.ts` model to tell us for itself. We'll simply make the existence of an email address good enough to make the user authenticated:

```
export class User {
  constructor(
    public firstName: string = "",
    public lastName: string = "",
    public email: string = ""
  ) {}

  getName() {
    return this.firstName + ' ' + this.lastName;
  }

  isAuthenticated() {
    return this.email !== "";
  }
}
```

We can simply return our observable as a property from our service. The best practice when working with Observables in Angular is to append a `$` symbol to denote that the property is an Observable. Here, we will make our user property to be `currentUser$`. We can also set up a logout method to allow a user to sign out after they are authenticated:

```
import { Component } from '@angular/core';
import {CurrentUserService} from "./current-user.service";
import {User} from "./user";
import {Observable} from "rxjs/Observable";

@Component({
  selector: 'app-root',
  templateUrl: './app.component.html',
  styleUrls: ['./app.component.scss']
})
export class AppComponent {
  public authorCount: Number = 3;
  public currentUser$: Observable<User>;
```

```
    constructor(private currentUserService: CurrentUserService) {
      this.currentUser$ = currentUserService.getUser();
    }

    logout(): void {
      this.currentUserService.logout();
    }
}
```

Hooking up our Observable `currentUser$` property to our application navigation is done easily through the use of the `async` pipe helper. Async knows how to watch for changes on properties so that when data changes in the Observable, it is also automatically updated in our template. We can simply use a `ngIf` or `else` statement to toggle between different display modes based on the state of the `isAuthenticated` property of our user:

```
<nav class="navbar navbar-expand navbar-light bg-light">
  <a class="navbar-brand" href="#">MEAN Stack Blog</a>
  <ul class="navbar-nav mr-auto">
    <li class="nav-item">
      <a class="nav-link" routerLink="/posts" routerLinkActive="active"
i18n="A collection of blog posts|Primary link to list of blog
posts">Posts</a>
    </li>
    <li class="nav-item">
      <a class="nav-link" routerLink="/authors" routerLinkActive="active"
i18n="People who write blog posts|Primary link to list of blog authors">
        {authorCount, plural, =1 {Author} other {Authors}}
      </a>
    </li>
  </ul>
  <div class="navbar-nav">
    <span *ngIf="(currentUser$ | async).isAuthenticated(); else
unauthenticated">
      <span class="nav-link">{{(currentUser$ | async).getName()}} | <a
href="#" (click)="logout()">logout</a></span>
    </span>
    <template #unauthenticated>
      <a routerLink="/login" routerLinkActive="active" class="nav-link
pull-right">Login</a>
    </template>
  </div>
</nav>

<main class="container main-content">
  <router-outlet></router-outlet>
</main>
```

By default, `isAuthenticated` is `false` because the user's email defaults to an empty string. However, after a user logs in, the service updates this value to true. By using an Observable, our user interface receives this change and automatically updates our interface to correct state, showing the user their name and a logout button.

Using JWT authentication with Express and Angular

Managing authentication state via a session cookie is a valid strategy, but an increasingly common approach is to use a compact JSON Web Token or JWT to manage authentication state between the back-end and frontend layers of our web application. We can store our user information inside a JWT so that the client can restore its authenticated state upon reload.

Getting ready

To use JWT in our application, we will need to install a library both in our Express web server and in our Angular application. For our web server, we will use **jwt-express**, a very handy and easy-to-use JWT library for Express. We will use this library to create our JWT, as well as refresh it automatically when we get follow-up requests within a 15-minute expiration window:

```
npm install jwt-express --save
```

For Angular, we will install the popular `angular2-jwt` library. We will use this library to decode our JWT and read our user details from it, as well as make sure that its not expired:

```
npm install angular2-jwt --save
```

Finally, we will configure `angular2-jwt` and add some custom utilities in a new module. We should create this module using Angular CLI's generate command:

```
ng generate module jwt
```

How to do it...

Let's follow the steps below to add JWT authentication to our Angular and Express applications:

1. First, we will import `jwt-express` into our `/app.js` Express configuration and initialize it right after our `cookieParser` middleware. JWT works with `cookieParser` by default, but we want to customize its cookie options so that our JWT is not an `httpOnly` cookie, unlike our session cookie. That way, our client application can perform a logout operation by destroying the JWT itself:

```
...
var auth = require('./middleware/auth');
var jwt = require('jwt-express');

...
app.use(cookieParser(process.env.cookieSecret));
app.use(jwt.init(process.env.jwtSecret, {
  cookieOptions: {httpOnly: false}
}));
...
```

2. Next, we will update our `/routes/login.js` route configuration to generate a new JWT upon login instead of our user model. We will include the JWT-serialized attributes so that we are only sending the data back to the frontend that it needs to know about. We'll also append an expiration time to this token for 10 minutes (600 seconds) from the current time:

```
...
router.post('/', login, function(req, res, next) {
  req.session.save(function (err) {
    var user = serializer.serialize(req.session.user);
    var userJSON = user.data.attributes;
    userJSON.exp = new Date().getTime() + 600;
    var jwt = res.jwt(userJSON);
    res.json(jwt.token);
  });
});

module.exports = router;
```

3. With our Express application updated and restarted, we will now need to update our Angular application to use JWT. In our newly created `/src/app/jwt/jwt.module.ts` module, we will include and configure our `angular2-jwt` module and create two utility methods, called `getToken` and `deleteToken`, reading and writing from our JWT cookie:

```
import { NgModule } from '@angular/core';
import { Http, RequestOptions } from '@angular/http';
import { AuthHttp, AuthConfig } from 'angular2-jwt';

const tokenName = 'jwt-express';
export function getToken():string {
  let ca: Array<string> = document.cookie.split(';');
  let caLen: number = ca.length;
  let cookieName = `${tokenName}=`;
  let c: string;
  for (let i: number = 0; i < caLen; i += 1) {
    c = ca[i].replace(/^\s+/g, '');
    if (c.indexOf(cookieName) == 0) {
      return c.substring(cookieName.length, c.length);
    }
  }
  return '';
}

export function deleteToken() {
  document.cookie = `${tokenName}=; expires=-1`;
}

export function authHttpServiceFactory(http: Http, options:
RequestOptions) {
  return new AuthHttp(new AuthConfig({
    tokenGetter: (() => getToken()),
  }), http, options);
}

@NgModule({
  providers: [
    {
      provide: AuthHttp,
      useFactory: authHttpServiceFactory,
      deps: [Http, RequestOptions]
    }
  ]
})
export class JwtModule {}
```

4. Next, we will update our `/src/app/current-user.server.ts` service to look for a JWT token on start up. We will read the token's contents using the `JwtHelper` class from `angular2-jwt`. We can also use this library to check whether the token has expired. From the decoded token, we now have everything we will need to create a user record and provide that to our `setUser` method:

```typescript
import {Injectable} from '@angular/core';
import {User} from "./user";
import {Http, Headers, Response, RequestOptions} from
'@angular/http';
import {Observable, BehaviorSubject} from "rxjs";
import 'rxjs/add/operator/toPromise';
import {JwtHelper} from "angular2-jwt";
import {getToken, deleteToken} from "./jwt/jwt.module";

@Injectable()
export class CurrentUserService {
  private user = new BehaviorSubject<User>(new User());
  private jwtHelper: JwtHelper = new JwtHelper();

  constructor(private http: Http) {
    let token = getToken();
    if (token && !this.jwtHelper.isTokenExpired(token)) {
      this.setUser(this.decodeUserFromToken(token));
    }
  }

  getUser(): Observable<User> {
    return this.user.asObservable();
  }

  decodeUserFromToken(token): User {
    let userJSON = this.jwtHelper.decodeToken(token);
    return new User(userJSON.firstName, userJSON.lastName,
userJSON.email);
  }

  setUser(user:User) {
    this.user.next(user);
  }

  login(username: string, password: string): Promise<User> {
    let headers = new Headers({ 'Content-Type': 'application/json'
});
    let options = new RequestOptions({ headers: headers });
    return this.http.post('/api/login', JSON.stringify({ username:
username, password: password }), options)
```

```
        .toPromise()
        .then((response) => {
          let token = response.json();
          let user = this.decodeUserFromToken(token);
          this.setUser(user);
          return user;
        }).catch((error) => {
          let errorJSON = JSON.parse(error._body).errors[0];
          return Promise.reject(errorJSON);
        })
    }

    logout(): void {
      this.setUser(new User());
      deleteToken();
    }
  }
```

5. Finally, we will simply include our `JwtModule` in our
   `/src/app/app.module.ts` module:

```
...
import { LoginComponent } from './login/login.component';
import { JwtModule } from './jwt/jwt.module';
...

@NgModule({
  ...
  imports: [
    ...
    Angular2FontawesomeModule,
    JwtModule
  ],
  ...
})
export class AppModule {}
```

6. With this, we now have fully switched over to use JWT for our user
   authentication model. This will automatically show users as authenticated until
   they manually logout, or their session expires with no activity on the back-end
   server for 15 minutes.

How it works...

The jwt-express middleware works very similarly to how our cookie middleware in Express does; the main difference is that the JWT is only written if the user goes through our `/login` route successfully. Whenever a user makes a request to our application, the JWT is evaluated for whether it's genuine and not yet expired. By setting the JWT token so that it is not sent as a http-only cookie, we can allow Angular to read and parse the token using `JwtModule`. By parsing the token's contents and using that to set our current user service, we can keep our users logged in via a valid JWT token stored in their browser.

Likewise, deleting the token effectively signs the user out of our application.

6
Cloud Service Integrations

This chapter will provide guidance for some advanced integrations that can only be handled securely through the server layer of a MEAN Stack application. We will provide examples for implementing these integrations in a secure manner that won't expose vulnerable data to the frontend client application.

For many of our integrations, we will connect to external cloud-based services. Some services, such as **Cloudinary**, offer great image hosting and management services that make it easy to decouple working with image files from our backend server's filesystem. There are also services that enable a wide range of business critical functionality that you really should not implement on your own, such as enabling payment processing using **Stripe**.

In this chapter, we will cover the following recipes:

- Uploading large multi-part files with Express
- Uploading images to Cloudinary from Express
- Securing image downloads from Cloudinary
- Resizing images and transformations with Cloudinary
- Working with Stripe payment processor in Express
- Accepting credit card payments in Angular with Stripe

Introduction

Many modern web applications have external cloud services that they depend on to function. Using monolithic web servers to handle all an application's services and features has given way to a service-oriented approach, which distributes an application's needs to dedicated micro-services. Often, whole sections of micro-services can be replaced with external cloud services via API integrations. This shift trades control and flexibility of a given service for scalability and availability.

Popular cloud platforms, such as Amazon Web Services, guarantee 99.95% uptime of their services across all their geographic zones. That's a mere 4 hours, 22 minutes, and 48 seconds of downtime in an entire year, which is considerably mitigated if you diversify your application across more than one geographical zone. Having a 99.9% or better uptime is very common for most popular cloud services, and when you compare that with the cost and risk of maintaining your own custom solution, it's clear why so much of the web these days has moved to the cloud.

From a developer standpoint, the main benefit of leveraging cloud services is to rapidly expand the capabilities and features of your application in exchange for the modest transactional cost of the service. In the rapid paced world of JavaScript web application development, choosing the right service will often come down to evaluating their documentation and deciphering how to properly integrate the service to achieve your goal.

Let's explore how to build some advanced cloud service integrations into our web application.

Uploading large multi-part files with Express

Before we wade into adding dependencies for external services and APIs in application, let's start with understanding how to implement the basics of a feature without any external dependencies. It's always worth considering the trade-offs involved in building your own solution to a problem versus leveraging an external cloud service to assist.

File uploading is a very common feature in web applications. From documents to images, files that need to be transferred from a user's desktop to any web service have to go through a `multipart/form-data` file upload. In this recipe, we will add a backend API to upload images to our Express application, which we could then use to add a cover image to our blog posts.

Getting ready

We will continue to use an API client, such as Postman, for this chapter to test and develop our API endpoints. If you haven't installed Postman, or another client, I recommend that you do so to help make the cycle of retesting your requests much easier. Postman specifically supports the ability to set a form-data field to a file value, which is what we will need to test our multipart/form-data upload:

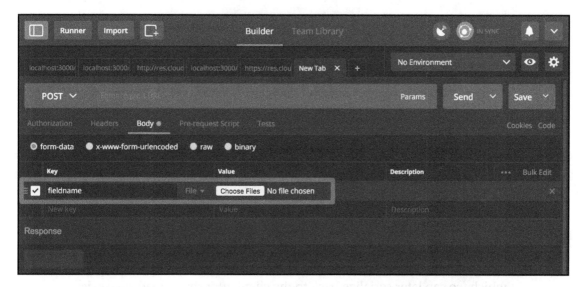

To parse our file uploads, we will also need a file upload parsing library called **Multer**. You must install Multer to your Express application's `package.json` file:

```
npm install multer --save
```

How to do it...

Let's follow these instructions to add a `multipart/form-data` file upload to our application so that we can add cover images to our blog posts:

1. First, we will create a new route configuration called `/routes/api/images.js`. This will contain all the configuration for uploading and storing references for our uploaded images in a simple `images` array:

```
var express = require('express');
var router = express.Router();
var multer  = require('multer');
```

```
var upload = multer({ dest: 'uploads/' });

var images = [];

module.exports = router;
```

2. We will continue to use `jsonapi-serializer` to serialize our uploaded objects so that we can consistently return JSON API responses to our API clients:

```
var express = require('express');
var router = express.Router();
var multer  = require('multer');
var upload = multer({ dest: 'uploads/' });
var JSONAPISerializer = require('jsonapi-serializer').Serializer;
var JSONAPIError = require('jsonapi-serializer').Error;

var images = [];

var serializer = new JSONAPISerializer('images', {
  id: 'filename',
  attributes: ['originalname', 'mimetype', 'path', 'size']
});

module.exports = router;
```

3. We will create a `coverUpload` method, which will construct an upload callback using Multer. This will create a `req.file` object on our Express request object, which we can later serialize back to the client after the upload succeeds:

```
var express = require('express');
var router = express.Router();
var multer = require('multer');
var upload = multer({ dest: 'uploads/' });
var JSONAPISerializer = require('jsonapi-serializer').Serializer;
var JSONAPIError = require('jsonapi-serializer').Error;

var images = [];

var serializer = new JSONAPISerializer('images', {
  id: 'filename',
 attributes: ['originalname', 'mimetype', 'path', 'size']
});

var coverUpload = function(req, res, next) {
  upload.single('cover')(req, res, function (err) {
    if (err) {
      return res.status(422).json(new JSONAPIError({
```

```
        status: 422,
    title: 'Image Upload Error',
    detail: err.message
        }));
    }
      next();
    });
};

router.post('/', coverUpload, function(req,res) {
  images.push(req.file);
  res.json(serializer.serialize(req.file));
});

module.exports = router;
```

4. Now, we can simply update our /routes/api.js route configuration to include our images route configuration and attach it to our /images route. We should also ensure that we include multipart/form-data in our enforceContentType middleware, or else our upload will be rejected by our API based on its Content-Type header:

```
...
var images = require('./api/images');
...
router.use(enforceContentType({
  type: ['application/json', 'multipart/form-data']
}));

router.get('/', function (req, res, next) {
  res.send('API is running');
});

router.use('/login', login);
router.use('/images', jwt.require('role', '===', 'admin'), images);
router.use('/posts', jwt.require('role', '===', 'admin'), posts);
...
```

5. Now we are able to post an image with the field name `cover` to our Express application's `/images` route, and have it return a reference to where the image is stored on our web server, and other metadata on it. We will be able to see that the file's contents are renamed and copied into an `/uploads` directory in our Express project.

How it works...

Multer is Express middleware that provides everything that we need to parse a `multipart/form-data` upload by its field name. By default, it writes the file to our operating system's disk, which we can configure by providing a destination file path during initialization.

The `req.file` object is a reference object that Multer leaves on the Express request option, with which we can interrogate the file that was uploaded. There are many different properties in this object, each containing different information we might want to know about the file:

Property	Description
`fieldname`	The `multipart/form-data` field that contains the uploaded image
`originalname`	The uploaded image's original filename
`encoding`	The encoding type of the uploaded file
`mimetype`	The mime type of the uploaded image
`size`	The file size of the uploaded image in bytes
`destination`	The name of the directory where the uploaded image is saved
`filename`	The renamed filename of the uploaded image in your upload directory
`path`	The relative file path where the uploaded image is saved
`buffer`	The raw file buffer for the uploaded image

We will also be doing a bit more advanced configuration with Multer in the next recipe - *Uploading images to Cloudinary from Express.*

There's more...

We have developed this file upload feature purely from a backend Express application perspective. However, supporting `multipart/form-data` encoding as part of a `<input type="file">` isn't very complicated to implement on the frontend:

```
<form action="http://localhost:3000/api/login" method="post"
enctype="multipart/form-data">
  <input type="file" name="cover">
  <button type="submit">Submit</button>
</form>
```

This sort of file upload support has existed in web browsers since the HTML 4 spec, so there is a lot of supplemental information available online about this topic.

> If you are interested in learning more about the frontend aspect of this topic, check out the official W3 documentation for multipart/form-data:
> `https://www.w3.org/TR/html401/interact/forms.html#h-17.13.4`

Uploading images to Cloudinary from Express

Offloading image handling from our back-end web server's filesystem has many advantages. From a performance perspective, not having to rely on the bandwidth, memory, and raw disk I/O for all the image operations originating from a single web server is much more scalable. Another big advantage is that your web server's environment can be treated as disposable, because the important resources can be persisted in a separate service. This makes the complexities of deploying web applications much more straightforward, as there isn't any need to migrate content across deployment environments. Images and other large files can quickly become difficult to manage without a dedicated service of some sort.

There are many different services that allow you to upload images to the cloud. They range in terms of services, complexity, pricing, and support for different frameworks. Cloudinary provides a nice middle ground in terms of these concerns. Although other services such as **Amazon Simple Storage Service (S3)** may be very popular, they also require considerably more setup and expertise to configure than a dedicated image management platform such as Cloudinary. We will use Cloudinary to upload our images to a dedicated cloud storage service separate from our Express web server.

Getting ready

For the next few recipes, we will use Cloudinary (`http://cloudinary.com/`) to work with images uploaded to our Express web server. To get access to the services Cloudinary provides, we will need to create a free account to get an API key and secret key.

To get set up with your free Cloudinary account, perform the following steps:

1. Go to `http://cloudinary.com/`, and click on the **SIGN UP FOR FREE** button:

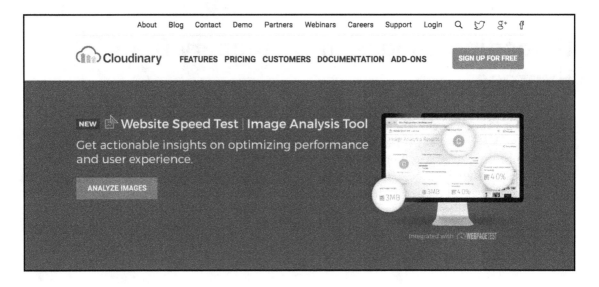

2. You will need to fill out the sign up form with the required information, and if you wish, you can choose a name for your cloud account, which will be visible in any `HTTP` requests to Cloudinary that we will create:

3. After signing up, you can choose whether you want to go through the Cloudinary tutorial or not. After you close the tutorial dialog, you will be presented with your **Cloudinary** dashboard, which has all the API key information we will need:

4. Finally, Cloudinary supports its own Node.js module that works with its services. We should install the Cloudinary module in our Express application's `package.json` file, as follows:

```
npm install cloudinary --save
```

How to do it...

Let's go through the following steps to store our uploaded cover images in Cloudinary:

1. First, we will need to configure Cloudinary by creating a new `/middleware/cloudinary.js` middleware:

 We will load our private API credentials from Cloudinary. It is important to keep these a secret. I recommend that you use Node.js environment parameters to remain hidden from your source code. `https://nodejs.org/api/process.html#process_process_env`

```
var cloudinary = require('cloudinary');
var JSONAPIError = require('jsonapi-serializer').Error;

cloudinary.config({
  cloud_name: process.env.cloudinaryCloudName,
  api_key: process.env.cloudinaryAPIKey,
  api_secret: process.env.cloudinaryAPISecret
});

var self = module.exports = {};
```

2. Next, we will implement two methods; one to construct Express middleware to upload a file using a file from Multer called `uploadFromFilePath` and the other to actually process the upload with Cloudinary called `upload`. Both of these methods will need to have error handling in case our request fails in either of them. In the case of our Cloudinary error handling, we will rely on Cloudinary's own error object formatting to return more intelligent failure messages from their service, including its HTTP status code:

```
...
var self = module.exports = {
  upload: function(image, options) {
    if (!options) options = {};
    return function(req, res, next) {
      cloudinary.v2.uploader.upload(image, options, function(error,
result) {
        if (error) {
          return res.status(error.http_code).json(new
JSONAPIError({
            status: error.http_code,
            title: 'Cloudinary Upload Error',
            detail: error.message
          }));
        }
        req.cloudinary = result;
        next();
      });
    }
  },

  uploadFromFilePath: function(req, res, next) {
    if (req.file && req.file.path) {
      let path = req.file.path;
      return self.upload(path)(req, res, next);
    } else {
      return res.status(500).json(new JSONAPIError({
        status: 500,
```

```
            title: 'Invalid File Path',
            detail: 'There is no file path available to upload to
    Cloudinary.'
        }));
    }
  }
};
```

3. We can now update our `/routes/api/images.js` route configuration to use our new Cloudinary middleware. We will now serialize our Cloudinary object instead of our `Multer` object. Note that we are still using `jsonapi-serializer`'s serializer configuration to whitelist which properties map to the object's ID and which properties are sent back to our API client:

```
var express = require('express');
var router = express.Router();
var multer  = require('multer');
var upload = multer({ dest: 'uploads/'});
var cloudinary = require('../../middleware/cloudinary');
var JSONAPISerializer = require('jsonapi-serializer').Serializer;
var JSONAPIError = require('jsonapi-serializer').Error;

var images = [];

var serializer = new JSONAPISerializer('images', {
  id: 'public_id',
  attributes: ['url', 'secure_url', 'bytes', 'created_at', 'width',
'height']
});
...
router.post('/', coverUpload, cloudinary.uploadFromFilePath,
function(req,res) {
  var image = req.cloudinary;
  images.push(image);
  res.json(serializer.serialize(image));
});

module.exports = router;
```

4. Now when we upload an image, we will get a JSON API response that contains reference URLs to Cloudinary for our images. If we visit these URLs, we can see that our uploaded image is actually hosted on and returned from Cloudinary's service instead of our own web server:

```
https://res.cloudinary.com/cloud-name/image/upload/***********/****
****************.jpg
```

How it works...

Cloudinary, as a service, provides us with a Node.js module full of ready-made tools to use to communicate with their service. After initializing the module with our secret API credentials, we will simply need to invoke the APIs within their module, and the details of the work are done for us.

The upload method takes a local file reference and uploads it to Cloudinary with a callback when it succeeds or fails in this operation, as follows:

```
cloudinary.v2.uploader.upload(file, options, callback);
```

It can also support an options object, which can be used to customize several aspects of the uploaded image. One of the great things about Cloudinary is the remarkable amount of customization options available for working with images. The following is a sample of the sort of robust documentation available for configuring image uploads in Cloudinary:

Property	Type	Description
public_id	String	Indicates the name used for the image in Cloudinary; it will be visible in the URL for the resource and can also be provided as a folder path. It should not include the file extension.
folder	String	A folder on Cloudinary where the image can be stored.
use_filename	Boolean	Indicates whether the original filename of the image should be used for its public_id property.
unique_filename	Boolean	Can be used in conjunction with use_filename to allow multiple instances of the same filename to be uploaded.

resource_type	String	Indicates the type of file being uploaded to Cloudinary; it can be `image`, `raw`, `video`, or `auto`.
type	String	Indicates the authentication type for the uploaded image; it can be `upload`, `private`, or `authenticated`.
access_mode	String	Used in conjunction with type to allow an image to act as if it's a different authentication type while still keeping the default URL structure; it can be `public` or `authenticated`.
discard_original_filename	Boolean	Indicates whether to keep the original image filename on upload.
overwrite	Boolean	Indicates whether images with a matching `public_id` should overwrite an existing image or not.
tags	Array | String	This is used to append an array or a comma-separated list of tag metadata to an image upload.
context	String	An alternative way to attach key-value pairs of metadata to an image upload.
colors	Boolean	Scans the uploaded image for its primary colors and writes them as metadata values.
faces	Boolean	Scans the uploaded image for any faces contained in it and writes their coordinates as metadata values.
image_metadata	Boolean	Scans the image for IPTC, XMP, and Exif metadata and writes them as metadata values.
phash	Boolean	Scans the image to generate a perceptual hash (pHash) and writes it as a metadata value.

responsive_breakpoints	JSON	Allows automatic generation of responsive breakpoints for images based on provided breakpoint definitions, which will be written as metadata values.
auto_tagging	Decimal	Scans the image to assign automatic tags using image recognition with a confidence score as metadata values.
categorization	String	An advanced version of auto_tagging that works with Cloudinary's imagga_tagging add-on.
detection	String	An advanced version of facial detection using Cloudinary's advanced facial attribute detection add-on.
ocr	String	Scans image to extract text from it using OCR image recognition using Cloudinary's OCR text detection and extraction add-on.
exif	Boolean	Extracts Exif metadata as Cloudinary image metadata.
eager	Array | String	Indicates an array or a pipe-separated list of transformations to run on an uploaded image in sequence; generates these transformations upon upload instead of when requesting the image for the first time.
eager_async	Boolean	Works in conjunction with eager to allow transformations to occur in the background after upload.
eager_notification_url	String	Works in conjunction with eager to allow a webhook callback when transformations on an uploaded image are completed.
transformation	Object | Array	Defines a series of transformations to run on an uploaded resource before saving it to Cloudinary; can be an array of multiple transformations to be run in series.

format	String	Indicates the format to convert an uploaded image to before saving in Cloudinary, such as `jpeg`, `png`, or `gif`.
custom_coordinates	String	Saves a set of coordinates for the purpose of working in conjunction with a custom `gravity` transformation.
face_coordinates	String	Saves a set of face coordinates as metadata to an uploaded image manually.
background_removal	String	Scans an image and automatically clears the background using Cloudinary's Remove-The-Background Editing add-on.
raw_convert	String	Scans a file and automatically converts it to a PDF file or other image format using Cloudinary's Aspose document conversion add-on.
allowed_formats	Array | String	An array or a comma-separated list of file formats that will be allowed to be uploaded.
async	Boolean	Indicates whether Cloudinary should perform this upload in the background asynchronously.
backup	Boolean	Indicates whether Cloudinary should create a backup of the uploaded image.
callback	String	Allows the setup of a URL to redirect to upon successful upload of an image. Usually only used in frontend upload workflows.
headers	String	Allows setting custom HTTP headers to be provided on delivery of images to clients.
invalidate	Boolean	Invalidates CDN cached copies of previously uploaded images and all transformations when overwriting an image with the same `public_id`.

moderation	String	Allows you to use Cloudinary's management console to manually approve image uploads first, or use Cloudinary's WebPurify image moderation add-on.
notification_url	String	Allows the setup of a webhook callback when the upload operation is completed.
proxy	String	Allows Cloudinary to upload remote images through a proxy.
return_delete_token	Boolean	Returns a deletion token in the upload response that can be used within 10 minutes to delete the given image.
upload_preset	String	Allows you to process a image using a predefined Cloudinary preset from the management console.

For its part, Cloudinary offers extensive documentation for all its services, including image upload. We will dive into many more parts of configuring Cloudinary for use in our web application in this chapter, but if you are interested, you can find much more detail concerning its upload capabilities from the following official documentation:

```
http://cloudinary.com/documentation/upload_images
```

There's more...

One detail about our change to using a cloud storage service such as Cloudinary for our images still remains. We are still writing our images to our local filesystem before uploading them. An easy solution to this problem is to move away from relying on the file system of our operating system entirely and using a memory-based solution instead. Luckily, Multer provides simple drop in support for such a solution.

First, we will create two new methods in our `/middleware/cloudinary.js` middleware. These methods will added support to Cloudinary's `upload_stream` API by passing a file buffer from Multer to it:

```
...
uploadBuffer: function(buffer, options) {
  if (!options) options = { discard_original_filename: true };
  return function(req, res, next) {
    cloudinary.v2.uploader.upload_stream(options, function(error, result) {
      if (error) {
```

```
            return res.status(500).json(new JSONAPIError({
               status: 500,
               title: 'Cloudinary Upload Error',
               detail: error.message
            }));
         }
         req.cloudinary = result;
         next();
      }).end(buffer);
   }
},

uploadFromFileBuffer: function(req, res, next) {
   if (req.file && req.file.buffer) {
      let buffer = req.file.buffer;
      return self.uploadBuffer(buffer)(req, res, next);
   } else {
      return res.status(500).json(new JSONAPIError({
         status: 500,
         title: 'Invalid File Buffer',
         detail: 'There is no file buffer available to upload to Cloudinary.'
      }));
   }
}
}
...
```

To get the file buffer and stop Multer from writing files to disk, we will need to invoke the memoryStorage object and configure Multer to use it. We will also change our Cloudinary middleware from depending on the req.file.path property to using req.file.buffer instead:

```
var multer  = require('multer');
var storage = multer.memoryStorage();
var upload = multer({ storage: storage });
...
router.post('/', coverUpload, cloudinary.uploadFromFileBuffer,
function(req,res) {
   var image = req.cloudinary;
   image.originalname = req.file.originalname;
   images.push(image);
   res.json(serializer.serialize(image));
});

module.exports = router;
```

This change will shift from writing uploaded images to the filesystem to using a memory-based stream instead. This process guarantees after upload to Cloudinary that there are no lingering artifacts consuming your web servers disk space while still consuming the same amount of memory.

> You can learn more about **Multer** and how it can be used for file uploads in Express from its GitHub documentation:
> `https://github.com/expressjs/multer`

Securing image downloads from Cloudinary

Uploading images to cloud storage for the purpose of hosting public images is very useful, but what about resources that we want to handle in a more private manner? Cloudinary supports several different types of resource authentication, including the signing of asset URLs.

Getting ready

Let's change our uploaded cover images to be private by default when they are uploaded. We can then make an API endpoint that will automatically sign and redirect to authenticated images that we will only be able to view if we are logged in as an admin user.

How to do it...

Let's perform the following steps to add authentication requirements to view our uploaded Cloudinary images:

1. First, we will update our upload functions in `/middleware/cloudinary.js` to default the authentication type of our uploaded images to the `authenticated` type. This will guarantee that they will be inaccessible without a signed URL to access them:

```
...
upload: function(image, options) {
  if (!options) options = {};
  options.type = "authenticated";
  ...
},
...
```

```
uploadBuffer: function(buffer, options) {
  if (!options) options = {};
  options.type = "authenticated";
  options.discard_original_filename = true;
  ...
},
...
```

2. We'll also add a new method for getting all our image resource information from Cloudinary using the `cloudinary.v2.api.resources` API. This API will return a list of images that we have stored in Cloudinary, including the URLs to access them. Using this API, we will be able to get the `public_id` property needed to fetch a specific image resource from Cloudinary:

```
...
getImages: function(options) {
  return function(req, res, next) {
    cloudinary.v2.api.resources(options, function(error, result) {
      if (error) {
        return res.status(error.http_code).json(new JSONAPIError({
          status: error.http_code,
          title: 'Cloudinary Error',
          detail: error.message
        }));
      } else {
        req.cloudinary = result.resources;
        next();
      }
    })
  };
},
...
```

3. We can now add two other methods for working with images. The first `getSignedImageById` will look for an Express request parameter ID and pass that to our next method `getSignedImage`, which will actually generate a signed request URL to Cloudinary for the image:

```
...
getSignedImage: function(name, options) {
  if (!options) options = {};
  options.sign_url = true;
  options.type = "authenticated";
  return function(req, res, next) {
    var image = cloudinary.url(name, options);
    req.cloudinary = image;
    next();
```

```
    }
  },

  getSignedImageById: function(req, res, next) {
    if (req.params && req.params.id) {
      let name = req.params.id;
      return self.getSignedImage(name)(req, res, next);
    } else {
      return res.status(500).json(new JSONAPIError({
        status: 500,
        title: 'Invalid Image Request',
        detail: 'There is no Cloudinary public_id provided.'
      }));
    }
  }
}
...
```

4. We can now update our `/routes/api/images.js` route configuration to add a fetch route for all images, as well as a nested route to return a specific image by its `public_id`. We will make the `cloudinary.getImages` route return our resources in the JSON API format. We will also make the specific image request actually perform a redirect to the returned Cloudinary signed URL:

```
...
var serializer = new JSONAPISerializer('images', {
  id: 'public_id',
  attributes: ['url', 'secure_url', 'originalname', 'bytes',
'created_at', 'width', 'height', 'type']
});
...
router.get('/', cloudinary.getImages({type: "authenticated"}),
function(req, res) {
  res.json(serializer.serialize((req.cloudinary)));
});

router.get('/:id', cloudinary.getSignedImageById, function(req,
res) {
  res.redirect(req.cloudinary);
});

module.exports = router;
```

5. Now, if we restart our Express web server and navigate to `localhost:3000/api/images`, we will see a list of images we have uploaded to Cloudinary. If we copy the `id` property out from one of those entries and make a request to `localhost:3000/api/images/:id`, we will see that an image from Cloudinary is returned to us if we are authenticated as an admin for our backend. If we are not authenticated, we will get an error from our Express web server instead.

How it works...

When we consider the role security plays in our application, it is easy to see how to control our own resources, but easy to forget about the security resources we rely on external cloud services for. Fortunately, services such as Cloudinary have easy built-in tools to secure resources using the authentication `type` option upon upload.

The secure signing of our images with Cloudinary relies on the secret key information we initially configured in our `/middleware/cloudinary.js` middleware. Signing provides an effective mechanism to encrypt the parameters of the request, including its `public_id` and options, into a format that can't be changed by the client making the API request. Ultimately, it provides a modicum of protection from users being able to guess an image resource's URL for Cloudinary, even if they know the `public_id` of the image in Cloudinary and the `cloud-name` property for our Cloudinary account. Instead, the only reliable source for these URLs comes from our Express API, which through a redirect response effectively masks the URL for Cloudinary from the user. It appears that the image is taken from our Express web server instead of an external cloud storage service.

There's more...

There are actually three different types of authentication provided by Cloudinary. A signing URL is the only option available to free Cloudinary accounts. They also support more sophisticated auth token and cookie-based options, which require Enterprise plans, but which offer much more robust configuration options, including time limiting and IP access restrictions. If you have image privacy needs beyond what Signed URLs can provide for your application, you will need to upgrade your Cloudinary account:

	Signed URL	Token	Cookie
Time limited	No	Yes	Yes
IP restriction	No	Yes	Yes

User-session limited	No	No	Yes
Pattern-based access (ACL)	No	Yes	Yes
Customizable access per image	No	Yes	Yes
CDN caching	Yes	Yes	Yes
Plan availability	Free	Enterprise	Enterprise
Setup required	No	Yes	Yes
Private CDN distribution required	No	Yes	Yes
CNAME required	No	No	Yes

You can learn more about authentication options in Cloudinary's official authenticated images documentation:
`http://cloudinary.com/documentation/image_`
`transformations#authenticated_images`

Resizing images and transformations with Cloudinary

Having integrated with Cloudinary to take advantage of our basic image uploading and serving needs, we may turn our attention to leveraging some of its more powerful features to make building our web application easier. One of Cloudinary's best strengths is its image processing transformation options, which provide a sophistication rarely found in most cloud storage systems that make tailoring assets for specific web application purposes very easy. Let's explore how we can leverage these transformation options to automatically optimize our images after upload to Cloudinary.

Getting ready

Let's create a middleware layer to our Express web server to customize our requested image styling. We will load images from our `localhost:3000/api/images/:id` route, but will pass through some customization options as URL parameters to change the width, height, crop, and even format of the image result returned to us.

For this recipe, we will need to install **Lodash**, a very popular micro-library that works with arrays and objects in JavaScript and Node.js:

```
npm install --save lodash
```

We'll be using Lodash to do property filtering for our Cloudinary image transformation options. If you are interested in learning more about Lodash and its capabilities, you can check out the official documentation for more details:

```
https://lodash.com/docs
```

How to do it...

Let's add image transformation URL parameters to our image API using Cloudinary's transformation options by following these steps:

1. First, we will need to create a whitelist of the URL query parameters we want to pick out for specific transformations in Cloudinary. We will use Lodash's pick method to filter out only the specific query keys and values that we want to allow. We will turn these into a set of options, which we will pass through to Cloudinary:

```
var cloudinary = require('cloudinary');
var JSONAPIError = require('jsonapi-serializer').Error;
var _pick = require('lodash/pick');

var self = module.exports = {
  ...
  getTransformation: function(req, res, next) {
    let transforms = _pick(req.query, ['width', 'height', 'crop',
'radius', 'gravity', 'format']);
    req.transformation = transforms;
    next();
  },
  ...
  getSignedImageById: function(req, res, next) {
    if (req.params && req.params.id) {
      let name = req.params.id;
      let options = req.transformation;
      return self.getSignedImage(name, options)(req, res, next);
    } else {
      return res.status(500).json(new JSONAPIError({
        status: 500,
        title: 'Invalid Image Request',
        detail: 'There is no Cloudinary public_id provided.'
```

```
              }));
           }
        }
     };
```

2. Now, all we need to do is add our middleware to our
   `cloudinary.getSignedImageById` route:

   ```
   router.get('/:id', cloudinary.getTransformation,
   cloudinary.getSignedImageById, function(req, res) {
     res.redirect(req.cloudinary);
   });
   ```

3. After restarting our web server, when we make requests to fetch an image, we
   can also include optional URL parameters to set the size and various other
   options for our image. Try uploading an image with a face to Cloudinary and
   returning it via our API with the following parameters. You will get a very
   attractive user avatar image with no need to do complicated CSS or other manual
   image manipulations:

   ```
   localhost:3000/api/images/*****************?width=200&height=200&gr
   avity=face&crop=thumb&radius=max&format=png
   ```

How it works...

Manipulating images in Cloudinary is the sort of best-in-class feature set that can make you
consider why you would ever want to roll your own image hosting service to begin with. Its
robust image transformation API can enable application user experiences and automation
that would require considerable investment without it. It's also one of Cloudinary's most
extensive APIs with many options available for manipulating your image resources:

Property	Example values	Description
width	100, 0.4, and auto	The width of the image
height	100, 0.4, and auto	The height of the image
crop	scale, fit, limit, mfit, fill, lfill, pad, lpad, mpad, crop, imagga_crop, and imagga_scale	How to crop content to fit within the image's dimensions
aspect_ratio	1.3 and 16:9	Sets the aspect ratio for the image
gravity	north_west, north, north_east, west, center, east, south_west, south, south_east, xy_center, face, faces, body, ocr_text, adv_face, adv_faces, adv_eyes, custom, and auto	Provides guidance to crop images
zoom	0.75 and 2.5	A zoom factor applied to the image
x	90 and 0.3	Sets a horizontal position for the image
y	420 and 0.4	Sets a vertical position for the image

`format`	`pg, jpe, jpeg, jpc, jp2, j2k, wdp, jxr, hdp, png, gif, webp, bmp, tif, tiff, ico, pdf, ps, ept, eps, eps3, psd, svg, ai, djvu,` and `flif`	The format the image should be converted into
`fetch_format`	`auto, webp,` and `jpeg-xr`	Defines the format to be served during general purpose fetch requests to save bandwidth
`quality`	`90, auto,` and `jpegmini`	The quality of image compression that should be used
`radius`	`50, 10:0:0:10,` and `max`	A border radius applied to the image
`angle`	`90, auto_right, auto_left, ignore, vflip,` and `hflip`	Rotates or mirrors the image
`effect`	`hue:30, red:100, green:-40, blue:10, negate, brightness:30, brightness_hsb:50, sepia:90, grayscale, blackwhite, saturation:30, colorize:53, replace_color, tint, contrast:-30, vibrance:20, auto_color, improve, auto_brightness, full_light:20, outline:outer:10:100, cartoonify:20:50, art:icognito, gamma:50, multiply, screen, make_transparent, trim, shadow:20, distort, shear, displace, oil_paint, red_eye, adv_redeye, vignette, gradient_fade, pixelate, pixelate_region, blur, blur_region, blur_faces, sharpen, unsharp_mask,` and `ordered_dither`	Applies a wide range of visual filters and effects to images
`opacity`	`40`	The transparency of the image
`border`	`4px_solid_red, 4px_solid_rgb:00a0be,` and `4px_solid_rgb:00a0be40`	Adds a border around the image
`background`	`green, rgb:00a0be, auto:border, auto:predominant, auto:border_contrast,` and `auto:predominant_contrast`	Adds a background color to a transparent image
`overlay`	`public_id, text:default_style:My+Overlay,` and `text:Arial_30:Tada!`	Adds an overlay of another image by public_id or text on top of the image
`underlay`	`public_id`	Adds a background image by public_id under the image
`default_image`	`public_id`	A placeholder image to use if the requested image does not exist
`delay`	`15`	Sets the frame-rate for animated images
`color`	`green, rgb:00a0be`	Colorizes the image with a specified color
`color_space`	`srgb, no_cmyk, tinysrgb,` and `cs_icc:public_id`	Sets the color space that should be used for the image
`dpr`	`auto, 2.0`	Sets the pixel ratio for the image that should be used
`page`	`12`	When generating an image from a file, chooses the page to be returned
`density`	`72`	Sets the resolution density to be used when generating an image from a file
`flags`	`any_format, attachment, apng, awebp, clip, clip_evenodd, cutter, force_strip, ignore_aspect_ratio, keep_iptc, layer_apply, lossy, no_overflow, preserve_transparency, png8, png24, png32, progressive, progressive:semi, progressive:steep, progressive:none, rasterize, region_relative, relative, strip_profile, text_no_trim, tiff8_lwz,` and `tiled`	Optional advanced processing flags for Cloudinary image processing
`transformation`	`my_cloudinary_predefined_transformation`	Applies a predefined Cloudinary transformation from the management console to the image
`if`	`w_gt_100` (width greater than 100 px), `h_lt_50` (height less than 50px)	Applies conditional logic to do the transformation only if provided criteria are true
`variable`	`$height_60/my_cloudinary_predefined_transformation`	Allows you to pass configuration parameters to predefined cloudinary transformations

It's also worth noting that any of these transformations can be applied in a series through the use of the `transformations` option in Cloudinary's upload API. With this many options available, we can do virtually any kind of image manipulation we could imagine in our application.

There's more...

One of Cloudinary's biggest strengths as a cloud service provider is their detailed and consistent documentation. There is much more to learn about Cloudinary, but if you are interested, their transformation documentation has many examples of how images look after being manipulated, and how to chain multiple transformations together to get more elaborate image results:

```
http://cloudinary.com/documentation/image_transformations
```

Working with Stripe payment processor in Express

Finally, in these last two sections, let's shift gears and implement a cloud service solution that we almost certainly couldn't build ourselves: a payment gateway. To do this, we will use the popular payment processor **Stripe** to configure a simple payment route. For our blog application, we might use such a feature to allow user donations or potentially offer premium features to paid users. The most important part of our implementation is keeping our user's payment information secure and safe from exposure to outside parties.

Getting ready

Very similar to Cloudinary, our first step before getting started is to set up our Stripe account:

1. You can create a test account for free by visiting `https://stripe.com/` and clicking on **CREATE ACCOUNT**:

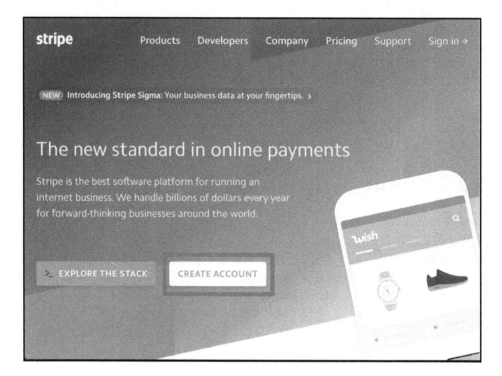

2. After you have signed up and verified your email address, you will have access to the Stripe management dashboard. You can find the API credentials we will need to integrate with Express in the API section of the sidebar, in fields labeled **Publishable key** and **Secret Key**:

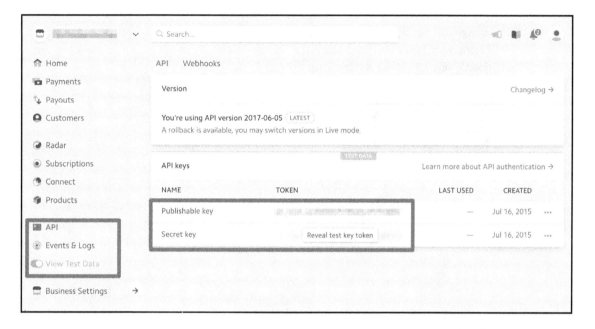

3. You will want to toggle the **View Test Data** switch **on** to make sure that we are working with test credentials instead of full production keys. Otherwise, you may accidentally pay with real money and incur a Stripe processing fee.

4. We will also want to install the Stripe NPM module for working with the Stripe API, similar to how we integrated with the Cloudinary API:

```
npm install stripe --save
```

With our Stripe test API keys acquired and our Stripe module installed, we are ready to begin setting up our payment processor integration.

How to do it...

Let's perform the following steps to get integrated with **Stripe** as a payment processor; we will add a simple test route to add customers to our account and return customer data from it:

1. First, we will need to create a new /middleware/stripe.js middleware, which will contain all our configuration for Stripe. We will define two middleware methods, one to create a customer record in Stripe using our JWT's email property and another to return a full customer list from Stripe:

```
const keyPublishable = process.env.stripeAPIPublishableKey;
const keySecret = process.env.stripeAPISecretKey;
const stripe = require("stripe")(keySecret);

var self = module.exports = {
  createCustomer: function(req, res, next) {
    return stripe.customers.create({
      email: req.jwt.payload.email
    }).then(function(customer) {
      req.stripe = { customer: customer };
      next();
    })
  },

  getCustomers: function(req, res, next) {
    stripe.customers.list()
      .then(function(customers) {
        res.json(customers);
      })
  }
};
```

2. We will want to provide thorough error handling whenever working with third-party APIs, so we'll add jsonapi-serializer's error serializer and add an errorHandler middleware, which we will use for parsing any errors returning from the Stripe API:

```
var JSONAPIError = require('jsonapi-serializer').Error;
const keyPublishable = process.env.stripeAPIPublishableKey;
const keySecret = process.env.stripeAPISecretKey;
const stripe = require("stripe")(keySecret);

var self = module.exports = {

  errorHandler: function(error) {
```

```
        return function(req, res) {
          res.status(500).json(new JSONAPIError({
            status: 500,
            title: error.type,
            detail: error.message
          }));
        };
      },

    createCustomer: function(req, res, next) {
      return stripe.customers.create({
        email: req.jwt.payload.email
      }).then(function(customer) {
        req.stripe = { customer: customer };
        next();
      }).catch(function(error) {
        return self.errorHandler(error)(req, res);
      });
    },

    getCustomers: function(req, res, next) {
      stripe.customers.list()
        .then(function(customers) {
          res.json(customers);
        })
        .catch(function(error) {
          return self.errorHandler(error)(req, res);
        });
    }
  };
```

3. Now that we have created our Stripe middleware, we can import it into our
   `/routes/api.js` route configuration. We'll create a route that checks whether
   there is an active JWT token first for authentication protection, before creating a
   customer and returning our customer list to us in a JSON format:

```
...
var stripe = require('../middleware/stripe');
...
router.use('/login', login);
router.use('/customers', jwt.active(), stripe.createCustomer,
stripe.getCustomers);
router.use('/images', jwt.active(), jwt.require('role', '===',
'admin'), images);
router.use('/posts', jwt.active(), jwt.require('role', '===',
'admin'), posts);
...
```

```
module.exports = router;
```

4. Now, we can log in to our API, and visit `http://localhost:3000/api/customers` to get a record from Stripe of all our customers. If we repeat this request, we will see our total number of customer entries increment by one, and if we attempt to access this endpoint without having a valid JWT, we will get a JWT unauthenticated error instead.

How it works...

The Stripe API is integrated into our express application in a very similar manner as Cloudinary. It's primary difference is the domain of concerns it has with our data because it deals with payments and customers instead of images.

The **Stripe customer API** is just one of many APIs in Stripe for working with the Stripe payment processor service. You can see your customer records within Stripe's administrative dashboard within the Customers section. This is a great way to make sure that your API creates and persists the correct customer data to Stripe.

 You can learn more about Stripe's customer API by checking out the following official documentation:
`https://stripe.com/docs/api#customers`

Accepting credit card payments in Angular with Stripe

Creating and reading customer records from Stripe is great, but what we really want is to use Stripe to allow credit card payments through our web application. Let's add a credit card form from Stripe into our web application to accept donation payments for all the hard work it takes to keep our Mean Stack blog working.

Getting ready

We will need to create a new Angular payment component for all the payment-specific UI and logic we will be setting up in this section. The fastest way to do so is to use the Angular CLI `generate` command for this:

```
ng generate component payment
```

How to do it...

Let's perform the following steps to add a Stripe powered credit card donation form to our Angular web application:

1. First, we'll need to update our `/middleware/stripe.js` middleware to change the way we identify customers to rely on parameters from Stripe's form submission. We will also need to add a new method to create a charge within Stripe for the amount of money that will be displayed on our donation form:

```
...
var self = module.exports = {

  ...
  createCustomer: function(req, res, next) {
    return stripe.customers.create({
      email: req.body.stripeEmail,
      source: req.body.stripeToken
    }).then(function(customer) {
      res.stripe = { customer: customer };
      next();
    }).catch(function(error) {
      return self.errorHandler(error)(req, res);
    });
  },
  ...
  charge: function(amount) {
    return function(req, res, next) {
      if (res.stripe && res.stripe.customer) {
        var customer = res.stripe.customer;
        stripe.charges.create({
          amount,
          description: "Donation",
          currency: "usd",
          customer: customer.id
        }).then(function (charge) {
          res.stripe.charge = charge;
```

```
            next();
        }).catch(function(error) {
            return self.errorHandler(error)(req, res);
        });
    } else {
        var error = new Error("Must provide customer for purchase
transaction");
        return self.errorHandler(error)(req, res);
    }
    };
    }
};
```

2. Next, we'll add a new /donate route, which will automatically read our Stripe customer information and process the charge. We will also need to extend our enforcedContentType Content-Types configuration in /routes/api.js to include application/x-www-form-urlencoded:

```
. . .

router.use(enforceContentType({
    type: ['application/json', 'multipart/form-data', 'application/x-
www-form-urlencoded']
}));

. . .
router.use('/donate', stripe.createCustomer, stripe.charge(500),
function(req, res) {
    res.send('thank you');
});
router.use('/customers', jwt.active(), stripe.getCustomers);
. . .
```

3. With our back-end charges set up, we will next need to flesh out /src/app/payment/payment.component.ts in our Angular application to add Stripe's payment form to our application. We can achieve this using Angular's Renderer2 core library to dynamically insert the scripts necessary to generate the Stripe form. This form will require several data attributes to configure it as well, including our public key. The best way to include this public key is to add it to the /src/environments/environments.ts file:

```
import { Renderer2, OnInit, Component, Inject } from
'@angular/core';
import { DOCUMENT } from '@angular/platform-browser';
import { environment } from '../../environments/environment';
```

```
@Component({
  selector: 'app-payment',
  templateUrl: './payment.component.html',
  styleUrls: ['./payment.component.scss']
})
export class PaymentComponent implements OnInit {

  constructor(private renderer: Renderer2, @Inject(DOCUMENT)
private document) {}

  public ngOnInit() {
    var s = this.renderer.createElement('script');
    s.type = "text/javascript";
    s.src = "https://checkout.stripe.com/v2/checkout.js";

    this.renderer.addClass(s, 'stripe-button');
    this.renderer.setAttribute(s, 'data-key',
environment.stripeAPIKey);
    this.renderer.setAttribute(s, 'data-amount', '500');
    this.renderer.setAttribute(s, 'data-name', 'Angular Blog');
    this.renderer.setAttribute(s, 'data-description', 'Donation');
    this.renderer.setAttribute(s, 'data-locale', 'auto');
this.renderer.appendChild(this.document.getElementById('stripeForm'
), s);
  }
}
```

4. For the `/src/app/payment/payment.component.html` template, we will only need a simple form with the ID `stripeForm` and an action that points to our Express `/api/donate` route. On initialization, our component will find our form element using an ID and append the Stripe button script to it, and it will self-initialize as a Stripe payment button:

```
<section class="row">
  <div class="col col-sm-12">
    <div class="card">
      <div class="card-header">
        <h1>Donations</h1>
      </div>
      <div class="card-body">
        <p class="card-text">This blog is made possible due to the
generous
          donations from users like you!</p>
        <form id="stripeForm" action="/api/donate" method="POST">
        </form>
      </div>
    </div>
```

```
      </div>
    </section>
```

5. Finally, we will simply need to add our `PaymentComponent` to our `/src/app/app.module.ts` module and define a route to it:

```
...
import { PaymentComponent } from './payment/payment.component';

const ROUTES = [
  ...
  {
    path: "payment",
    component: PaymentComponent,
  },
  {
    path: "**",
    component: PageNotFoundComponent
  }
];

@NgModule({
  declarations: [
    ...
    PaymentComponent
  ],
  ...
})
export class AppModule {}
```

6. Now, if we visit `http://localhost:4200/payment` and click on the **Pay with Card** button displayed on the page, Stripe will automatically launch a payment window we can input credit card information into. Submitting a payment will result in the charge being processed by our Express back-end and ending with a simple thank-you message rendered by Express.

How it works...

The addition of the Stripe Pay with Card button is done by manipulating the DOM of the component using Angular's `Renderer2` core library. This library is necessary because Angular, by default, strips out any script tags from component templates, which would prevent simply including the script from functioning. However, when we use `Renderer2`, we can actually dynamically generate and insert the script tag and necessary data attributes needed by Stripe to properly initialize this UI.

Since it's a routable component, when we leave this page, it will tear down all its template views, including its Stripe button configuration and script tag, leaving no mess for us to clean up afterward. If we had appended the button to the body of the document, however, it would still remain, and every subsequent visit to `http://localhost:4200/payment` would cause a new instance to appear. It's important to remember when working with `Renderer2` to keep content within the template of the component so that it's properly cleaned up upon the user's exit from the page.

For local testing with the test mode toggle enabled in your Stripe dashboard, you can simply enter the credit card number `4242 4242 4242 4242`, a future expiration date, and a three-digit confirmation code to test the payment workflow with Stripe:

This payment will be visible within the **Payments** section of the Stripe administrative dashboard as well.

You can learn more about charges and how they work in Stripe by checking out the following official documentation:
`https://stripe.com/docs/api#charges`

7
MongoDB and Mongoose

This chapter is an in-depth guide to configuring the database layer of our MEAN stack web application using **MongoDB** and the **Mongoose** framework. We will cover some common issues with modeling and validating data, as well as how to query our database for exactly what we are looking for.

The recipes covered in this chapter are as follows:

- How to set up and create a MongoDB database
- Connecting to MongoDB through Mongoose
- Working with data model in MongoDB and Mongoose
- Querying for data using Mongoose query selectors

Introduction

Persisting data in a web application usually means the involvement of a **structured query language** (**SQL**) database to handle the structure and relationships of data. This approach, for many applications, provides a common answer to the modeling of application data and their relationships to each other. However, the nature of data in SQL databases is one of highly-structured schemas with clearly defined field types. In contrast to the flexible, semi-structured objects of JavaScript, this approach can sometimes make it burdensome to work with data structures between the web server and database.

The relationship of the data between the application and SQL databases is managed by serialization and deserialization between the database structures and the web server's model. The gap between what the data is when it's in the database and what it's transformed into on the web server can cause unwanted context shifting between different **domain specific languages** (**DSLs**) for querying that data. This can sometimes lead to mistakes and unexpected frustration when maintaining a large or complex web application.

The most common solution to these issues is to rely on an **object-relational mapping (ORM)** library to manage interactions between the web application and the database. However, no ORM can completely erode the need to intrinsically understand what is being serialized and deserialized between the database and web server.

To this end, many developers have turned towards no-SQL database solutions, such as **MongoDB**, to provide an alternative answer for how to persist and work with data in their web applications. The capabilities of MongoDB to work natively with JSON object structures for application data allow developers a more natural relationship between their objects on the web server, and even the front-end application, with its persisted state in the database. This, combined with many other features related to alternative architectures for scaling database performance, and the prevalence of document data structures over relational ones in many applications, has made MongoDB a very popular answer for teams looking to capitalize on an all JavaScript-based web application stack.

How to set up and create a MongoDB database

Before we dive headlong into working with MongoDB in our Express web server, let's cover the basics of how to set up MongoDB and create a simple database using the MongoDB `mongod` process and the `mongo` shell. After we create our database, we will write a simple test record to the database to explore what writing data to MongoDB looks like. One of the unique aspects of MongoDB is its ability to read and write values natively in the JSON format. This makes working with MongoDB data through tools like Mongoose very easy, as we will see in-depth in further sections.

Getting ready

We need to install MongoDB locally to use it in our application. The MongoDB team provides extensive documentation for installing MongoDB on every conceivable operating system and, often, with several examples of different ways to install based on your preferences for how you want MongoDB to run as a process.

You can visit the following link for more information on it:

```
https://docs.mongodb.com/manual/administration/install-community/
```

For an example of how simple MongoDB can be to install, the following is an example of how Mac OS users can use *homebrew* to install MongoDB via their terminal:

```
brew install mongodb
```

You can check that mongoDB is properly installed and accessible to run by simply checking its version in your terminal:

```
mongo --version
```

How to do it...

Follow these steps to initialize MongoDB and create a new database called `mean-db`:

1. First we will need to start the MongoDB process locally, so we can connect to it. This process will need to remain running for all the sections of this chapter:

    ```
    mongod
    ```

2. This will spawn a new live process in our terminal for mongoDB. We can watch this process to see events and updates sent to MongoDB. In another terminal, we can enter the MongoDB shell:

    ```
    mongo
    ```

3. This will bring up a command prompt for MongoDB that we can use to send commands to it. We will use this shell to create a new database for our project. The `use` command will tell Mongo this is the name of the database we want to work with. By providing a new database name to MongoDB, we will create a new database once we insert a document into it:

    ```
    use mean-db
    ```

4. By default, MongoDB doesn't create the database until it stores some sort of record within it. Let's create a simple test post record in our `mean-db` database:

    ```
    db.posts.insert({"title":"Learning MongoDB"})
    ```

5. We can confirm that our `mean-db` database exists by querying for all the databases within MongoDB:

    ```
    show dbs
    ```

How it works...

MongoDB runs as a process on your local file system. By default, it stores files in `/data/db`. This process must be running in order for you to read or write any content from MongoDB. In the coming sections of this book, it's important to make sure you are running the process. One easy way to make sure that MongoDB is always running is to create a process daemon to run in the background. You can create such a daemon using the following command on Mac OS:

```
mongod --fork --logpath /var/log/mongodb.log
```

This starts the a MongoDB process, and logs all its events to a log file on your machine.

The `mongo` command activates a special MongoDB shell that you can use to send commands to your MongoDB process. Following are the most common types of commands you will run in the mongo shell.

Mongo shell commands

Command	Examples	Description
help	`help`, `help admin`, `help connect`, `help keys`, `help misc`, `help mr`	Provides help for the different commands accessible in mongo shell.
use	`use mean-db`, `use <name>`	Sets the active database within the current mongo shell.
show	`show dbs`, `show collections`, `show users`, `show profile`, `show logs`, `show log <name>`	Show lists of types of available content within the mongo shell.
exit	`exit`	Exits the mongo shell.
db	`db.posts.insert(<json>)`, `db.<name>.<command>`	Allows you to use commands to interact with the currently active database.

Most of our interactions with MongoDB moving forward will be in Express through Mongoose. However, if you are interested in learning more about what you can do with the MongoDB shell, there is a lot more information available in the official MongoDB shell documentation:
https://docs.mongodb.com/manual/reference/mongo-shell/

There's more...

For a long time, the MongoDB development community has created various database GUI clients to assist working with MongoDB. Many of these clients have very similar feature sets and focus on providing a GUI interface to manage your MongoDB databases and records. Recently, the MongoDB team has provided their own official GUI toolkit called **MongoDB Compass**. If you are interested in having a GUI client to manage your database in conjunction with the sections in this chapter, you can download and install the client from MongoDB's official download page, at no cost for developers:

```
https://www.mongodb.com/download-center?filter=enterprise#compass
```

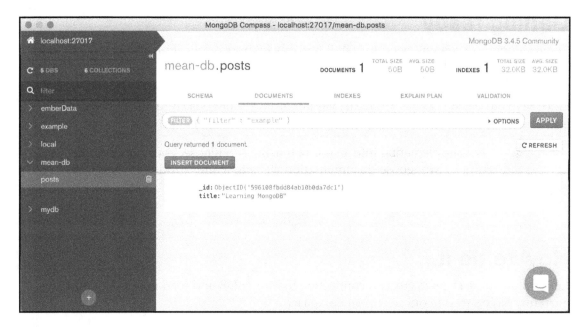

This utility can be a very useful reference to see exactly what data is persisted to MongoDB. You can even use it to test queries and create documents outside of your application. If you are ever in doubt about the state of your MongoDB database, you should use **MongoDB Compass** to investigate.

Connecting to MongoDB through Mongoose

Mongoose is a popular **object document mapper** (**ODM**) for Node.js that provides a natural interface for working with MongoDB documents, collections, and databases. You can think of Mongoose as a superset of MongoDB functionality that is tailored to work inside Node.js. We will use Mongoose for all the details of connecting to MongoDB, defining our model schemas, and retrieving documents. One of the strengths Mongoose shares with Express is its very lightweight, flexible, and compossible approach to database queries.

Getting ready

To use Mongoose, we will need to install it to our Express application's `package.json` file:

```
npm install mongoose --save
```

Once saved to our `package.json` file, we can import Mongoose into our Express application in order to communicate with our running MongoDB process.

 For supplemental information on using Mongoose, you check out the official Mongoose documentation website while working through this section:
`http://mongoosejs.com/`

How to do it...

Let's follow these steps to create a connection to MongoDB and read how many posts we currently have saved in our `mean-db` database:

1. First, we will need to import Mongoose into our Express application. We will do this by creating a new `database.js` file in the root of our project that we will use to configure our database configuration between our application and MongoDB. We will simply connect to MongoDB through a path to our local machine, and the specific database we want to use: `mongodb://localhost/mean-db` . We will also export this reference to our `mean-db` connection in case we may need it in other parts of our application:

   ```
   var mongoose = require('mongoose');
   mongoose.connect('mongodb://localhost/mean-db');

   module.exports = mongoose.connection;
   ```

2. Connecting to MongoDB is an asynchronous process, so we will use a promise to notify us when the connection succeeds or fails:

```
var mongoose = require('mongoose');
mongoose.connect('mongodb://localhost/mean-db').then(function() {
  console.log('connected to mongodb!');
}, function(error) {
  console.error('failed to connect to MongoDB...', error);
});

module.exports = mongoose.connection;
```

3. Now, after we get connected, we can request content from our databases, such as how many posts are saved in it:

```
var mongoose = require('mongoose');
mongoose.connect('mongodb://localhost/mean-db').then(function() {
  console.log('connected to mongodb!');
  db.collection('post').count().then(function(count) {
    console.log("post count: " + count);
  });
}, function(error) {
  console.error('failed to connect to MongoDB...', error);
});

module.exports = mongoose.connection;
```

4. To use our new MongoDB database connection, we simple need to add it to our app.js Express configuration file in the root of our project:

```
...
var db = require('./database');
...
```

5. By restarting our Express application, we will see our connection status and post count logged to the console. If there is a connection error, or if our connection is terminated while our application is running, we will also see an error for that:

```
connected to mongodb!
post count: 1
```

How it works...

Mongoose is a node module similar to the many other node modules we have used within Express in this book. Its main role is to handle the connection to the MongoDB database. This connection is asynchronously resolved through the URI `mongodb://localhost/mean-db`. This same request can be modified to connect to different servers or databases. In our case, we are simply connecting to our localhost MongoDB process, and loading the `mean-db` database:

```
mongodb://<server>/<data-base>
```

The connection object we get back from Mongo can bound to event listeners for startup and failure callbacks from Mongoose. Attempting to make requests before MongoDB is connected will simply queue them in Mongoose until a connection is established. Exiting our Express application effectively terminates our connection to MongoDB, and will restart the connection every time we restart Express. This is very handy if using a process manager, such as Forever, to automatically restart our Express application.

There's more...

MongoDB supports many different configuration options that can be set up when connecting to your MongoDB database with Mongoose. These options can provide support for database authentication, working with multiple databases, and database replication. These options are provided through a configuration object to `mongoose.connect`, or the imported `mongoose` node module itself:

```
var mongoose = require('mongoose');

var options = {
  db: { native_parser: true },
  server: { poolSize: 5, socketOptions: { keepAlive: 1} },
  replset: { rs_name: 'myReplicaSetName' },
  user: 'myUserName',
  pass: 'myPassword',
  auth: { authdb: 'admin'}
  mongos: false
}

mongoose.Promise = require('bluebird');
mongoose.connect('mongodb://localhost/mean-db', options);
```

- For learning how to configure the parsing and serialization functions of your mongoDB connection, use the `db` property:

  ```
  http://mongodb.github.io/node-mongodb-native/2.1/api/Db.html
  ```

- For configuring your connection to your MongoDB database process, you can use the `server` property:

  ```
  http://mongodb.github.io/node-mongodb-native/2.1/api/Server.html
  ```

- If you are using replication with your MongoDB database, the `replset` property is what you would use to configure this operation:

  ```
  http://mongodb.github.io/node-mongodb-native/2.1/api/ReplSet.html
  ```

- For user authentication, you can use the `user`, `password`, and `auth` property to configure how you authenticate users in MongoDB:

  ```
  http://mongodb.github.io/node-mongodb-native/api-generated/db.
  html#authenticate
  ```

- By default, Mongoose uses `mpromise` as its built-in promise library, but you can replace this with your own promise library using the `promiseLibrary` property on the Mongoose node module itself. If you want to use another promise library, such as **bluebird**, you will have to install it and save it to your Express application's `package.json` file first:

  ```
  npm install --save bluebird
  ```

  ```
  http://mongoosejs.com/docs/promises.html
  ```

- Finally, if you are working with multiple MongoDB connections, you can set the `mongos` flag and provide multiple URIs as a comma-separated list:

  ```
  http://mongodb.github.io/node-mongodb-native/2.1/api/Mongos.html
  ```

Working with data model in MongoDB and Mongoose

Models control how the documents we save to the database are structured. Mongoose allows us to define and work with models in our application even before our connection to MongoDB is completed. When working with particular objects, such as a blog post or user record, it is the schema we define with Mongoose that provides the mapping between what our application understands our data looks like, and what is actually written to the database. Mongoose does more than simply provide tools to modeling data though; it also provides many useful utility methods to assist in manipulating documents and storing them in MongoDB.

How to do it...

Let's follow these steps to upgrade our Express /api/posts REST API to use Mongoose to read and write data from MongoDB:

1. First, let's create a new Mongoose model called /models/posts.js. Separating our model definitions from our route configurations and middleware will make referencing models in multiple parts of our application much easier:

```
var mongoose = require('mongoose');
var Schema = mongoose.Schema;

var postSchema = new Schema({
  title:   String,
  content: String,
  published: { type: Date, default: Date.now }
});

module.exports = mongoose.model('post', postSchema);
```

2. Next, we'll replace our simple store array in /routes/api/posts.js to import and use our Mongoose posts model instead. We need to map our _id Mongoose model ID in our serializer configuration, as well as make sure it transforms our models into normal JSON objects, so any unexpected model properties don't interfere with serialization. For now, we will also drop the author field; we will bring it back in Chapter 8,*Relationships* when we discuss how to work with relationships in Mongoose:

```
var restFactory = require('../../middleware/rest');
```

```
var Posts = require('../../models/posts');

var serialize = {
  transform: function(post) {
    return post.toObject();
  },
  id: '_id',
  attributes: ['title', 'content', 'published']
};

var deserialize = {
  keyForAttribute: 'dash-case'
};

module.exports = restFactory('posts', Posts, serialize,
deserialize);
```

3. Our `/middleware/rest.js` middleware is currently configured to work as a simple array-based data store. Instead, let's replace these references with queries to MongoDB's model API to find and update content. All of these methods will be asynchronous requests that MongoDB will process, so we will need to restructure each HTTP hook to use the appropriate Mongoose model API method:

```
...
module.exports = function(resourceId, store, serialize,
deserialize) {
  ...

  return resource({
    id : resourceId,

    load : function(req, id, callback) {
      store.findById(id, function(error, item) {
        callback(null, item);
      });
    },

    list : function(req, res) {
      store.find({}, function(error, items) {
        res.json(serializer.serialize(items));
      });
    },

    read : function(req, res) {
      res.json(serializer.serialize(req[resourceId]));
    },
```

```
    create : function(req, res) {
      deserializer.deserialize(req.body).then(function(item) {
        var doc = new store(item);
        doc.save(function(error, savedDoc) {
          res.json(serializer.serialize(savedDoc));
        });
      })
    },

    update : function(req, res) {
      var id = req.params[resourceId];

      deserializer.deserialize(req.body).then(function(itemReplace)
{
        store.replaceOne({ _id: id }, doc, function(error) {
          res.status(204).send();
        });
      });
    },

    modify: function(req, res) {
      var id = req.params[resourceId];
      deserializer.deserialize(req.body).then(function(itemModify)
{
        store.updateOne({ _id: id }, itemModify, function(error) {
          res.status(204).send();
        });
      })
    },

    delete : function(req, res) {
      var id = req.params[resourceId];
      store.remove({ _id: id }, function (error) {
        res.status(204).send();
      });
    }
  });
};
```

4. Because these requests are relying on an external service, it's a good idea to pay extra attention to the error handling on our asynchronous requests. We'll provide simple utility methods for catching JSON API deserialize, MongoDB, and resource *404* errors, and formatting them consistently using the JSON API error format. Our deserializer errors are written as **try/catch** statements due to the complexities related to parsing JSON body content:

```
...
module.exports = function(resourceId, store, serialize,
deserialize) {
  var serializer = new JSONAPISerializer(resourceId, serialize);
  var deserializer = new JSONAPIDeserializer(deserialize);

  var apiError = function(status, title, description) {
    return new JSONAPIError({
      status: status,
      title: title,
      detail: description
    });
  };

  var deserializeError = function(error) {
    error = error || {};
    return apiError(400, error.title || "Invalid Request Format",
error.detail || "Requests must use JSON API format.");
  };

  var storeError = function(error) {
    error = error || {};
    return apiError(400, error.name || "Database Request Failed",
error.message || "Unable to handle requested database operation.");
  };

  var fileNotFound = function(id) {
    return apiError(404, 'Not found', 'Resource ' + id + ' does not
exist.');
  };

  return resource({
    id : resourceId,

    load : function(req, id, callback) {
      store.findById(id, function(error, item) {
        if (error) return callback(storeError(error));
        if (!item) return callback(fileNotFound(id));
        callback(null, item);
      });
```

```
  },

  list : function(req, res) {
    store.find({}, function(error, items) {
      if (error) return res.status(400).json(storeError(error));
      res.json(serializer.serialize(items));
    });
  },

  read : function(req, res) {
    res.json(serializer.serialize(req[resourceId]));
  },

  create : function(req, res) {
    try {
      deserializer.deserialize(req.body).then(function(item) {
        var doc = new store(item);
        doc.save(function(error, savedDoc) {
          if (error) return
res.status(400).json(storeError(error));
          res.json(serializer.serialize(savedDoc));
        });
      })
    } catch(error) {
      return res.status(400).json(deserializeError(error));
    }
  },

  update : function(req, res) {
    var id = req.params[resourceId];
    try {
deserializer.deserialize(req.body).then(function(itemReplace) {
        store.replaceOne({ _id: id }, itemReplace,
function(error) {
          if (error) return
res.status(400).json(storeError(error));
          res.status(204).send();
        });
      });
    } catch(error) {
      return res.status(400).json(deserializeError(error));
    }
  },

  modify: function(req, res) {
    var id = req.params[resourceId];
    try {
deserializer.deserialize(req.body).then(function(itemModify) {
```

```
                store.updateOne({ _id: id }, itemModify, function(error)
  {
           if (error) return
res.status(400).json(storeError(error));
             res.status(204).send();
        });
       })
     } catch(error) {
       return res.status(400).json(deserializeError(error));
     }
   },

   delete : function(req, res) {
     var id = req.params[resourceId];
     store.remove({ _id: id }, function (error) {
       if (error) return res.status(400).json(storeError(error));
       res.status(204).send();
     });
   }
 });
};
```

5. Now, we can restart our Express application and make requests to our
   `http://localhost:3000/api/posts` REST endpoint to read and write content
   from MongoDB with the results returning in a sanitized JSON API format.
   Attempting to write data in an invalid format or non-existing ID will result in a
   JSON API error instead.

How it works...

Our `/middleware/rest.js` middle already had a means of reading from, and writing to, a
generic array-based model store. We have simply updated those places of the application to
rely instead on Mongoose's model API to do the same operations. In many ways, this
simplifies some of the operations we were previously doing, but the added complexity of
the callbacks for the asynchronous requests to the database adds some new nuances to our
middleware. The PUT (update), PATCH (modify) and DELETE (delete) HTTP method hooks,
in particular, are worth a second look:

```
... // update
store.replaceOne({ _id: id }, itemReplace, function(error) {
 if (error) return res.status(400).json(storeError(error));
 res.status(204).send();
});
```

```
... // modify
store.updateOne({ _id: id }, itemModify, function(error) {
  if (error) return res.status(400).json(storeError(error));
  res.status(204).send();
});

... // delete
store.remove({ _id: id }, function (error) {
  if (error) return res.status(400).json(storeError(error));
  res.status(204).send();
});
...
```

`update` and `modify` are very similar except for using different Mongoose API methods. In compliance with the difference between the PUT and PATCH HTTP verbs, the former is totally replacing this record with a new object (including potentially omitting fields), while the latter is applying changes on top of the last version of the record. To facilitate this, some optional flags are provided to update that tell MongoDB what the desired update behavior is.

Another interesting characteristic is that they do not return any content back with them; they simply return a successful HTTP status code. This is a default behavior of MongoDB for these API methods, because if successful, the expectation for these requests would be that returning the whole model state to the client is unnecessary. If we really did want to return this record, we would simply add another callback to find the updated record and return it.

Mongoose's model API provides many ways to interact with model data in MongoDB. Its API broadly falls into two parts: `model` methods and `document` methods.

Mongoose Model API

Mongoose's model API provides tools for working with predefined Mongoose Model's. It's the primary API that you will use to manipulate documents in MongoDB:

Property	Example	Description
remove	`Posts.remove({title: 'foobar'});`	Removes matching documents from the db.

aggregate	`Posts.aggregate() .group({}) .select({});`	Performs data aggregations on the models collection.
bulkWrite	`Posts.bulkWrite([{ insertOne: {} }, { updateOne: {} }, { deleteOne: {} }]);`	Combines multiple create, update, and delete operations into a single MongoDB request.
count	`Posts.count({});`	Retrieves the count of items that match.
create	`Posts.create(new Post({}));`	Creates and saves one or more documents passed to it.
deleteMany	`Posts.deleteMany({});`	Very similar to `remove`, but will always remove any matches regardless of options provided.
deleteOne	`Posts.deleteOne({});`	Very similar to `remove`, but will always only remove a single document.
discriminator	`Posts.discriminator('Review', ReviewSchema);`	Defines a discriminator for a model, a way to map different schema models to the same collection.

`distinct`	`Posts.distinct('title');`	Defines a distinct query that will return a list of unique values for the field on the same collection.
`ensureIndexes`	`Posts.ensureIndexes();`	Requests that MongoDB confirm it has created indexes for all the indexed fields in the collection.
`find`	`Posts.find({title: 'foobar'});`	Returns any documents that match, but default returns all records in the collection.
`findById`	`Posts.findById(123);`	Returns a specific document that matches the ID provided.
`findByIdAndRemove`	`Posts.findByIdAndRemove(123);`	Finds and removes a specific document that matches the ID provided.
`findByIdAndUpdate`	`Posts.findByIdAndUpdate(123, {});`	Finds and updates a specific document that matches the ID provided, with the provided update object.

findOne	`Posts.findOne({});`	Returns the first matching document, with the provided update object.
findOneAndRemove	`Posts.findOneAndRemove({});`	Removes the first matching document, with the provided update object.
findOneAndUpdate	`Posts.findOneAndUpdate({}, {});`	Updates the first matching document, with the provided update object.
geoNear	`Places.geoNear([4,5], { maxDistance : 5, spherical : true });`	Performs a geospatial-based nearby query for documents in a collection.
geoSearch	`Places.geoSearch({ type : "restaurant" });`	Performs a geospatial-based search for documents in a collection.
hydrate	`var post = Posts.hydrate({ _id: '54108337212ffb6d459f854c', title: 'foobar' });`	Creating a new document from existing raw data. Mostly used for converting fixture data into Mongoose documents.
insertMany	`Posts.insertMany([]);`	Very similar to `create`, but will add all the documents as one MongoDB request.

mapReduce	`Posts.mapReduce({ map: {}, reduce: {}});`	Executes a map reduce command.
populate	`Posts.populate(post, {path: 'author'});`	Populates a subdocument reference inside the provided document. We will discuss this feature in detail in Chapter 8.
replaceOne	`Posts.replaceOne({});`	Very similar to update, except it will completely replace the document.
translateAliases	`Posts.find(Posts.translateAliases({'alias': 'foobar' });`	Converts alias values for purposes of making a query to MongoDB.
update	`Posts.update({}, {});`	Updates the matching documents with the provided object.
updateMany	`Posts.updateMany({}, {});`	Updates all the matching documents with the provided object, regardless of options provided.

updateOne	`Posts.updateOne({}, {});`	Updates the first matching document with the provided object, regardless of options provided.
where	`Post.where('title', 'foobar');`	Allows you to provide a query for a field and value.
$where	`Post.$where('this.title !== "foobar"');`	Allows you to provide a JavaScript expression as a query to MongoDB.
base	`Post.base;`	If using discriminators, this is the base model instance for this model.
baseModelName	`Post.baseModelName;`	If using discriminators, this is the base model name for this model.
collection	`Post.collection;`	The collection for this model.
db	`Post.db;`	The current MongoDB database connection.
discriminators	`Post.descriminators;`	A list of discriminators for this model.
modelName	`Post.modelName;`	The name of this model.

schema	Post.schema;	The schema for this model.

Mongoose Document API

Mongoose's document API provides tools for working with retrieved documents from the model API. These APIs are in some ways very similar to the model API but are scoped to the specific document:

Property	Example	Description
increment	post.increment();	Will increment a document's version upon save.
model	post.model('Author')	Returns another model instance.
remove	post.remove();	Removes this document from the db.
save	post.save();	Saves this document in its current state to MongoDB.
$where	post.$where('this.title !== "foobar"').exec(function (error, docs) {});	Allows you to provide a JavaScript expression as a query to MongoDB.
base	post.base;	If using discriminators, this is an instance of the base model for this document.
baseModelName	post.baseModelName;	If using discriminators, this is the base model name for this document.
collection	post.collection;	Instance of the collection this document uses.
db	post.db;	Instance of the database connection this document uses.
discriminators	post.descriminators;	A list of discriminators associated with this document's model.
modelName	post.modelName;	The name of the model for this document.

| schema | `post.schema;` | Instance of the schema for the model of this document. |

The document API also has methods for working with document relationship references, which we will discuss in `Chapter 8`, *Relationships*.

There's more...

Now that our API is fully functional with MongoDB, it's very easy to create documents and have them available between application restarts. However, sometimes when working with an application, it's more desirable to make sure the data reverts to a consistent state so that development changes and experimentation don't result in unexpected database states.

One solution to this problem is to generate mock data, and to allow the application to reset its state to this mock data state upon start up. We can use the fabulous library `faker.js` to help us create some mock post records in our application:

```
npm install faker --save
```

All we need to do is use our NODE_ENV process variable as a flag for managing this behavior. We will make a simple mock generator method that will purge our database of stored records and generate a defined number of mock models for it. This way, upon restart, our database will be in a reliable state for any testing or functionality we need:

```
var Post = require('./models/posts');
var env = process.env.NODE_ENV || 'development';

var mongoose = require('mongoose');
mongoose.Promise = require('bluebird');
mongoose.connect('mongodb://localhost/mean-db');

var generateMock = function(model, count, generateFake) {
  console.log("purging all " + model.modelName + "...");
  model.deleteMany({}, function() {
    let mocks = [];
    for (var i=0; i < count; i++) {
      mocks.push(generateFake());
    }

    model.insertMany(mocks, function (error) {
      if (error) return console.error('Failed to create mock ' +
model.modelName);
      console.log(count + " mock " + model.modelName + " created");
    });
```

```
    });
};

var mongo = mongoose.connection;
var db = mongo.db;
mongo.on('error', console.error.bind(console, 'failed to connect to
mongodb:'));
mongo.once('open', function() {
  if (env == 'development') {
    var faker = require('faker');
    generateMock(Post, 30, function() {
      return {
        title: faker.lorem.words(),
        content: faker.lorem.sentences(),
        published: faker.date.past()
      }
    });
  }
});

module.exports = db;
```

Faker allows us to create randomly generated content for our posts that, while distinct from each other, is still the same type of content from post to post. This makes it much easier to have a reliable psuedo-realistic dataset in our database while still keeping things very consistent after each application restart.

Querying for data using Mongoose query selectors

Instead of SQL to query data from the database, Mongoose relies on using the JavaScript method chaining to build logical queries, which will be sent over to MongoDB once executed. The model API already exposed us to some rudimentary queries through methods like `find` and `where`, but we can expand upon those greatly with Mongoose's query API methods.

How to do it...

Let's follow these steps to add query parameters to our Express `/api/post` REST endpoint to support pagination. We will also implement some advanced filtering queries, including date range filtering to our API:

1. First, we'll extend the list method of our /middleware/rest.js middleware to parse query parameters for _size and _page from our REST API URL parameters. The underscores are useful to denote that these properties are URL parameters, instead of Mongoose Query API parameters. Whether these properties are provided or not, we will set default values for them using a ternary operator, and append them sequentially to our main query operation:

```
...
module.exports = function(resourceId, store, serialize,
deserialize, middleware) {
...

    return resource({
      ...

      list : function(req, res) {
        var query = store.find();
        var size = req.query._size ? parseInt(req.query._size) : 10;
        var page = req.query._page ? parseInt(req.query._page) : 1;
        query.limit(size);
        query.skip(size * (page - 1));

        query.exec(function(error, items) {
          if (error) return res.status(400).json(storeError(error));
          res.json(serializer.serialize(items));
        });
      },

      ...
    });
};
```

2. To expand the range of query options available, we will filter out the _size and _page query parameters and pass the rest through to a where query. This provides a very direct, very powerful option for querying through our REST API to MongoDB. We will include a middleware method option that we will use in the next step to secure this query API:

```
...
var _omit = require('lodash/omit');

module.exports = function(resourceId, store, serialize,
deserialize, middleware) {
  ...
  return resource({
    ...
```

```
    middleware: middleware,

  list : function(req, res) {
    var query = store.find();
    var size = req.query._size ? parseInt(req.query._size) : 10;
    var page = req.query._page ? parseInt(req.query._page) : 1;
    var filters = _omit(req.query, ['_size', '_page']);
    query.where(filters);
    query.limit(size);
    query.skip(size * (page - 1));

    query.exec(function(error, items) {
      if (error) return res.status(400).json(storeError(error));
      res.json(serializer.serialize(items));
    });
  },

    ...
  });
};
```

3. Having such a wide open API is very useful, but it can also be very exploitable from a security standpoint. Let's create a passthrough middleware in our /routes/api/posts.js configuration that will secure it. We'll use Lodash's pick operation to build a whitelist of what query parameters we allow through. This way, we can allow users to query certain parts of our database, but only those that we explicitly allow. We can also use this middleware to do some advanced parsing to support a date-range query for our published dates. URL parameters will always come through Express as strings, so to create a valid date-range query for Mongoose, we will need to parse it into JSON:

```
var restFactory = require('../../middleware/rest');
var Posts = require('../../models/posts');
var _pick = require('lodash/pick');

var serialize = {
  attributes: ['title', 'content', 'published', 'author'],

  author: {
    ref: function (user, author) {
      return author.id;
    },
    attributes: ['firstName', 'lastName', 'email']
  }
};

var deserialize = {
```

```
      keyForAttribute: 'dash-case'
};


module.exports = restFactory('posts', Posts, serialize,
deserialize, function(req, res, next) {
  req.query = _pick(req.query, ['_size', '_page', 'title',
'published']);
  if (req.query.published) {
    try {
      req.query.published = JSON.parse(req.query.published);
    } catch(error) {
      console.error('unable to parse published date format');
    }
  }
  next();
});
```

4. Now, we can restart our Express application and start making requests to our `http://localhost:3000/api/posts` REST endpoint.

How it works...

With our URL parameters passed through to Mongoose, we can make a variety of queries, including pagination pages and sizes, and finding posts by title:

```
http://localhost:3000/api/posts?page=3

http://localhost:3000/api/posts?size=10&page=1

http://localhost:3000/api/posts?title=foobar
```

Even more impressive, for published dates, we can actually send an entire date range query in the JSON format as a URLEncoded query parameter, and it will return to us only the posts with publish dates between these two ISO dates. For this date range filter to work, the dates must already be formatted in **ISO 8601 standard** to be successfully parsed by MongoDB:

```
http://localhost:3000/api/posts?published={"$gte":
"2017-05-11T00:08:38.317Z", "$lt": "2017-06-08T11:57:14.963Z"}

http://localhost/api/posts?published=%7B%22$gte%22:%20%222017-05-11T00:08:3
8.317Z%22,%20%22$lt%22:%20%222017-06-08T11:57:14.963Z%22%7D
```

These parameters are fed to Mongoose's query API, which provides a way of composing requests for documents data together into a single request to MongoDB. This query API is perhaps Mongoose's most powerful toolkit. It provides a robust way to associate different queries together and then execute them as a single request. It contains dozens of methods, covering everything from filtering, sorting, and manipulating document results, to geospatial, optimization, and functional utilities for querying MongoDB. Its breadth encompasses many of the features you would expect in a fully featured database without the need for an underlying structured query language.

Mongoose Query API

Mongoose's query API provides some of the most powerful search tools available in MongoDB, and are available as chainable methods to any Mongoose model API query such as `find`, `findOne`, or `where`:

Property	Example	Description
all	`query.all('tags', ['person', 'place']);`	Returns documents where the value of a field is an array that contains all the specified elements.
and	`query.and([{ status: 'priority' }, { title: 'foobar' }]);`	Performs a logical *and* operation on an array of expressions and returns the documents that match them.
batchSize	`query.batchSize(100)`	Sets the number of documents to be returned in each batch by MongoDB. Unlike `limit`, which sets the total number or results returned, batch is simply how the total matches will be broken apart.
box	`query.box({ ll : [40, -24], ur :[43, -25] });`	Sets a geospatial query result using a provided rectangle definition.

cast	`query.cast(Post);`	Sets the query schema to that of a defined model or document.
catch	`query.catch();`	A promise catch for failed queries.
circle	`query.circle('locations', { center: [20, 20], radius: 10});`	Sets a geospatial query result using a provided circle definition.
collation	`query.collation({ 'locale': 'fr_CA' });`	Allows language-specific rules for string comparison, such as rules for lettercase and accent marks.
comment	`query.comment('title search');`	Attach a comment to a query that can be retrieved in any context that it is used.
count	`query.count();`	Sets query to only return the count of matches.
cursor	`query.cursor(). on('data', function(doc) {});`	Returns a reference to the MongoDB driver cursor; useful for doing stream operations with MongoDB queries.
deleteMany	`query.deleteMany();`	Sets query to execute a `deleteMany` operation on the matches.
deleteOne	`query.deleteOne();`	Sets query to execute a `deleteOne` operation on the first match.

distinct	`query.distinct('title');`	Sets query to execute a `distinct` operation, which will return a list of unique values for the field on the same collection.
elemMatch	`query.elemMatch('score', { $gte: 75, $lt: 100 });`	Returns documents with an array field that matches one or more queries.
equals	`query.where('title').equals('foobar');`	Adds a complementary comparison value to another query operation for equality.
exec	`query.exec();`	Executes the query.
exists	`query.exists('title', true);`	When provided with a field and a `true` Boolean, returns documents that have that field set to `null`. When Boolean is `false`, returns documents that do not have that field.
find	`query.find();`	Returns documents that match a provided query; can be chained with other `find` and `where` query results to act as a filter.
findOne	`query.find();`	Returns a single documents that matches a provided query.
findOneAndRemove	`query.findOneAndRemove();`	Removes a single document that matches a provided query.

findOneAndUpdate	`query.findOneAndUpdate();`	Updates a single document that matches a provided query.
geometry	`query.geometry({ type: 'Point', coordinates: [100, 200] }`	Sets a geospatial query using a $geoJSON definition.
getQuery	`query.getQuery();`	Returns the current query conditions.
getUpdate	`query.getUpdate();`	Returns the current update operations on this query.
gt	`query.gt('score', 2000);`	Performs a logical *greater than* operation on this query.
gte	`query.gte('score', 2000);`	Performs a logical *greater than or equal* operation on this query.
hint	`query.hint({title: 1});`	Sets a preferred index for MongoDB to use in resolving the query.
in	`query.in('tags', ['person', 'place', 'thing']);`	Returns documents where the value of a field equals any value in the specified array.
intersects	`query.intersects({ type: 'LineString', coordinates: [[150.0, 30.0], [150, 19.0]] })`	Sets a geospatial intersection query using a $geoJSON definition.
lean	`query.lean();`	Optimization flag for returning normal JSON objects instead of Mongoose documents.
limit	`query.limit(20)`	Sets the total number of documents returned with the query.

lt	`query.lt('score', 2000);`	Performs a logical *less than* operation on this query.
lte	`query.lte('score', 2000);`	Performs a logical *less than or equal* operation on this query.
maxDistance	`query.maxDistance('location', 200);`	Sets a geospatial maximum distance query.
maxScan	`query.maxScan(70);`	Constrains a query to only scan a specified number of documents. Useful for preventing long running queries.
merge	`query.merge(anotherQuery);`	Merges another query onto the current query.
mod	`query.mod('score', [5, 2]);`	Returns documents using a modulo operation on a provided field, by a provided devisor, that matches the provided remainder.
mongooseOptions	`query.mongooseOptions();`	Returns Mongoose-specific options for the current query.
ne	`query.ne('title', 'foobar');`	Performs a logical not equal operation on this query.
near	`query.near({ center: [10, 10] });`	Sets a geospatial nearby query.
nin	`query.nin('tags', ['people', 'places']);`	Returns documents that do not have any of the provided values for a field, or the field does not exist.

nor	`query.nor([{ status: 'priority' }, { title: 'foobar' }]);`	Performs a logical *nor* operation using the provided expressions and returns the documents that match none of them.
or	`query.or(([{ status: 'priority' }, { title: 'foobar' }]);`	Performs a logical or operation using the provided expressions and returns the documents that match any of them.
polygon	`query.polygon('location', [10,20], [51, 35], [70,15])`	Sets a geospatial polygon query.
populate	`query.populate('author');`	Similar to `Model.populate`, allows you to populate subdocument fields of query results.
read	`query.read('primary');`	If using replicas, allows you define the MongoDB nodes to read from.
regex	`query.regex('title', /foobar/);`	Returns documents with field values that return matches from a provided regular expression.
remove	`query.remove();`	Similar to `Model.remove`, will remove documents that match the query.
replaceOne	`query.replaceOne({});`	Similar to `Model.replaceOne`, will replace the first matched document from the query with the provided one.

select	`query.select('title published');`	Provides query projection to MongoDB for which fields to include in matched document results. Fields to be included are provided as a string of fieldnames. Fields can also be prefixed with -- to exclude specific values from results.
selected	`query.selected();`	Returns whether a `select` query projection has been defined on this query.
selectedExclusively	`query.selectedExclusively();`	Returns whether a `select` query project was used exclusively ('-field') on this query.
selectedInclusively	`query.selectedInclusively();`	Returns whether a `select` query project was used inclusively ('field') on this query.
setOptions	`query.setOptions({});`	An alternative way to set the `tailable`, `sort`, `limit`, `skip`, `maxScan`, `batchSize`, `comment`, `snapshot`, `hint`, `read`, `lean`, and `safe` properties.
size	`query.size('tags', 5);`	Returns documents that match the length for a provided field.

skip	`query.skip(20);`	Sets an offset for the documents to be returned. Usually used in conjunction with `limit` to implement pagination.
slice	`query.slice('tags', [20, 10]);`	Returns a subset of elements within the provided property for the documents returned using a skip and limit parameter.
snapshot	`query.snapshot();`	Notifies MongoDB to prevent returning a document more than once if an intervening write operation moved a document. This is mostly used in sensitive multiuser session transactions.
sort	`query.sort('-published');`	Sets a sort order for the documents returned using a provided field in ascending order. Can be prefixed with a '-' to return values in descending order instead.
stream	`query.stream().on('data', function (item) {});`	Exposes a Node.js stream interface for the current query.
tailable	`query.tailable();`	Tells MongoDB to use a tailable cursor for this query.
then	`query.then();`	A promise catch for successful queries.

`toConstructor`	`var DoIt = query.toConstructor();`	A factory method for converting the current query state into a reusable query method.
`update`	`query.update({});`	Same as `Model.update`, will update documents that matches the query with the provided properties.
`updateMany`	`query.updateMany({});`	Same as `Model.updateMany`, will update all the documents that match the query with the provided properties.
`updateOne`	`query.updateOne({});`	Same as `Model.updateOne`, will update the first document that matches the query with the provided properties.
`where`	`query.where('title', 'foobar');`	Same as `Model.where`, allows you to provide a query for a field and value.
`$where`	`query.$where('this.title !== "foobar"');`	Same as `Model.$where`, allows you to provide a JavaScript expression as a query to MongoDB.
`within`	`query.within().geometry()`	Sets a geospatial query within a predefined geospatial query shape, such as `circle`, `rectangle`, `geometry`, or `polygon`.

$geoWithin	query.$geoWithin = false;	Flag to tell MongoDB to opt out of using $geoWithin.

There's more...

Returning a document by its title is very useful, but what if we want to do a full text search for any blog post that contains a specific word in it? For instance, what if we wanted to have a search input that a visitor could type **MongoDB** into and get back a list of all the blog posts that contain that keyword in the title? To support such a feature, we can simply add a text index to our model Schema's title attribute to tell MongoDB that we want it to generate an index for our text in our post titles:

```
var mongoose = require('mongoose');
var Schema = mongoose.Schema;

var postSchema = new Schema({
  title:  { type: String, index: 'text' },
  content: String,
  published: { type: Date, default: Date.now }
});

module.exports = mongoose.model('post', postSchema);
```

To add a search option to our API, let's simply add a `new _search` URL parameter to our URL parameter whitelist in `/routes/api/posts.js`:

```
module.exports = restFactory('posts', Posts, serialize, deserialize,
function(req, res, next) {
  req.query = _pick(req.query, ['_size', '_page', '_search', 'title',
'published']);
  ...
});
```

Then, we can use this URL parameter, if it exists, to append a text search query to our `/posts` API endpoint that requests that data from our MongoDB index:

```
...
list : function(req, res) {
  var query = store.find();
  var size = req.query._size ? parseInt(req.query._size) : 10;
  var page = req.query._page ? parseInt(req.query._page) : 1;
  var filters = _omit(req.query, ['_size', '_page', '_search']);

  if (req.query._search) {
```

```
    query.where({$text: {$search: req.query._search}});
  }

  query.where(filters);
  query.sort({ 'published': -1 });
  query.limit(size);
  query.skip(size * (page - 1));

  query.exec(function(error, items) {
    if (error) return res.status(400).json(storeError(error));
    res.json(serializer.serialize(items));
  });
},
...
```

Now, we will send our API a search URL parameter for a keyword:

```
http://localhost:3000/api/posts?_search=MongoDB
```

We will get back a list of items from MongoDB that contain the word **MongoDB** in their title.

8
Relationships

In this chapter, we will cover the range of data relationships available within MongoDB and Mongoose. This will include inner-model relationships, such as validations, virtual properties, and pre-save hooks. We will also cover document relationships, such as embedding sub-documents and using object references to model parent and child relationships.

In this chapter, we will cover the following recipes :

- Working with data validations and virtuals in Mongoose
- Creating sub-documents in Mongoose models
- Using pre-save hooks and custom methods in Mongoose models
- Creating embedded documents in MongoDB with objectId
- Creating relational documents in MongoDB with population

Introduction

MongoDB is what is known as a **document database**, which means that its approach to data management is geared towards working with rich documents with multi-leveled schema. That doesn't mean we can't use a document database for the same sorts of data we might expect to see from a traditional **relational database**, but it's important to note the differences in how that data is composed within the database.

For example, two different tables in a relational SQL database might simply be best represented as a single document in a document database:

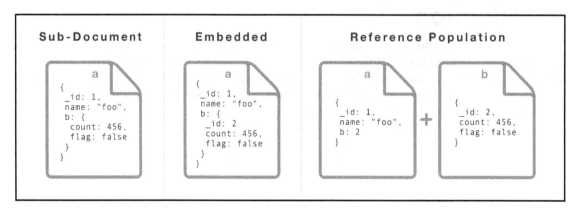

One of the main distinctions between a **NoSQL** document database, such as MongoDB, and a traditional **SQL** relational database is the manner with which relationships between documents are managed. Relational databases traditionally use *JOIN* operations to merge normalized tables of data together as part of a query operation. Documents in MongoDB take a different approach to data management, expecting objects to more closely resemble self-contained structures than sprawling normalized tables of information. However, there are many ways to work with relationships in MongoDB and Mongoose, including document relationships that look very similar to how you would work with a traditional SQL relational database.

In this chapter we will explore the three primary ways we can model document relationships in MongoDB; **sub-documents**, **embedded documents**, and **reference population**:

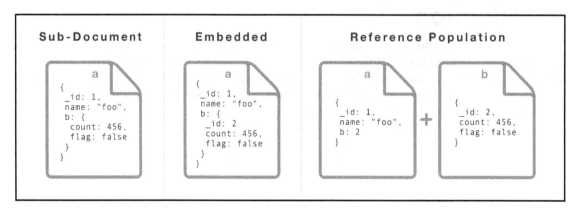

In this chapter, we will grapple with the possibilities of how to best model relationships in our MEAN Stack web application using each of these different approaches and discussing the merits of each approach.

Working with data validations and virtuals in Mongoose

Before we start dealing with relationships between different models, let's cover how to build relationships between the properties of our model and Mongoose.

One of the most common property relationships is validation of what we are saving in our model. This relationship between the value input to the model, and what the model's schema is predefined to allow, helps us by providing an easy to use mechanism to make sure only valid data is saved to MongoDB. Mongoose provides a rich and extensible validation toolkit for handling virtually any type of validation you would want to perform, before persisting it to the database. Validation errors can also be returned in API responses to provide feedback when mistakes are made from the client.

Another powerful feature for extending the capabilities of our models is the use of Mongoose virtual properties. This creates a relationship between a normal property on a model, and provides a hook for applying a transformation to that property that can be returned as a new computed property on the model. As we will see, this is a very powerful way to extend model capability without actually storing any extra data in our database.

Getting ready

Let's add validation to our blog post model so that we won't save values that don't match our expectations. We will add validations for required fields and character lengths for our title. We will also add a custom validation that will use a regular expression to validate a property.

We will also extend the functionality of our blog post by adding support for markdown. **Markdown** is a common format for rich text content, such as blog posts. We will use a Mongoose virtual property to convert our markdown content to normal HTML for the purposes of displaying posts in our application.

To work with markdown and make sure we perform our HTML conversion in a safe manner, we will need to install the popular markdown library, `showdown`, and the `showdown-xss-filter` module to our application's `package.json` dependencies:

```
npm install showdown showdown-xss-filter --save
```

For the rest of this chapter, we will also continue to rely on a REST API client for testing our Express API and its new MongoDB relationships. If you haven't done so yet, downloading a REST API client, such as **Postman**, can be very helpful for following along in this chapter.

How to do it...

Let's follow these steps to add a few different model validations and a new virtual `html` property to our blog post schema:

1. First, let's update our `/models/posts.js` model configuration to add validations for required fields and minimum and maximum character lengths. We will also create a custom validation to not allow our blog post content that starts with a markdown header:

```
var mongoose = require('mongoose');
var Schema = mongoose.Schema;

function markdownValidator (value) {
  var regex = new RegExp(/^#*\s/);
  return !regex.test(value);
}

var postSchema = new Schema({
  title:  { type: String, index: 'text', required: true, minlength:
5, maxlength: 64 },
  content: { type: String, required: true, validate: [
markdownValidator, 'cannot start post content with a title' ]},
  published: { type: Date, default: Date.now }
});


module.exports = mongoose.model('post', postSchema);
```

2. Next, we will add a virtual property to our blog posts schema. We will use the Showdown library to convert the content property into HTML. We will also need to configure Showdown to use `showdown-xss-filter` to help protect against cross-site scripting attacks within the markdown content:

Cross-site scripting attacks are caused by vulnerabilities that allow an attacker to insert malicious code from a client into your application. In this case we are protecting against an attacker inserting malicious JavaScript into their markdown that would be potentially saved into MongoDB and served by our web application.

```
var mongoose = require('mongoose');
var Schema = mongoose.Schema;

var showdown  = require('showdown');
var xssFilter = require('showdown-xss-filter');
var converter = new showdown.Converter({extensions: [xssFilter]});
converter.setOption('requireSpaceBeforeHeadingText', 'true');

function markdownValidator (value) {
   var regex = new RegExp(/^#*\s/);
   return !regex.test(value);
}

var postSchema = new Schema({
   title:   { type: String, index: 'text', required: true, minlength:
5, maxlength: 64 },
   content: { type: String, required: true, validate: [
markdownValidator, 'cannot start post content with a title' ]},
   published: { type: Date, default: Date.now }
});

postSchema.virtual('html').get(function () {
   return converter.makeHtml(this.content);
});

postSchema.set('toObject', { getters: true });

module.exports = mongoose.model('post', postSchema);
```

3. We will also need to update our `/routes/api/posts.js` route configuration to add our new html property to our JSON API serializer configuration:

```
...
var serialize = {
  transform: function(post) {
    return post.toObject();
  },
  id: '_id',
  attributes: ['title', 'content', 'published', 'html']
};
...
```

4. Finally, to test out our new html virtual, we will upgrade our `/database.js` mock configuration to generate some sample markdown content:

```
...
var mongo = mongoose.connection;
var db = mongo.db;
mongo.on('error', console.error.bind(console, 'failed to connect to
mongodb:'));
mongo.once('open', function() {
  if (env == 'development') {
    var faker = require('faker');
    generateMock(Post, 30, function() {

      var markdown = faker.lorem.sentences();
      markdown += "## " + faker.lorem.sentence() + "\n";
      markdown += "[" + faker.lorem.words() + "](" +
faker.internet.url() + ")\n";

      return {
        title: faker.lorem.words(),
        content: markdown,
        published: faker.date.past()
      }
    });
  }
});

module.exports = db;
```

5. Now, when we POST blog post content to `http://localhost:3000/api/posts`, and the content property starts with a # character, it will fail validation due to starting with a header. Putting a header anywhere other than the beginning will pass validation:

```
{ "data": { "type": "posts", "attributes": { "title": "Invalid",
"content": "## starting with a header will fail" } } }{
  "data": { "type": "posts", "attributes": { "title": "Valid",
"content": "however
  \n## having a header afterwards is fine" } } }
```

How it works...

Schema validation is a part of the `SchemaTypes` API in Mongoose. It provides many options for configuring validations on properties of a model and can be composed together on a given field.

SchemaTypes API

Property	Type	Accepts	Description
required	any	boolean, function	If true, adds a required validator for this property.
default	any	any	Sets a default value for the path. If the value is a function, the return value of the function is used as the default.
select	any	boolean	Specifies default projections for queries.
validate	any	function	Adds a validator function for this property.
get	any	function	Defines a custom getter for this property using `Object.defineProperty()`
set	any	function	Defines a custom setter for this property using `Object.defineProperty()`
alias	any	string	Defines a virtual with the given name that gets/sets this path.
index	any	boolean	Whether to define a index on this property.
unique	any	boolean	Whether to define a unique index on this property.
sparse	any	boolean	Whether to define a sparse index on this property.
lowercase	string	boolean	Whether to always call `.toLowerCase()` on the value.
uppercase	string	boolean	Whether to always call `.toUpperCase()` on the value.
trim	string	boolean	Whether to always call `.trim()` on the value.
match	string	regular expression	Creates a validator that checks whether the value matches the given regular expression.
enum	string	array	Creates a validator that checks whether the value is in the given array.
maxlength	string	number	Specifies a maximum character length on this property.
minlength	string	number	Specifies a minimum character length on this property.

max	date, number	date, number	Specifies a maximum date or number on this property.
min	date, number	date, number	Specifies a minimum date or number on this property.
expires	date	date	Specifies an expiration date on this property.

To learn more about the schema API in Mongoose, you can check out the official documentation page:

```
http://mongoosejs.com/docs/schematypes.html
```

There's more...

It's worth pausing to reflect on how similar our Mongoose model schema configuration, and our model schema inside a client application like our Angular application, are to one another:

- **Mongoose Post Schema**:

```
var postSchema = new Schema({
  title:  String,
  content: String,
  published: { type: Date, default: Date.now }
});
```

- **Angular Post Schema**:

```
export class BlogPost {
  constructor(
    public title: string = "",
    public content: string = "",
    public published: Date = new Date(),
  ) {}
}
```

You may be wondering if there is some logical way to simplify our application to create our model schema once, and simply load it into both places, considering they are both JSON representations of the same object. If a model was simply a collection of properties and types, this sort of approach would be trivial. However, due to the complexity of converting default values, validation, and virtuals from one format to another, this approach is quite complicated.

> While we will not dive into this topic in the scope of this book, if you do find the concept of isomorphic model definitions intriguing and are interested in experimenting with the concept yourself, I recommend checking out the *Advanced Schema's section* of Mongoose's official API documentation.
>
> It provides guidance on how to convert your Mongoose schemas to ES6 classes that are much more compatible with Angular's build system and could provide an avenue for code reuse across the backend and frontend of your application.
>
> For more information on this, you can visit the following link:
> `http://mongoosejs.com/docs/advanced_schemas.html`

Creating sub-documents in Mongoose models

Sub-documents are a common way to compose a child model into a parent model's schema. Consider, for example, the creation of an order record in an e-commerce system. This record would contain references to a user model, a list of product models, and a payment and shipping model. In an SQL database, each of these entities would have a referenced ID within their own normalized table, using several `JOIN` operations to merge the necessary parts together into this new order model construct. By default, MongoDB approaches this problem radically differently, with the entirety of the schema simply embedding the sub-document references directly into its own order schema definition.

This approach is a trade-off. It gives you expressive, flexible JSON model representations that remain performant while still allowing rich querying and searching capabilities. However, the loss is that embedded data is written in place without being updated when values change outside itself. In practice, this makes sub-documents best for modeling many-to-one relationships. Think of items such as comments, on a blog post. There can be many comments, but they can only relate to a single blog post. Such a relationship can be effectively handled as a sub-document relationship in MongoDB.

Getting ready

Let's create an embedded sub-document relationship between our blog post and a new author model. We will save the author object within our blog post and will also serialize its relationship into our JSON API response.

How to do it...

Let's follow these steps to embed an author model as a sub-document into our blog post schema:

1. First, we will create a new /models/authors.js model configuration:

```
var mongoose = require('mongoose');
var Schema = mongoose.Schema;

var authorSchema = new Schema({
  firstName:  String,
  lastName: String,
  email: { type: String, required: true }
});

module.exports = mongoose.model('author', authorSchema);
```

2. We will include our new Author model into our /models/posts.js schema configuration as a new author property:

```
...
Author = require('./author');
...
var postSchema = new Schema({
  title:  { type: String, index: 'text', required: true, minlength:
5, maxlength: 64 },
  content: { type: String, required: true, validate: [
markdownValidator, 'cannot start post content with a title' ]},
  published: { type: Date, default: Date.now},
  author: Author.schema
});
...
```

3. Next, in our `/routes/api/posts.js` route configuration, we will need to update our JSON API serializer configuration to include our new `author` property as a relationship reference in our response:

```
...
var serialize = {
  transform: function(post) {
    return post.toObject();
  },
  id: '_id',
  typeForAttribute: function(attribute) {
    if (attribute === 'author') return 'users';
  },
  attributes: ['title', 'content', 'published', 'author', 'html'],
  author: {
    ref: '_id',
    attributes: ['firstName', 'lastName', 'email']
  }
};
...
```

4. To see this new relationship in action, let's upgrade our `/database.js` mocks to generate an author for each blog post:

```
...
var Author = require('./models/authors');
...
mongoose.connect('mongodb://localhost/mean-db').then(function() {
  if (env == 'development') {
    var faker = require('faker');

    generateMock(Post, 30, function() {
      var markdown = faker.lorem.sentences();
      markdown += "## " + faker.lorem.sentence() + "\n";
      markdown += "[" + faker.lorem.words() + "](" +
faker.internet.url() + ")\n";

      return {
        title: faker.lorem.words(),
        content: markdown,
        published: faker.date.past(),
        author: new Author({
          firstName: faker.name.firstName(),
          lastName: faker.name.lastName(),
          email: faker.internet.email()
        })
      }
```

```
        });

      }
  }, function(error) {
    console.error('failed to connect to MongoDB...', error);
  });

  module.exports = mongoose.connection;
```

How it works...

Sub-documents are effectively just objects embedded directly into your model. Their main advantage is that you can reuse schema definitions from another model, including validations and even indexes for better querying performance.

In our JSON API serializer, we configure our embedded author model to be treated as a relationship. This is useful because, in the event of the same author writing several blog posts, the author object would only be included once. This can be an incredibly efficient way to send data with relationships through your REST API, and is one of the major advantages of using JSON API over just serializing JSON objects from Mongoose into a response:

```
...
"included": [
  {
    "type": "users",
    "id": "597167ff46a61445e35ce65c",
    "attributes": {
      "first-name": "Arnold",
      "last-name": "Marquardt",
      "email": "Kenyon.Dach@yahoo.com"
    }
  },
...
```

Using pre-save hooks and custom methods in Mongoose Models

Often, we need to transform values between what is written to the model and what we want to persist in our database. One of the most common uses for this kind of transformation is for password security. Saving a password in any format other than a **salted hash** to your database is a serious security vulnerability. The best way to handle this with Mongoose is to simply use the built in pre-save hook to perform this operation using an encryption library, such as `bcrypt`.

In cryptography, a *salt* is just random data that is used in conjunction with a one-way function known as a *hash*. A hash is a mathematical algorithm that maps a piece of data like a password, to a string of a fixed size. The main use of salts is to defend against a hashing vulnerability known as a rainbow table attack.

If you are interested in learning more about the nuances of password hashing and best security practices, I recommend checking out this article on the topic:
`https://crackstation.net/hashing-security.htm`

Getting ready

Let's replace our simple `Author` model implementation with a full `User` model. This means we will need to add support for handling and authenticating the password property. For this, we will need to install and save as a dependency in our application's `package.json` file the `bcrypt` encryption library to perform salting and hashing on our saved passwords:

```
npm install bcrypt --save
```

How to do it...

Let's follow these steps to add a User model to our application with secure password handling:

1. First, we will replace our `/models/authors.js` model configuration with a slightly enhanced `/models/users.js` model configuration:

   ```
   var mongoose = require('mongoose');
   ```

```
var Schema = mongoose.Schema;

var userSchema = new Schema({
  firstName:  String,
  lastName: String,
  email: { type: String, unique: true, required: true },
  password: { type: String, required: true },
  role: String,
});

module.exports = mongoose.model('user', userSchema);
```

2. Next, we will include bcrypt and configure a pre-save method to perform a password hashing function on our password before writing it to the database. We will also implement a custom function for comparing a provided password with this hash to check whether it's a match, without ever requiring us to save the actual password to our database:

```
var bcrypt = require('bcrypt');
var mongoose = require('mongoose');
var Schema = mongoose.Schema;

var userSchema = new Schema({
  firstName:  String,
  lastName: String,
  email: { type: String, unique: true, required: true },
  password: { type: String, required: true },
  role: String,
});

userSchema.pre('save', function(next) {
  var user = this;
  if (!user.isModified('password')) return next();

  bcrypt.genSalt(function(error, salt) {
    if (error) return next(err);

    bcrypt.hash(user.password, salt, function(error, hash) {
      if (error) return next(err);

      user.password = hash;
      next();
    });
  });
});

userSchema.methods.comparePassword = function(testPassword,
```

```
callback) {
  bcrypt.compare(testPassword, this.password, function(error,
isMatch) {
    if (error) return callback(error);
    callback(null, isMatch);
  });
};

module.exports = mongoose.model('user', userSchema);
```

3. We will need to upgrade our `/routes/api/login.js` route configuration to use our new User model to validate that the username and password are still a match:

```
...
var Users = require('../../models/users');

...
var login = function(req, res, next) {
  var username = req.body.username;
  var password = req.body.password;

  if (username && password) {
    Users.findOne({ email: username }, function(error, user) {
      if (error || !user) return
res.status(401).json(authError('Invalid username or password for
user authentication.'));

      user.comparePassword(password, function(error, match) {
        if (error) return res.status(401).json(authError('Invalid
username or password for user authentication.'));
        if (match) {
          req.session.user = user;
          next();
        } else {
          res.status(401).json(authError('Invalid username or
password for user authentication.'));
        }
      });
    });
  } else {
    res.status(401).json(authError('Must provide username or
password for user authentication.'));
  }
};

...
```

4. Finally, we can update our `/database.js` mocks to use our new `User` model. We will also manually create an admin user that is guaranteed to have the same username and password:

```
...
var User = require('./models/users');
...
mongoose.connect('mongodb://localhost/mean-db').then(function() {
  if (env == 'development') {
    var faker = require('faker');

    generateMock(Post, 30, function() {
      var markdown = faker.lorem.sentences();
      markdown += "## " + faker.lorem.sentence() + "\n";
      markdown += "[" + faker.lorem.words() + "](" +
faker.internet.url() + ")\n";

      return {
        title: faker.lorem.words(),
        content: markdown,
        published: faker.date.past(),
        author: new User({
          firstName: faker.name.firstName(),
          lastName: faker.name.lastName(),
          email: faker.internet.email(),
          password: faker.internet.password(),
          role: 'author'
        })
      }
    });

    User.deleteMany({}, function() {
      var admin = new User({
        firstName:  faker.name.firstName(),
        lastName: faker.name.lastName(),
        email: 'nmcclay@nickmcclay.com',
        password: 'Secret',
        role: 'admin'
      });

      admin.save().then(function(user) {
        console.log("created new admin: " + user.email);
      });
    });
  }
}, function(error) {
  console.error('failed to connect to MongoDB...', error);
```

```
  });

  module.exports = mongoose.connection;
```

How it works...

Our pre-save hook is called whenever we call the save method on our document. This hook operates very similarly to our express middleware, allowing us to transform the document before saving it to MongoDB. For password security, we use `bcrypt` to create a salted hash of the provided password and save that to the database, instead of the original string. This helps protects our user's privacy in the event of a security breach that had access to our database.

To compare the password, we simply added a new comparison function to generate a new hash with a provided password and compare the results. The actual internals of `bcrypt` are fairly complicated and are based on a JavaScript implementation of the blowfish encryption algorithm. For our purposes, it simply provides a mechanism to compare two hashes and determine if they match each other, which is all we need to authenticate a user.

Creating embedded documents in MongoDB with objectId

Sometimes, there is no substitute for a genuine multi-document relationship in your models. The main method for accomplishing this in MongoDB is through **objectId references**. These allow for implementation of *one-to-one*, *one-to-many*, and *many-to-many* relationships through reference IDs in models. This type of relationship is very common in web applications. Consider, for instance, our blog post and user relationship. While we could embed the user as a sub-document, if the user ever changes their name, our blog post would still show the name they had when they originally authored the blog post. A true relationship is the best way to model these separate documents.

Getting ready

Let's implement an objectId reference relationship between our user model and blog post model. We'll extend our API to include a `/api/users` endpoint that will allow us to work with users in the same way as our blog posts.

How to do it...

Let's follow these steps to add an objectId reference relationship between users and posts:

1. First, let's create a /routes/api/users.js route configuration for working with users. We will also configure its JSON API serialization configuration, including a reference post that will just contain a list of IDs to blog posts written by this user:

```
var express = require('express');
var router = express.Router();
var restFactory = require('../../middleware/rest');
var Users = require('../../models/users');

var serialize = {
  transform: function(post) {
    return post.toObject();
  },
  id: '_id',
  attributes: ['firstName', 'lastName', 'email', 'role', 'posts'],
  posts: {
    ref: true
  }
};

var deserialize = {
  keyForAttribute: 'dash-case'
};

module.exports = restFactory('users', Users, serialize,
deserialize);
```

2. We will need to include and add our users route to our /routes/api.js route configuration as well:

```
...
var users = require('./api/users');

...
router.use('/customers', jwt.active(), stripe.getCustomers);
router.use('/images', jwt.active(), jwt.require('role', '===',
'admin'), images);
router.use('/posts', jwt.active(), jwt.require('role', '===',
'admin'), posts);
router.use('/users', jwt.active(), jwt.require('role', '===',
'admin'), users);

...
```

3. To make working with multiple document models that have relationships more straightforward, we will extract our /database.js mocks to its own /mocks.js configuration. This will make maintaining and configuring our mocks more easy in our application:

```
var faker = require('faker');
var Post = require('./models/posts');
var User = require('./models/users');

var makePost = function() {
  var markdown = faker.lorem.sentences();
  markdown += "## " + faker.lorem.sentence() + "\n";
  markdown += "[" + faker.lorem.words() + "](" +
faker.internet.url() + ")\n";

  return new Post({
    title: faker.lorem.words(),
    content: markdown,
    published: faker.date.past(),
  });
};

var makeUser = function() {
  return new User({
    firstName: faker.name.firstName(),
    lastName: faker.name.lastName(),
    email: faker.internet.email(),
    password: faker.internet.password(),
    role: 'author'
  });
};

module.exports = {
  generateAuthorAndPosts: function(postCount) {
    var user = makeUser();

    let posts = [];
    for (var i=0; i < postCount; i++) {
      var post = makePost();
      post.author = user;
      posts.push(post);
    }

    user.posts = posts;
    user.save().then(function(user) {
      console.log('created new author: ' + user.email);
      return Post.insertMany(posts).then(function() {
```

```
            console.log('created ' + postCount + ' new posts');
        }).catch(function(error) {
          throw error;
        });
      }).catch(function(error) {
        throw error;
      });
    },

    generateAdmin: function() {
      var admin = new User({
        firstName:  faker.name.firstName(),
        lastName: faker.name.lastName(),
        email: 'nmcclay@nickmcclay.com',
        password: 'Secret',
        role: 'admin'
      });

      return admin.save().then(function(user) {
        console.log("created new admin: " + user.email);
      }).catch(function(error) {
        throw error;
      });
    }
  };
```

4. In our `/database.js` configuration, we will simply include our new `/mocks.js` configuration and use it to set up new authors and posts, as well as our admin account:

```
var env = process.env.NODE_ENV || 'development';
var mongoose = require('mongoose');
mongoose.Promise = require("bluebird");
mongoose.connect('mongodb://localhost/mean-db').then(function() {
  if (env == 'development') {
    var mocks = require('./mocks');
    mongoose.connection.db.dropDatabase().then(function() {
      mocks.generateAuthorAndPosts(3);
      mocks.generateAuthorAndPosts(3);
      mocks.generateAuthorAndPosts(3);
      mocks.generateAdmin()
    });
  }
}, function(error) {
  console.error('failed to connect to MongoDB...', error);
});

module.exports = mongoose.connection;
```

5. Finally, in our `/models/users.js` model configuration, we will add our new posts property that will be mapped as a placeholder for an array of ObjectId references for our posts model:

```
...
var userSchema = new Schema({
  firstName:  String,
  lastName: String,
  email: { type: String, unique: true, required: true },
  password: { type: String, required: true },
  role: String,
  posts: [{ type: Schema.Types.ObjectId, ref: 'posts' }]
});
...
```

How it works...

The format for our JSON API requests from `http://localhost:3000/api/posts` will now contain a fully embedded user object, but with an ID that matches an independent user record:

```
"data": [
  {
    "type": "posts",
    "id": "596aafb6aede86ed94d5261d",
    "attributes": {
      "title": "dolores earum et",
      "content": "Tempora qui est sed minima cupiditate...",
      "published": "2016-08-09T13:56:03.378Z",
      "html": "<p>Tempora qui est sed minima cupiditate...."
    },
    "relationships": {
      "author": {
        "data": {
          "type": "users",
          "id": "596aafb6aede86ed94d5261c"
        }
      }
    }
  },
  ...
"included": [
  {
    "type": "users",
    "id": "596aafb6aede86ed94d5261c",
    "attributes": {
```

```
            "first-name": "Merl",
            "last-name": "Bahringer",
            "email": "Jaime_Herman@hotmail.com"
        }
    },
    ...
```

The JSON API response for our `http://localhost:3000/api/users` endpoint will include our user details, but will not include anything more than a list of post document objectId references:

```
{
  "data": {
    "type": "users",
    "id": "596aafb6aede86ed94d5261c",
    "attributes": {
      "first-name": "Merl",
      "last-name": "Bahringer",
      "email": "Jaime_Herman@hotmail.com",
      "role": "author"
    },
    "relationships": {
      "posts": {
        "data": [
          {
            "type": "posts",
            "id": "596aafb6aede86ed94d5261d"
          },
          {
            "type": "posts",
            "id": "596aafb6aede86ed94d5261e"
          },
          {
            "type": "posts",
            "id": "596aafb6aede86ed94d5261f"
          }
        ]
      }
    }
  }
}
```

We can actually access the properties of the referenced post documents using another operation called `populate`. In the next recipe, we'll learn how to use `populate` with these sorts of object references in Mongoose.

Creating relational documents in MongoDB with population

Having an objectId reference can be useful. However, we often want to return a whole model as if it were an embedded sub-document, but have it contain the updated data from the referenced document. This operation is possible using Mongoose's `populate` method. With populate, we can retrieve the additional document details required, similar to a *JOIN* operation in a relational database, and merge the result into the referencing document.

Getting ready

Let's update our `/middleware/rest.js` middleware to support Mongoose population for retrieving documents that contain embedded objectId references. We will be able to retrieve our full post details in our `/api/users/<user id>` API endpoint requests by populating the included posts property on our user document.

How to do it...

Let's follow these steps to learn how to populate our user's blog post list with their blog post content:

1. First, we will need to restructure our `/middleware/rest.js` middleware to allow a full set of override methods, not just the middleware callback. We will do that using the `lodash` default to allow us to merge our custom methods with the rest of the default REST API callbacks defined below it:

```
...
var _defaults = require('lodash/defaults');

module.exports = function(resourceId, store, serialize,
deserialize, overrides) {
  ...
  return resource(_defaults(overrides, {
    ...
  }));
};
```

2. To make sure we don't break our `/routes/api/posts.js` route configuration, we should update `restFactory` to use this new override option for our middleware hook:

```
...
module.exports = restFactory('posts', Posts, serialize,
deserialize, {

  middleware: function(req, res, next) {
    req.query = _pick(req.query, ['_size', '_page', '_search',
'title', 'published']);
    if (req.query.published) {
      try {
        req.query.published = JSON.parse(req.query.published);
      } catch(error) {
        console.error('unable to parse published date format');
      }
    }
    next();
  }
});
```

3. Next, in our `/routes/api/users.js` route configuration, we will override the load and read options of our `restFactory` REST API callbacks, so that we can target specific fields in a user record for population. To do this, we will create a new custom serializer that will recognize the attributes for the nested post model properties and properly serialize them in our JSON API response:

```
var express = require('express');
var router = express.Router();
var restFactory = require('../../middleware/rest');
var Users = require('../../models/users');
var JSONAPISerializer = require('jsonapi-serializer').Serializer;
var _clone = require('lodash/clone');

var serialize = {
  transform: function(user) {
    return user.toObject();
  },
  id: '_id',
  attributes: ['firstName', 'lastName', 'email', 'role', 'posts'],
  posts: {
    ref: true
  }
};
```

```
var deserialize = {
  keyForAttribute: 'dash-case'
};

var populatedSerialize = _clone(serialize);
populatedSerialize.posts = {
  ref: '_id',
  attributes: ['title', 'content', 'html', 'published']
};
var populatedSerializer = new JSONAPISerializer('users',
populatedSerialize);

module.exports = restFactory('users', Users, serialize,
deserialize, {
  load: function(req, id, callback) {
    var query = Users.findById(id);
    query.populate('posts');
    query.exec(function(error, item) {
      callback(null, item);
    });
  },

  read: function(req, res) {
    res.json(populatedSerializer.serialize(req['users']));
  }
});
```

4. Because we are overriding the default method for handling finding and loading an individual user record, we will also need to add our own error handling here:

```
...
var JSONAPIError = require('jsonapi-serializer').Error;
...
module.exports = restFactory('users', Users, serialize,
deserialize, {
  load: function(req, id, callback) {
    var query = Users.findById(id);
    query.populate('posts');
    query.exec(function(error, item) {
      if (error) return callback(new JSONAPIError({
        status: 400,
        title: error.name || 'Database Request Failed',
        detail: error.message || 'Unable to handle requested
database operation.'
      }));

      if (!item) return callback(new JSONAPIError({
        status: 404,
```

```
            title: 'Not found',
            detail: 'Resource ' + id + ' does not exist.'
        }));

        callback(null, item);
    });
},
...
}));
```

5. Now when we make requests for individual users, we can see that the included
    property contains posts that have all their details, including their virtual
    properties, serialized into it:

```
...
"included": [
  {
    "type": "posts",
    "id": "596ac2d78624af295aa08d81",
    "attributes": {
      "title": "dolores qui eum",
      "content": "Aut voluptas velit quis incidunt...",
      "html": "<p>Aut voluptas velit quis incidunt..."
      "published": "2016-11-07T03:28:58.649Z"
    }
  },
  ...
```

How it works...

By limiting population to our load and read method, we guarantee we will only invoke
population when we make requests for a specific user. This is important, because
population can be a source of performance loss if our database performs population too
often. Much like an SQL query with too many JOIN operations, having too many populate
operations can slow down your query time significantly. By limiting our populate query to
only when we are fetching a single user record, we are providing some built-in limits to the
scope of how many documents will be populated in any given request.

The `populate` method is a very powerful tool for composing different documents together
in MongoDB, and provides the closest option to how a relational database would approach
data modeling. Use it carefully, and it will be an invaluable tool in modeling your objects in
a way that matches the needs of your application.

For more information, you can visit the following link:

```
http://mongoosejs.com/docs/populate.html
```

There's more...

There are many ways to work with documents in MongoDB. One other tool worth mentioning is that, similar to the Query API, returned documents have their own Document API. We started exploring some of this API in Chapter 7, *MongoDB and Mongoose*. This API also provides a range of tools for manipulating, serializing, and working with document relationships. It even provides options for populating document properties after they have been returned:

Document API

Property	Example	Description
$ignore	`post.$ignore('content');`	Prevents validation and saving the provided property upon save.
$isDefault	`post.$isDefault('published');`	Checks whether the provided property is set to its default value.
depopulate	`post.depopulate('user');`	Takes a populated field and returns it to its unpopulated state as an objectId.
equals	`post.equals(anotherPost);`	Checks whether the document contains the same data as another provided document.
execPopulate	`let promise = post.populate('user').execPopulate();`	Performs a population query as a promise.
get	`post.get('html');`	Returns the specified property from the document as a getter.
init	`post.init(mockPost, function() {});`	Initializes a document.

inspect	`post.inspect();`	Logs the contents of the document to the console.
invalidate	`post.invalidate('title', 'must not contain foobar', 'foobar');`	Marks the provided property as invalid, causing validation to fail.
isDirectModified	`post.isDirectModified('content');`	Checks whether document's provided property was directly set and modified, otherwise is false.
isDirectSelected	`post.isDirectSelected('user.email');`	Checks whether document's provided property was explicitly selected. When there is no projection, will always return true.
isInit	`post.isInit('html');`	Checks whether the provided property has been initialized.
isModified	`post.isModified('title');`	Checks whether the provided property has been modified.
isSelected	`post.isSelected('user.email');`	Checks whether the provided property was selected in the query, which initialized this document.
markModified	`post.markModified('title');`	Marks the provided property as having changes to save to the db.

modifiedPaths	`post.modifiedPaths(['title', 'content']);`	Same as markModified, but takes an array of properties.
populate	`post.populate('user', function() {});`	Performs a population on the provided property in the document.
populated	`post.populated('user');`	Returns the objectId reference used for population.
set	`post.set('title', 'foobar');`	Sets the specified value to the specified property on the document as a setter.
toJSON	`post.toJSON({ getters: true });`	Same as toObject, but is called when JSON.stringify is used on the document.
toObject	`post.toObject({ getters: true });`	Converts the document into a vanilla javascript object. Can be provided options for configuring usage of virtual properties in serialization.
toString	`post.toString();`	A console.log-friendly way to serialize a document for logging.
unmarkModified	`post.unmarkModified('content');`	Clears the modified state on the specified path.
update	`post.update({ title: 'foobar' }, function(error) {});`	Sends an update command with this document's ID as the query selector.

validate	`post.validate(function(error) {} );`	Executes registered validation rules for this document.
validateSync	`let error = post.validateSync();`	Synchronous version of `validate`.
errors	`post.errors();`	Returns all the current validation errors on this document.
id	`post.id();`	Returns this document's ID as a string.
isNew	`post.isNew();`	Check whether the document is new.
schema	`post.schema();`	Returns a reference to the document's schema.

If you are interested in learning more about working with documents, and document relationships, you can check out the official Mongoose documentation page:

`http://mongoosejs.com/docs/api.html#document-js`

9
Build Systems and Optimizations

In this chapter, we will cover some of the most important client-side optimizations that you can make use of in your web application through build system configuration with WebPack. We will expand our ES6 and TypeScript compilation to include the other JavaScript layers of our MEAN Stack. Once we have a common build system across our full-stack environment, we will explore common types of optimizations we can apply through our build system to greatly decrease the file size of our application and increase its loading performance.

In this chapter, we will cover the following recipes:

- Using ES6 and Typescript with Express and Node.js
- Configuring WebPack for use in Node.js applications
- Optimizing asset delivery with gzip compression in Express
- Optimizing images for delivery with WebPack
- Optimizing Font-Awesome with custom font generation

Introduction

Web applications serve content over a network connection that can vary considerably in connection speed. Developers who optimize the size and number of resources needed to serve their application, will see performance benefits for all their users, especially those having poor connections.

Compounding this, most users expect to see content from a website load in 2 seconds or less. Most users aren't aware of their network connection speed, so it's up to the developer to make an application load as fast as possible to keep up with user expectations.

According to surveys done by Akamai and Gomez.com, nearly half of web users expect a site to load in 2 seconds or less, and they tend to abandon a site that isn't loaded within 3 seconds. 79% of web shoppers who have trouble with web site performance say they won't return to the site to buy again and around 44% of them would tell a friend if they had a poor experience while shopping online. You can visit the following link for more information:
`https://blog.kissmetrics.com/loading-time/`

Optimizations for modern web application loading performance can generally be broken down into three different categories: reducing the number of asset requests, the overall size of assets, and the latency for retrieval for assets. In this chapter, we will explore each of these different ways to increase the performance of our web application through alteration of the configuration of our various build systems.

We will also explore how to leverage build systems to optimize our development performance. Build systems can help augment our ability to write better code, more quickly and consistently. Using consistent JavaScript cross compilation with tools, such as **Babel.js** and **TypeScript**, we can more easily keep both our back-end and front-end code bases stylistically consistent.

Using ES6 and Typescript with Express.js and Node.js

Node.js out of the box has virtually full support for ES6 (also known as ES2015) in version 6 and later versions. That means that even the long-term supported versions of Node.js now fully support ES6 syntax and features. However, many of the advanced language features used in Angular, such as optional typing, decorators, and interfaces are only available by using TypeScript. Using the same flavor of JavaScript helps you reduce the cost of context shifting between the backend and frontend of our web application. TypeScript will also help us prevent common typing errors and better modularization of our code. Luckily, TypeScript had first-class support for Node.js since the beginning. Let's explore how to convert our Express web server to use TypeScript.

Getting ready

To use TypeScript in Node.js, we will need to install the **typescript** library via NPM and save it in our Express `package.json` file. You will also want to install TypeScript globally so that we can use the `tsc` command to manually compile our TypeScript files:

```
npm install typescript --save
npm install typescript -g
```

Working with TypeScript will also require us to import type definitions for the various libraries we are using for our project. When first getting started, can seem a bit daunting to convert to using TypeScript. If you are already working with many external libraries, you should check out to the **definitelyTyped** project, to see whether any of the libraries you are using already have type definitions provided:

`https://github.com/DefinitelyTyped/DefinitelyTyped/tree/master/types`

In our case, many of the modules we are using in Express already have type definitions available for them that we simply need to install them using NPM:

```
npm install @types/node @types/express @types/morgan @types/body-parser
@types/cookie-parser @types/express-session @types/helmet --save
```

How to do it...

Let's perform the following steps to convert our `Express.js` main application file to use TypeScript so that we can use the same JavaScript syntax between our frontend and backend applications:

1. First, we will want to create a new `/src` directory for all our application files; this makes compilation a bit more straightforward with our source TypeScript files taken from `/src`, while our compiled JavaScript output will be put into a generated `/dist` directory:

   ```
   mkdir src
   ```

2. Then, we will need to convert our `app.js` file into a new TypeScript-friendly class definition. We'll start with a new `/src/App.ts` class file, which will import all our needed libraries using the ES6 module style instead of Node.js's usual CommonJS (require) imports. We will also build the beginning of our `App` class and export a new application instance:

```
import * as express from 'express'
import * as morgan from 'morgan';
import * as cookieParser from 'cookie-parser';
import * as bodyParser from 'body-parser';
import * as session from 'express-session';
import * as jwt from 'jwt-express';
import * as helmet from 'helmet';
import * as auth from './middleware/auth';
import * as angular from './routes/angular';
import * as api from './routes/api';

import { Request, Response, Application } from 'express';
import { SessionOptions } from "express-session";

const env:string = process.env.NODE_ENV || 'development';
const secret:string = process.env.cookieSecret || 'secret';

class App {
    public app:Application;

    constructor() {
        this.app = express();
    }
}

export default new App().app
```

3. Next, we will break apart the logical parts of our Express application configuration and make them individual methods that we will run in sequence in our constructor. Some of these setup methods will also require flags for whether we are building in production mode or not. We can simply provide these as options:

```
...

const isProduction = env === 'production';

class App {
    public app:Application;
```

```
constructor() {
    this.app = express();
    this.enableLogging();
    this.setupParsing();
    this.setupCookies(isProduction);
    this.enableSecurity(isProduction);
    this.mountRoutes();
}

private enableLogging(): void {
    this.app.use(morgan('short'));
    this.app.use(auth.logger(morgan));
}

private setupParsing(): void {
    this.app.use(bodyParser.json());
    this.app.use(bodyParser.urlencoded({ extended: false }));
}

private setupCookies(inProdMode:boolean): void {
    this.app.use(cookieParser(process.env.cookieSecret));
    this.app.use(jwt.init(process.env.jwtSecret, {
        cookieOptions: { httpOnly: false }
    }));

    let sessionConfig:SessionOptions = {
        secret: secret,
        resave: false,
        name: 'express-project-session',
        saveUninitialized: true,
    };

    if (inProdMode) {
        sessionConfig.cookie = {
            secure: true,
            httpOnly: true,
            domain: 'localhost',
            expires: new Date(Date.now() + 60 * 60 * 1000)
        };
    }

    this.app.use(session(sessionConfig));
}

private enableSecurity(inProdMode:boolean): void {
    if (inProdMode) {
        this.app.use(helmet());
    }
```

```
    }

    private mountRoutes(): void {
        this.app.use('/', angular);
        this.app.use('/api', api);
        this.app.use(function(req:Request, res:Response) {
            var error:Error = new Error('Not Found');
            res.status(404).json({
                status: 404,
                message: error.message,
                name: error.name
            });
        });
    }
}

export default new App().app
```

4. Our `/src/App.ts` file will need to import some of our legacy route configurations and middleware. The easiest way to fix this is to simply move those files from their current root location to inside our new `/src` directory. We can easily continue to use these legacy JavaScript files in conjunction with our new TypeScript versions:

```
mv ./routes ./src/routes
mv ./middleware ./src/middleware
mv ./models ./src/models
mv ./database.js ./src/database.js
mv ./mocks.js ./src/mocks.js
```

5. Now that we have a new `App` class for our Express application and have moved all our other source files over, we will need to convert our `/bin/www` launcher script to initialize it. Instead of porting this file directly, we can make a simplified version for now that handles all the key parts required to launch our application. We will create this as a new `/src/index.ts` file in our source directory:

```
import app from './App'
import * as db from './database';

const port:number = Number(process.env.PORT) || 3000;

app.listen(port, (error:Error) => {
    if (error) {
        return console.log(error)
    }
```

```
        return console.log(`server is listening on ${port}`)
});
```

6. Although many of our modules have defined type definitions from
   `definitelyTyped`, our `jwt-express` library does not. If we use strict type
   checking in TypeScript, this omission will throw an exception during
   compilation. We can remedy this by simply declaring this module to TypeScript
   to let the compiler know that we are aware of it. To do that, we will simple create
   a new `declarations.d.ts` TypeScript definition file in the root of our project,
   as follows:

   ```
   declare module "jwt-express";
   ```

7. The default TypeScript looks for a `tsconfig.json` file in the root of a project to
   configure how TypeScript should function. We can create a simple configuration
   to tell TypeScript where our project files are, that we want to compile for Node.js,
   and where our type definitions, including our custom definitions, are in our
   project:

   ```
   {
     "compilerOptions": {
       "target": "es6",
       "module": "commonjs",
       "allowJs": true,
       "sourceMap": true,
       "declaration": false,
       "moduleResolution": "node",
       "emitDecoratorMetadata": true,
       "experimentalDecorators": true,
       "outDir": "./dist",
       "strict": true
     },
     "typeRoots": [
       "./node_modules/@types"
     ],
     "files": [
       "./declarations.d.ts"
     ],
     "include": [
       "src/**/*.ts"
     ],
     "exclude": [
       "node_modules"
     ]
   }
   ```

8. Now, to build our app, we can use the TypeScript command-line application, and then simply launch the built app from the /dist directory:

```
tsc
node ./dist
```

How it works...

The TypeScript compiler is a JavaScript cross-compiler that will convert TypeScript files with *.ts to a normal *.js version. This allows us to take advantage of new language features, such as strict type checking, variable scoping, and many other enhancements, while still reliably ending up with code that will run in any Node.js environment.

Since the TypeScript language is a superset language of ES6 JavaScript, we can mix the two freely in our project as necessary. While it would be optimal to convert our entire Node.js project using TypeScript, sometimes large project code bases or time limitations make it more convenient to convert portions of a project to TypeScript over time. This works wonderfully in TypeScript through the use of the allowJs flag in the TypeScript compiler. It allows us to import and use normal JavaScript files in conjunction with our new TypeScript files without any issues. This way, we can convert files to TypeScript, as we have the opportunity and, now, a prerequisite to use TypeScript in our project.

The tsconfig.json file is a configuration file that tells TypeScript where the root of a TypeScript project is and how to interact with its contents. This includes how to find and load files--where types definitions are stored, how to compile files, and where to put the generated result. There are quite a few ways to customize and configure your TypeScript environment, including enabling special language features and optimizations to your liking.

If you are interested in learning more about the available configuration options, you can check out the following official documentation: http://www.typescriptlang.org/docs/handbook/tsconfig-json.html

There's more...

Manually building our TypeScript files in our project adds an extra layer of complexity for what we need to do each time we restart our application. In Angular-CLI, this build system uses WebPack to configure and manage this build operation automatically. However, depending on the needs of your application, there are simple ways to automate a lightweight build process to compile TypeScript, and reload your application just using NPM scripts.

To do this, we will need to install a few additional modules to help us:

- `rimraf`: A simple utility to delete a nested directory of files
- `npm-run-all`: A utility to run npm scripts in a sequence
- `nodemon`: A process watcher to observe file changes

```
npm install --save-dev rimraf
npm-run-all nodemon
```

We can configure new scripts for various tasks we need our lightweight build system to do, such as clean our `/dist` directory, compile our TypeScript files, and, most importantly, watch for file changes and restart our application:

```
"scripts": {
  "clean": "rimraf dist",
  "start": "node ./dist/index.js",
  "build": "npm-run-all clean typescript --parallel watch:typescript
watch:server --print-label",
  "typescript": "tsc",
  "watch:typescript": "tsc --watch",
  "watch:server": "nodemon ./dist/index.js --watch ./dist --on-change-only"
},
```

Now, when we want to run our application, we can use `npm run build` to automatically rebuild our application and watch for changes in the `/src` directory. Any changes will automatically be recompiled by TypeScript, and our Express application will restart.

This approach is very lightweight, but relies on some less than obvious scripting that could be tricky to modify or enhance further. In the next section, we'll explore how to replace this with a robust WebPack-based approach that will make managing our build system much more configurable and customizable.

Configuring WebPack for use in Node.js applications

Reducing the number of asset requests means cutting down on the number of HTTP requests for resources the browser makes when loading the page. The fewer of these requests that are made, the better the overall application load speed, because HTTP as a protocol incurs a minor performance overhead, regardless of the size of the file itself. The most common approach to help this issue is through the use of JavaScript and CSS concatenation tools that merge multiple files in order to create fewer resources that are needed to load the page. With tools such as Angular-CLI, this is actually built into our application by default through the integrated WebPack build system. To do the same for our Express application, we will need to implement our own custom WebPack build system.

Getting ready

WebPack as a build system provides a robust configuration tool for bundling files together for web applications. It's most commonly used for front-end applications, such as Angular, but it can also be used for back-end applications, such as Express.

To configure WebPack for our Express application, we will need to install it and some other dependencies in our application. It is recommended that you save these as dev-dependencies since they are only relevant to the building of our application, and not the underlying business logic of our application itself:

```
npm install --save-dev webpack ts-loader copy-webpack-plugin webpack-node-externals
```

These modules provide tools that will make working with WebPack in Node.js much easier:

- `webpack`: The WebPack build system core library and CLI
- `ts-loader`: A WebPack TypeScript loader to work with TypeScript files
- `copy-webpack-plugin`: A Webpack plugin to copy a directory of files into WebPack build
- `webpack-node-externals`: A Webpack utility to work with `node_modules` dependencies

How to do it...

Let's follow these steps to create a custom WebPack configuration for building our Express application:

1. First, we will create a new `webpack.config.js` WebPack configuration file in the root of our application. This file will contain all the configuration needed to tell WebPack how to load and bundle our application files. Since our application uses a mixture of JavaScript and TypeScript files, we will need to provide the `ts-loader` TypeScript loader to transpile those files:

```
const path = require('path');

module.exports = {
  devtool: 'source-map',
  entry: path.resolve(__dirname, 'src/index.ts'),
  output: {
    path: path.resolve(__dirname, 'dist'),
    filename: 'express.bundle.js'
  },
  resolve: {
    extensions: ['.ts', '.tsx', '.js']
  },
  module: {
    rules: [
      {
        test: /\.tsx?$/,
        loader: 'ts-loader'
      }
    ]
  }
};
```

2. Since we are building our application for Node.js and not a web browser, we have some additional configuration options we must set up. We will make sure that our external `node_modules` dependencies are not bundled into our application and our output is configured to run as a proper Node.js application:

```
const nodeExternals = require('webpack-node-externals');

module.exports = {
  ...
  target: 'node',
  externals: [nodeExternals()],
  output: {
    path: path.resolve(__dirname, 'dist'),
```

```
        filename: 'express.bundle.js',
        libraryTarget: 'commonjs2'
    },
    ...
};
```

3. Since our application serves as a static file server for our Angular application's static resources, we should provide a means for our build process to handle this concern. The easiest way is to use `copy-webpack-plugin` to simply copy the resources from their current project directory to our new `/dist` build directory:

```
...
const CopyWebpackPlugin = require('copy-webpack-plugin');

module.exports = {
  node: {
    __dirname: false
  },
  ...
  plugins: [
    new CopyWebpackPlugin([
      {
        from: path.resolve(__dirname, '../my-angular4-project/dist'),
        to: 'angular'
      }
    ])
  ]
};
```

4. Since we changed how our WebPack resolves the application's current directory, it's important to make sure that the parts of our Express application that rely on `__dirname` are updated accordingly. There are two places in our application that reference the `__dirname` property : `/src/routes/angular.js` and `/src/middleware/auth.js`:

```
var adminLogFilePath = path.resolve(__dirname, filename);
var angularBuildPath = path.resolve(__dirname, 'angular');
```

5. Finally, to make working with WebPack as seamless as possible, we will update our NPM scripts in our `package.json` file to have dedicated `build` and `watch` scripts that we can use to run the WebPack build and enable a watch process with WebPack to automatically rebuild, whenever there are changes in our project's root directory:

```
"scripts": {
  "clean": "rimraf ./dist",
  "start": "node ./dist/express.bundle.js",
  "build": "webpack",
  "watch": "npm-run-all --parallel watch:server watch:build --
print-label",
  "watch:build": "webpack --watch",
  "watch:server": "nodemon ./dist/express.bundle.js --watch ./dist"
},
```

6. Now, we can run `npm run watch`, and our application will automatically compile our TypeScript and JavaScript files into a new `/dist/express.bundle.js` file, as well as the source from our Angular project into our build directory. Anytime we make a change to our `/src` directory file, the project will be recompiled through WebPack and reloaded with `nodemon`.

How it works...

Our WebPack configuration handles all our asset bundling needs for our Express application. Previously, our application was using Node.js's own module system to link different files together in our application. However, with WebPack bundling, our Express files are actually merged into a single `express.bundle.js` file that contains all our application's logic while still retaining their underlying relationships to each other. This also means that any processing done to our files, including TypeScript, can be applied consistently across all the assets of our project.

However, there are few unique things about our WebPack project's configuration that are important to point out. First is the `target` option, which tells WebPack what environment we are intending to build this project for. This is important because the manner in which Node.js and web applications bundle resources can be very different. For example, a big difference is that separate files in a web application are loaded via separate HTTP requests, but in our Node.js application, files are loaded only once into a Node.js process.

This is also why the `externals` option in our WebPack configuration is so important. Without this option, WebPack would build our `node_modules` dependencies into our bundle. This would create an unnecessarily large bundle file, and because we aren't in a browser, there is no overhead performance penalty to loading these dependencies normally with Node.js.

We will also want to ensure that we set the `_dirname: false` flag in our node options configuration. The reason for this is to separate the concern of our application for loading project, and the actual resolving of those project files in our filesystem. By setting this flag to false, we are telling our Node.js process that __dirname is equal to our /dist directory, as opposed to its default context of our project root.

Value	Description
true	`__dirname` is relative to the WebPack project context, usually, the project root directory; this is the default value
false	`__dirname` is relative to the output file location (/*dist* in our case)
mock	`__dirname` is the fixed value "/"

With these configuration changes in place, we can use WebPack to build a Node.js application that will allow us to easily manage and upgrade our build configuration as our application evolves.

There's more...

Since WebPack is a configuration-driven build system, there are many options available to customize the functioning of your build. The following is the high-level WebPack configuration API available for the `webpack.config.js` files:

Property	Values	Description
`entry`	string, object, and array	Path to where WebPack bundling starts; affected by `context`
`output`	object	Options related to how WebPack generates output results
`module`	object	Options regarding module loading and parsing; This option configures which loaders should handle certain file types within WebPack.

resolve	object	Options to resolve module requests, except for loaders, which is handled by `resolveLoaders`
performance	object	Options related to WebPack build performance
devtool	string	Enables and configures the style of source-map debugging for output resources
context	string	The current working directory for WebPack; defaults to the `webpack.config.js` location and also affects `entry` and `module` loaders
target	string, function	The environment in which the output bundle should run; changes chunk loading behavior and available modules; defaults to "web"
externals	string, regex, function, object, and array	A set of modules not to be bundled together into the output. Depending on `target`, this will request them at runtime from the environment
stats	string and object	Options for controlling what bundle information gets displayed in the console when running WebPack
devServer	object	Options related to `webpack-dev-server` used for local application development; very similar to Angular-CLI's development server
plugins	array	A list of additional plugins to process output with WebPack
resolveLoader	object	Same as `resolve`, but runs separately for loaders
profile	boolean	Enables capture of timing information to debug WebPack
bail	boolean	Enables exiting WebPack process upon the first exception encountered
cache	boolean	Enables caching of WebPack builds within watch process; defaults to `true`
watch	boolean	Enables watching of WebPack `context` for file changes to trigger rebuild
watchOptions	object	Options related to configuring `watch`
node	object	Options related to poly-fills for Node.js environments

`recordsPath`	string	Enables the generation of a JSON file containing webpack records for the build; useful for logging build information across multiple builds
`recordsInputPath`	string	The file path from which to read the last set of records for `recordsPath`
`recordsOutputPath`	string	The file path where the records should be written for `recordsPath`

This only covers the highest level of configuration options in WebPack. To dig into the detailed options for each, you should check out the excellent official documentation available on the WebPack website:

```
https://webpack.js.org/configuration/
```

Optimizing asset delivery with gzip compression in Express

Reducing the size of assets can mean a few different things in a web application. Commonly, minification tools remove whitespace and generally transform human-readable code into very efficient, but virtually unreadable minified code. This operation usually occurs in concert with file concatenation using utitlies such as `uglify.js`. The other way to reduce asset file size is through the use of asset compression, either by optimizing assets directly such as jpeg quality, or through the use of compression algorithms that can be sent over the network to be decoded by the browser. **Gzip** is a common solution that is supported by virtually every modern browser and provides huge file size savings for resources with lossless compression that can be up to 90% smaller than the uncompressed file. It works by applying a compression algorithm ahead of time to a resource's content, and then relying on a web server to serve it with a `Content-Encoding` header set that declares the resources as encoded to the browser. Once the browser receives the content, it inflates the content natively and loads it as if it received the original uncompressed resource.

Getting ready

To use compression on the assets served by our Express server, we will need to install a few modules:

- `compression-webpack-plugin`: A WebPack plugin to apply gzip compression to output assets
- `express-static-gzip`: Express middleware to serve gzip versions of assets, if they exist

```
npm install compression-webpack-plugin --save-dev
npm install express-static-gzip --save
```

We will also do some more TypeScript conversion, so we'll want to install a few more type definitions for modules we are using in our application. In this case, we should install the type definitions for our Cheerio html parser library:

```
npm install @types/cheerio --save-dev
```

Not installing these type libraries can cause TypeScript compilation errors, as TypeScript can't confirm what the source of these libraries and the typings of their various methods and properties are.

How to do it...

Let's perform the following steps to add gzip compression to our Angular static resources:

1. To make sure that we are getting the most out of our compression, it is also a good idea to ensure that our Angular application is built using production settings. This setting automatically minifies and does some optimizations to our code even before gzipping it:

   ```
   ng build -prod
   ```

2. We will need to add the `compression-webpack-plugin` WebPack plugin to our `webpack.config.js` configuration so that our JavaScript and CSS assets will be converted to the gzip format:

   ```
   ...
   const CompressionPlugin = require("compression-webpack-plugin");
   ...

   module.exports = {
   ```

```
  ...
  "plugins": [
    ...
    new CompressionPlugin({
      asset: "[path].gz[query]",
      algorithm: "gzip",
      test: /\.(js|css)$/
    })
  ],
  ...
};
```

3. Next, we will update our `/src/routes/angular.js` route configuration to use TypeScript, so we will replace it with a new `/src/routes/Angular.ts` file. When converting to TypeScript we will first change over our module imports and overall configuration file structure to use a TypeScript class. This `AngularRoute` class will have a constructor, which will run Cheerio's html parser to return our Angular application's `index.html` page:

```
import * as path from 'path';
import * as fs from 'fs';
import * as express from 'express';
import { NextFunction, Request, Response, Router } from "express";
import * as cheerio from 'cheerio';

class AngularRoute {
    public route: Router;
    private angularBuildPath: string;
    private indexPage: CheerioStatic;

    constructor() {
        this.route = express.Router();
        this.angularBuildPath = path.resolve(__dirname, 'angular');
        this.indexPage = this.getIndexPage(this.angularBuildPath);
    }

    getIndexPage(pathToAngular:string): CheerioStatic {
        const indexFile =  fs.readFileSync(
            path.join(pathToAngular, 'index.html'),
            {encoding: "utf8"});

        return cheerio.load(indexFile);
    }
}

export default new AngularRoute().route;
```

4. Similar to upgrading our /src/App.ts Express application configuration, we will break down the parts of our configuration file into logical methods in our new AngularRoute class. We will add our route serving logic out our constructor, and setup methods to inject the local configuring into the index.html file extracted by Cheerio:

```
...
class AngularRoute {
    public route: Router;
    private angularBuildPath: string;
    private indexPage: CheerioStatic;

    constructor() {
        this.route = express.Router();
        this.angularBuildPath = path.resolve(__dirname, 'angular');
        this.indexPage = this.getIndexPage(this.angularBuildPath);
        this.route.get('*', this.serveRoute.bind(this));
    }

    getIndexPage(pathToAngular:string): CheerioStatic {
        const indexFile =  fs.readFileSync(
            path.join(pathToAngular, 'index.html'),
            {encoding: "utf8"});

        return cheerio.load(indexFile);
    }

    getRequestLocale(req:Request):string {
        const acceptLanguage = req.get('Accept-Language') || 'en-us,en';
        return acceptLanguage.split(',')[0];
    }

    getIndexWithLocale(locale:string):string {
        this.indexPage('head script')
            .html('document.locale = "' + locale + '"');
        return this.indexPage.html()
    }

    serveRoute(req: Request, res:Response, next:NextFunction) {
        if (req.url.startsWith('/api')) return next();

        const locale = this.getRequestLocale(req);
        res.contentType('text/html; charset=UTF-8');
        res.send(this.getIndexWithLocale(locale));
    }
}
```

```
export default new AngularRoute().route;
```

5. To add compression, we will simply add a new method to our
   /src/Angular.ts file to add the express-static-gzip middleware to this
   route:

```
. . .
import * as expressStaticGzip from 'express-static-gzip';

class AngularRoute {
    . . .
    enableGzipCompression() {
        this.route.use(expressStaticGzip(this.angularBuildPath));
    }
    . . .
}
. . .
```

6. We will also need to update our route configuration import for our new
   /src/routes/Angular.ts file in our /src/App.ts imports:

```
. . .
import angular from './routes/Angular';
. . .
```

7. Since express-static-gzip doesn't have a definitelyTyped type definition, we
   will need to add this declaration to our declarations.d.ts file:

```
declare module "jwt-express";
declare module "express-static-gzip";
```

8. Now, when WebPack builds our application, we can see that it will generate gzipped versions of our JavaScript and CSS files in our /dist directory. When we visit http://localhost:3000/, Express will serve these new gzipped assets and provide a dramatic decrease in the file size for loading our web page which will help decrease our application's load time.

How it works...

The wonders of file minification and compression are truly remarkable when you compare the file sizes of assets at each stage of optimization. While in development mode, our entire application weighs in at nearly 4.5 megabytes of resources. Building our Angular application with production mode (ng build -prod) will yield significant improvements in the total file size of our application, reducing our overall page size to a reasonable 1.4 megabytes. These reductions in file size are mostly due to the removal of source maps and unnecessary development mode code from the application as well as file savings through file minification.

However, with Gzip added to the equation, we can further compress our assets to an even smaller ~600 KB size. This compression is a totally lossless optimization that is equivalent to the full version of our application, but at nearly a one-third of the size. Looking across the various gzipped files in our /dist directory, we can see a compression on some files with as much as 1/20th the size of the original file:

Assets	Development	Production	Gzip
main.bundle.js	73 KB	70 KB	13 KB
vendor.bundle.js	3,764 KB	797 KB	184 KB
styles.bundle.css	238 KB	165 KB	27 KB
total application	4,400 KB	1,400 KB	581 KB

This section also continues to demonstrate the flexibility afforded by upgrading parts of our application to TypeScript incrementally, instead of all at once. Something new that is worth noting about upgrading your legacy Express middleware TypeScript classes, is the need to manually bind the class's this property to the middleware:

```
constructor() {
    this.route = express.Router();
    this.angularBuildPath = path.resolve(__dirname, 'angular');
    this.indexPage = this.getIndexPage(this.angularBuildPath);
    this.route.get('*', this.serveRoute.bind(this));
}
```

Without this bind call on the method, we wouldn't have a reference to `this` inside our middleware when it is called by Express. The reason for this is that, while the middleware itself is defined once in our class, Express actually creates instances of this middleware when serving routes. This is due to the massively concurrent asynchronous approach to routing that makes Express so appealing as a web server. You could have multiple requests processing the same middleware in a sequence. However, it can be a tricky *gotcha* if you aren't careful when updating your Express middleware to use classes.

There's more...

Performing compression on our Angular application's compiled assets in our Express application's build system makes sense if you are serving them from an Express web server. However, what if you wanted to compress within your Angular application's own build system? It's possible to customize the configuration for an Angular application's build system by ejecting it from Angular CLI. This approach trades the ready-made, one-size-fits-all build functionality in Angular-CLI's default WebPack build system for a fully customizable and controllable WebPack setup. The choice to eject shouldn't be taken lightly, but it does offer the best way to take full control of your WebPack configuration.

 Ejecting your Angular-CLI operation is considered an advanced feature of Angular. The Angular-CLI core team has acknowledged the need for this feature given the current maturity of the Angular-CLI project, but they consider it a last resort, and offer limited support for such projects:

"Once you eject, you're on your own."
Filipe Silva - Angular CLI Core Team
`https://github.com/angular/angular-cli/issues/4907`

A detail of ejecting that can be tricky to deal with at first is that configuration options are *baked* into the output WebPack configuration during ejection. That means that, if we want to target both development and production environments, we either need to update our output configuration to support another type of environment flag or eject our project twice to get a production and development configuration. For the sake of simplicity, let's cover the multi-configuration solution to this problem.

First, we will need to remove the start script from our `package.json` file:

```
...
"scripts": {
  "ng": "ng",
  "start": "ng serve --proxy-config proxy.conf.json",
  "build": "ng build",
```

```
    "test": "ng test",
    "lint": "ng lint",
    "e2e": "ng e2e"
},
...
```

Then, we can run the ejection command with a configuration target for the production mode:

ng eject --prod

This will create a new `webpack.config.js` WebPack configuration that matches your default Angular CLI production configuration, but now with all the internals exposed for customization. Since we want to do this same process for development configuration also, we will want to rename this file `webpack.prod.config.js`:

mv webpack.config.js webpack.prod.config.js

To run the eject command again, we will have to delete the ejected flag from our `.angular-cli.json` configuration:

```
...
"project": {
  "name": "my-angular4-project",
  "ejected": true
},
...
```

We will also need to remove the `build`, `test`, `e2e` and `start` scripts from our `package.json` file:

```
...
"scripts": {
  "ng": "ng",
  "build": "webpack --config ./webpack.prod.config.js",
  "test": "karma start ./karma.conf.js",
  "lint": "ng lint",
  "e2e": "protractor ./protractor.conf.js",
  "start": "webpack-dev-server --port=4200",
  "pree2e": "webdriver-manager update --standalone false --gecko false --
quiet"
},
...
```

Now, we can rerun our ejection command without an environment flag to get the default WebPack development configuration. It's recommended that you run this command with the `--sourcemaps` flag as well, so we can make sure that our source maps are exported in our development WebPack configuration:

```
ng eject --sourcemaps
```

Now, we can fully customize our WebPack configuration in our Angular application to make any customizations we might want. Let's explore a few frontend application WebPack optimizations that might make sense in our application over the next few sections.

Optimizing images for delivery with WebPack

Over the past several years, the average size of websites has increased dramatically. The average web page today is 300% larger than their counterparts from 2013. The largest source of that increase in file size for websites can be found in images. In fact, images are responsible for over 50% of the file size of your average website, as seen in the following table:

Type of asset	2011	2013	2015	2017
HTML	37 KB	54 KB	54 KB	26 KB
Style sheets	28 KB	38 KB	64 KB	60 KB
Fonts	5 KB	22 KB	100 KB	97 KB
Scripts	135 KB	227 KB	337 KB	347 KB
Images	482 KB	915 KB	1332 KB</span>	1714 KB
Total page size	799 KB	1097 KB	2131 KB	3034 KB

> *From: HTTP Archive Project, Interesting Stats -* `http://httparchive.org/interesting.php`

Being able to optimize image resources is a critical tool to maintain the speed and performance of our websites and web applications. It's also something that a build tool such as WebPack can help us do as part of our build process by leveraging tools to compress and resize images. Let's explore how to include image optimization into our Angular application's build system using our ejected production WebPack configuration.

Getting ready

To perform our image optimization, we will need to install and save some new modules to our Angular project's `package.json` file:

```
npm install imagemin-webpack-plugin
image-maxsize-webpack-loader --save-dev
```

- `imagemin-webpack-plugin`: A WebPack plugin for compressing images
- `image-maxsize-webpack-loader`: A WebPack loader for resizing images

The `image-maxsize-webpack-loader` module also relies on an external library called `graphicsmagick` in order to resize our images. In order to use this module, we will need to install `graphicsmagick` to our environment as well. To install on macOS X, we can simply use `https://brew.sh/`:

```
brew install graphicsmagick
```

Windows users can similarly use the Windows package manager `https://chocolatey.org/` to install `graphicsmagick`:

```
choco install graphicsmagick
```

Linux users can use their package manager of choice to install `graphicsmagick`.

How to do it...

Let's perform the following steps to add image resizing and compression to the blog post cover images loaded by our Angular application:

1. First, let's add simple image compression to our Angular application's `webpack.prod.config.js` WebPack configuration. We will simply import the `imagemin-webpack-plugin` module and append it to the end of our plugins configuration. We will set up a filter to only apply compression to `.png` and `.jpg`/`.jpeg` image files, as well as some configurations for the quality of compression we want to use:

   ```
   ...
   const ImageminPlugin = require('imagemin-webpack-plugin').default;
   ...

   module.exports = {
     ...
   ```

```
  "plugins": [
    ...
    new ImageminPlugin({
      "test": /\.(png|jpe?g)(\?.*)?$/,
      "pngquant": {
        "quality": "50"
      }
    })
  ],
  ...
};
```

2. Our compression plugin is the last step of our build process. So, before compressing our resources, we can resize them for additional file size savings. To do that, we will need to add the `image-maxsize-webpack-loader` module as a loader for our `.png` and `.jpg`/`.jpeg` image files. We will also want to remove these files from the filter we use to load our other web assets with url-loader. This way, we will handle the processing of images from other web assets uniquely:

```
...
module.exports = {
  ...
  "module": {
    "rules": [
      ...
      {
        "test": /\.(webp|gif|otf|ttf|woff|woff2|cur|ani)$/,
        "loader": "url-
loader?name=[name].[hash:20].[ext]&amp;limit=10000"
      },
      {
        "test": /\.(png|jpe?g)(\?.*)?$/,
        "use": [
          "url-
loader?name=./assets/images/[name].[hash].[ext]&amp;limit=1000",
          "image-maxsize-webpack-loader?max-width=800&amp;max-
height=600"
        ]
      },
      ...
```

3. Since our `image-maxsize-webpack-loader` will automatically create new resized images for us, we don't need to copy the original images from assets anymore into our build. To do this, we will simply find and remove `"assets"` from the `GlobCopyWebpackPlugin` configuration, which copies it to our build directory. This way, only images we have resized will be copied to our build directory and processed by `imagemin-webpack-plugin`:

```
...
"plugins": [
  new NoEmitOnErrorsPlugin(),
  new GlobCopyWebpackPlugin({
    "patterns": [
      "assets",
      "favicon.ico"
    ],
    "globOptions": {
      "cwd": path.join(process.cwd(), "src"),
      "dot": true,
      "ignore": "**/.gitkeep"
    }
  }),
...
```

4. Since `image-maxsize-webpack-loader` is a WebPack loader, we need to actually import a resource in our application in order for WebPack to recognize it as a resource that needs optimization. By default, image paths that begin with `"/"` are ignored by our Angular WebPack configuration and will remain unaltered. However, absolute paths in styles are registered and processed by WebPack. We can use this to our advantage to configure our cover to use a `media-query` to responsively serve different sized versions of our cover image, based on the user's screen resolution. Add the following styles in the `/src/app/posts/post/post.component.scss` component style sheet:

```
.cover {
  background-image: url('../../../assets/images/dots.png?max-
width=1200&amp;max-height=600');
  background-size: cover;
  background-position: 50% 50%;
  min-height: 200px;
}

@media screen and (max-width: 991px) {
  .cover {
    background-image: url('../../../assets/images/dots.png?max-
```

```
width=720');
    min-height: 100px;
  }
}
```

5. In order to use this new responsive cover image, we will need to update our
    `/src/app/posts/post/post.component.html` component template also:

```html
<div class="row">
  <div class="card">
    <div class="card-img-top img-fluid cover" alt="Card image
cap"></div>
    <div class="card-header">
      <small class="pull-left">Posted - {{ postDate |
date:'shortDate' }}</small>
      <small class="pull-right">Matt DeLucas</small>
    </div>
    <div class="card-block">
      <h4 class="card-title">Blog Post - {{postId}}</h4>
      <p class="card-text">...</p>
      <a href="#" class="btn btn-primary">Go somewhere</a>
    </div>
  </div>
</div>
```

6. Now, we can build our new production WebPack configuration to see our image
    optimization in action. This configuration will automatically detect that
    `/assets/images/dots.png` is used twice at two different sizes and will
    automatically generate two different sized versions of this image as well as
    update their URL path in our style sheet to point to the correct one. At the end of
    the build, our image compression will also further optimize the output image
    files:

```
npm run build
```

How it works...

Our image optimization pipeline is a two-pass operation. The first pass is the `image-maxsize-webpack-loader`, which allows us to define, via URL parameters, exactly what the maximum allowed size for a given image should be. When WebPack loads this image, it will be passed over to `image-maxsize-webpack-loader`, which will use `graphicsmagick` to resize it using the parsed maximum size options:

```
background-image: url('../../../assets/images/dots.png?max-
```

```
width=1200&amp;max-height=600');
```

If there are no options provided, the default parameters provided on our loader will be used instead:

```
"image-maxsize-webpack-loader?max-width=800&amp;max-height=600"
```

The second pass of our image optimization is the `imagemin-webpack-plugin`, which automatically passes any images in our WebPack build output through its configured optimizers. Take a look at how our image optimization affects the size and quality of our image resources:

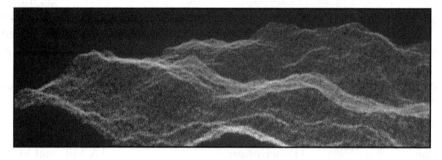

unoptimized original 2194x698 dots.png - 3.65 MB

Our original image is quite large and not well suited for the web outside of perhaps a premium stock photo site preview. If we compare this image to the average webpage sizes we reviewed earlier, it's clear that this resource is much too large and needs to be optimized:

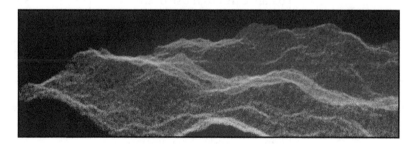

optimized and resized to 1200x382 dots.png - 110 KB

Can you tell the difference? If you inspect very closely, you may find some of the sharpness of the dots to be a slightly less sharp than the original, and the background gradient to be slightly less smooth.

However, our optimized image weighs in at a mere 110 KB. That's over 30 times smaller than our original resource for an image that is virtually visually identical. If we had only used image compression, we would get a file closer to 1 MB at the same resolution as the original. However, by resizing the image first and then applying compression, we get the best mix of image quality and file size for our asset.

There's more...

Since we are only working with `.png` files in this example, we are using the popular **pngquant** lossy png optimizer. For the context of our blog post cover image, this approach gives us a great image compression and quality trade-off. However, there are many different contexts for how you may want to optimize your images. Different image compressors make different trade-offs when it comes to image file types, quality, and file size. The `imagemin-webpack-plugin` supports a wide range of different image compression plugins you may be interested in using instead, based on the needs of your application. As long as the image compression plugin uses the `imagemin` plugin standard, it is compatible with `imagemin-webpack-plugin`.

Plugin Name	Description	Additional Materials
imagemin-pngquant	A lossy PNG compressor with an excellent file compression and alpha transparency support	https://pngquant.org/
imagemin-mozjpeg	A lossy JPG compressor with an excellent quality and file size balance through use of trellis quantization	https://research.mozilla.org/2014/03/05/introducing-the-mozjpeg-project/
imagemin-svgo	A Node.js-based SVG optimizer with a plugin-based architecture	https://github.com/svg/svgo#what-it-can-do
imagemin-gifsicle	A lossless GIF manipulation library that allows optimization of animated GIFs through use of Lempel-Ziv-Welch compression algorithm	https://github.com/kohler/gifsicle
imagemin-optipng	A lossless PNG compressor	http://optipng.sourceforge.net/pngtech/optipng.html

`imagemin-jpegtran`	A lossless JPG compressor	`http://jpegclub.org/` `jpegtran/`
`imagemin-jpeg-recompress`	A lossy JPG compressor that re-encodes to the smallest JPEG file size while keeping perceived visual quality through use of optimized huffman tables	`https://github.com/` `danielgtaylor/jpeg-` `archive#jpeg-` `recompress`
`imagemin-webp`	Converts JPG and PNG files into the much more efficient WEBP format	`https://developers.` `google.com/speed/` `webp/`
`imagemin-jpegoptim`	A JPG optimizer that provides lossless and lossy optimization based on setting maximum quality factor	`https://github.com/` `tjko/jpegoptim`
`imagemin-pngcrush`	A PNG optimizer that focuses on reducing the size of the PNG IDAT datastream by trying various compression levels and PNG filter methods	`https://pmt.` `sourceforge.io/` `pngcrush/`
`imagemin-zopfli`	A generic image optimizer that applies zopfli deflate compression to an asset	`https://github.com/` `google/zopfli`
`imagemin-giflossy`	A fork of Gifsicle with a lossy compression option	`https://github.com/` `pornel/giflossy`
`imagemin-gm`	A Node.js utility for using GraphicsMagick directly to manipulate images	`http://www.` `graphicsmagick.org/`
`imagemin-pngout`	A lossless PNG compressor that uses a custom deflate compressor	`http://advsys.net/` `ken/utils.htm`
`imagemin-guetzli`	A perceptual JPG compressor with compression density at high visual quality	`https://github.com/` `google/guetzli`
`imagemin-advpng`	A PNG re-compressor designed for use with the AdvanceMAME emulator	`http://www.` `advancemame.it/doc-` `advpng.html`

imagemin-pngquant-gfw	A fork of imagemin-pngquant optimized for working within China's great firewall	https://github.com/anhulife/imagemin-pngquant-gfw
imagemin-jpegtran-gfw	A fork of imagemin-jpegtran optimized for working within China's great firewall	https://github.com/anhulife/imagemin-jpegtran-gfw
imagemin-gif2webp	A utility for converting GIF files to the more efficient WEBP format	https://developers.google.com/speed/webp/docs/gif2webp

 You can find more information about these and other *imagemin* plugins by searching for *imageminplugin* query within the npmjs.com website: https://www.npmjs.com/browse/keyword/imageminplugin

Optimizing Font-Awesome with custom font generation

Icon fonts are a web development and design convenience that made a big splash through their use within the bootstrap CSS framework and the highly popular open source Font-Awesome icon font. However, these icon fonts can have a hidden file size cost, which is that they can contain hundreds of extra icons your application isn't using, but that are still being loaded in the browser by the user.

What we really want is the benefit and flexibility of using an icon font, that only includes the icons we actually need. Such a practice can be done manually through font generation tools such as icomoon.io. However, it is also possible to fully automate this process using our WebPack build system to automatically generate this custom icon font for us.

Getting ready

Let's build a custom web font to replace our full Font-Awesome library usage. We will continue to leverage all the advanced features of Font-Awesome, including our angular2-fontawesome module's custom directives, but without any additional icons that we don't need being loaded to our frontend application.

To do this, we will need to install a few modules to our Angular application's `package.json` file:

```
npm install webfonts-loader
font-awesome-svg-png --save-dev
```

- `webfonts-loader`: A WebPack loader for loading font files that allows generation of custom fonts
- `font-awesome-svg-png`: A collection of SVG and PNG files for each of the icons within `font-awesome`

How to do it...

Let's follow these steps to replace our full Font-Awesome icon font dependency with an automatically generated custom icon font that only includes the icons we are using:

1. First, we will need to create a new configuration file for `webfonts-loader` that will define a new font we will want it to build. We'll create a new `/src/font-awesome.font.js` configuration file, that is, a simple Node.js module that we will need to import into our WebPack build. It defines where all the files that make up our custom font live, what font file formats to export, what the name of the font will be, and even what template to use for generating the CSS that imports it:

```
module.exports = {
  "files": [
    "../node_modules/font-awesome-svg-png/white/svg/spinner.svg",
    "../node_modules/font-awesome-svg-png/white/svg/close.svg",
    "../node_modules/font-awesome-svg-png/white/svg/user.svg",
    "../node_modules/font-awesome-svg-png/white/svg/plus.svg",
    "../node_modules/font-awesome-svg-png/white/svg/newspaper-
o.svg"
  ],
  "cssTemplate": "./styles/font-awesome.hbs",
  "fontName": "FontAwesome",
  "classPrefix": "fa-",
  "baseSelector": ".fa",
  "types": [
    "eot",
    "woff",
    "woff2",
    "ttf",
    "svg"
  ],
```

```
      "fileName": "./assets/fonts/[fontname].[hash].[ext]",
      "fontHeight": 1792,
      "descent": 256,
      "centerHorizontally": true,
      "normalize": true
};
```

2. Next, we will need to import this configuration file into our
   `/src/app/app.module.ts` module configuration file near the top with our
   other imports. We only need it to be imported so that our WebPack build
   configuration will include it when we build our application:

   ```
   ...
   import '../font-awesome.font';
   ...
   ```

3. Now, for the tricky part, configure a custom loader to find our custom font
   configuration and feed it to `webfonts-loader`. Inside our
   `webpack.config.prod.js` configuration, we'll add a filter for any file matching
   the name `*.font.js` to be loaded by the `webfonts-loader`. We'll also
   configure it to pass the output to `sass-loader` and, finally, `css-loader`. This
   progressive series of loaders is important because each loader only handles
   certain parts of the preparation of the data for the build:

   ```
   ...
   module.exports = {
     ...
     "module": {
       "rules": [
         ...
         {
           test: /\.font\.js/,
           loader: ExtractTextPlugin.extract({
             fallback: 'style-loader',
             use: [
               {
                 "loader": "css-loader",
                 "options": {
                   "sourceMap": false,
                   "importLoaders": 1
                 }
               },
               {
                 "loader": "sass-loader",
                 "options": {
                   "sourceMap": false,
   ```

```
                    "precision": 8
                  }
               },
               'webfonts-loader'
             ]
          }),
        },
        {
          "test": /\.(webp|gif|otf|ttf|woff|woff2|eot|svg|cur|ani)$/,
          "loader": "url-
loader?name=[name].[hash:20].[ext]&amp;limit=10000"
          },
          ...
      ]
      ...
    }
};
```

4. In order to stop importing the entire Font-Awesome library, we will simply need to find and remove its import from our `/src/styles.scss`:

```
@import "~bootstrap/scss/bootstrap";

$fa-font-path: "~font-awesome/fonts";
@import "~font-awesome/scss/font-awesome";
```

5. Now, earlier we defined where the `cssTemplate` for our Font-Awesome custom font should come from. We will need to create this template as a custom handlebars file called `/src/styles/font-awesome.hbs`. This file is actually a template that will receive variables from `webfont-loader` and then return a sass file, which will be parsed by `sass-loader`. The key details for our icon font are provided inside the `{{ }}` brackets and the rest simply leverages the non-icon-specific parts of the original font-awesome sass library:

```
@import "~font-awesome/scss/variables";
@import "~font-awesome/scss/mixins";

@font-face {
  font-family: "{{fontName}}";
  src: {{{src}}};
}

@import "~font-awesome/scss/core";
@import "~font-awesome/scss/larger";
@import "~font-awesome/scss/fixed-width";
@import "~font-awesome/scss/list";
```

```
@import "~font-awesome/scss/bordered-pulled";
@import "~font-awesome/scss/animated";
@import "~font-awesome/scss/rotated-flipped";
@import "~font-awesome/scss/stacked";
@import "~font-awesome/scss/screen-reader";

{{#each codepoints}}
  .#{$fa-css-prefix}-{{@key}}:before {
    font-family: {{../fontName}};
    content: unquote("\"\\{{this}}\"");
  }
{{/each}}
```

6. Now, when we build our application in production mode, it will automatically create a custom font including the icons we reference in our /src/font-awesome.font.js configuration, and, because we continue to use the Font-Awesome library defaults, all the other styles will come through as expected without any need for alteration.

How it works...

The webfont-loader module allows us to create new fonts by loading configurations that define the content of that font. This operation creates an SVG-based font file, which is then, in turn, passed through various other font generators that convert the SVG font file into TTF, EOT, WOFF, and WOFF2 formats.

The key to keeping the font file's file size down is to limit the number of icons glpyhs included in the font. In this case, we only use Font-Awesome's spinner, close, user, plus, and newspaper-o icons. Compare that to the over 780+ icons in Font-Awesome's full library, and it's easy to see how much space we can save by only loading the icons we need.

File Type	Full font-awesome	Custom font-awesome
.eot	166 KB	3 KB
.svg	444 KB	3 KB
.ttf	166 KB	2 KB
.woff	98 KB	2 KB
.woff2	77 KB	1 KB

While these file savings aren't as high as those we gain through optimizing images, style sheets, or script files, they do help contribute to the overall efficiency of our web application's load performance.

There's more...

Icon fonts such as Font-Awesome work by carving out a space of key codes known as **code points** in a font, and mapping them to glyphs that are actually icons. It's a highly efficient way to pack many vector scalable icons into a convenient web browser-friendly asset. These code points aren't the usual keys accessible on your keyboard and are instead what is described in the unicode standard as *private use areas*. Normally, characters in unicode are addressed using the code point, such as U+004C , which is the code point for the latin character capital L. Each character has its own code point and is defined in the standard and must be interpreted the same way everywhere.

The exception to this are private use areas, which are special ranges of unicode code points that don't have a predefined purpose. Font-Awesome uses the code point range U+F0000–U+FFFFD to define its icons. This approach is identical to our custom-generated icon font, with webfont-loader simply starting at the beginning of this same private use area range and then just incrementing it with each icon added.

> You can learn more about private use areas and their relationship to the unicode standard via their wikipedia page at https://en.wikipedia.org/wiki/Private_Use_Areas.

10
Debugging

In this chapter, we will take a look at options related to debugging the backend parts of our MEAN Stack web application, focusing on Node.js application debugging tools. We will discuss using the native Node.js debug module, node inspector, and IDE-integrated debugging tools. We'll also discuss how to approach debugging beyond your development environment through the use of production monitoring services.

In this chapter, we will cover the following recipes:

- Debugging Node.js using the debug module
- Debugging Node.js using node-inspector in Google Chrome
- Debugging Node.js using JetBrain's WebStorm IDE
- Production error tracking and debugging with Sentry.io

Introduction

When it comes to JavaScript debugging, the humble `console.log` and logging-based debugging have long been a staple of JavaScript web development. However, one of the most amazing things to come with the revolution of JavaScript over the last decade has been the advancements made in tooling for better debugging of JavaScript. Most notably, the advances made in debugging Node.js have created a lot of attention on developing better ways to analyze and evaluate JavaScript applications while they are running.

Due to Node's underlying dependency on Google Chrome's V8 JavaScript engine, we now have more options available across both front-end and back-end application environments to debug complex JavaScript applications. Many improvements in V8's own JavaScript debugging capability have directly affected Node.js. In fact, with the recent Node.js 8 release, Node.js has recently undergone a significant upgrade to its debugging capabilities to rely more directly upon V8.

The legacy command-line debugger is being removed in Node.js 8. As a command-line replacement, **node-inspect** has been integrated directly into the *Node.js runtime*. Additionally, the V8 Inspector debugger, which was used previously as an experimental feature in Node.js 6, is being upgraded to a fully supported feature--you can refer to the following link for more information:

`https://nodejs.org/en/blog/release/v8.0.0/`.

This upgrade greatly affects developers because, depending on the nature of their application, they may only want to rely on long-term supported (LTS) versions of Node.js. As of now, Node.js 6 is the active LTS version until April 2018, with LTS support for Node.js 8 starting in November 2017:

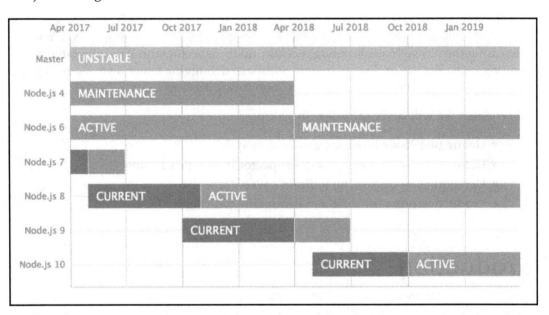

Due to the time-sensitive nature of this transition, we will cover both the approaches for debugging in Node.js 6 and the new features enabled in Node.js 8 in this chapter. This way, the choice of the version is up to the individual developer and their needs.

Debugging Node.js using the debug module

In Node 6, there are two primary tools for debugging with Node.js: the **debug module** and the **debugger utility**. The debug module is invoked using an environment parameter to define namespaces for logging debug messages from modules. It also can be imported into an application to implement your own custom namespace for debug logs. This feature is still fully available in Node 8 and later versions and is highly useful when tracking down issues in your application's behavior.

The built-in debugger utility is an interactive debugger in Node.js that, while not very sophisticated or full-featured, is an easily accessible and useful tool that many other more sophisticated debugging tools leverage as a foundation. It provides a basic, command-line driven debug tool that can be very handy when you don't want to rely on any other third-party tools. However, it has been deprecated in Node 8 and replaced with a new V8 inspect feature, which we will cover in the next section of this chapter.

Between these two different manners of debugger, we can explore that basics of debugging a Node.js application.

Getting ready

Most of the debugging we will be doing through the command line, and will require you to be able to run your Node.js application directly from the terminal. Due to the various environment keys required by the application, you will need to make sure that you export these environment variables so that your Node.js process will have them available:

```
export cookieSecret=xxxxxxx NODE_ENV=development jwtSecret=xxxxxxxx
cloudinaryCloudName=xxxxxxxxx cloudinaryAPIKey=xxxxxxxxxxxxxxxxxxxx
cloudinaryAPISecret=xxxxxxxxxxxxxxxxxxxx
stripeAPIPublishableKey=pk_test_xxxxxxxxxxxxxxxxxxxx
stripeAPISecretKey=sk_test_xxxxxxxxxxxxxxxxxxxx
```

We will also need to install the optional **debug** module in order to add our own custom debug logging to our application:

```
npm install debug --save
npm install @types/debug --save-dev
```

How to do it...

Let's perform the following steps to add some detailed debugging support to our Express application using the debug module:

1. First, we will create a new `debug` NPM script in our `package.json` file. This configuration is identical to our `start` script, except for providing node with the appropriate debug options:

```
{
  ...
  "scripts": {
    "clean": "rimraf ./dist",
    "start": "node ./dist/express.bundle.js",
    "debug": "DEBUG=express* node debug ./dist/express.bundle.js",
    "build": "webpack",
    "watch": "npm-run-all clean build --parallel watch:server
watch:build --print-label",
    "watch:build": "webpack --watch",
    "watch:server": "nodemon ./dist/express.bundle.js --watch
./dist --on-change-only"
  },
  ...
}
```

2. Next, we'll convert our `/src/database.js` Mongoose configuration to TypeScript and add a debugger command to it. If you encounter any issues with TypeScript, ensure that you also install the proper type definitions through NPM with `npm install @types/mongoose @types/bluebird --save-dev`:

```
import * as mongoose from 'mongoose';
import * as mocks from './mocks';
import * as bluebird from 'bluebird';

import {ConnectionBase} from "mongoose";

var env = process.env.NODE_ENV || 'development';
global.Promise = bluebird;

(<any>mongoose).Promise = bluebird;

mongoose.connect('mongodb://localhost/mean-db').then(function() {
  if (env == 'development') {
    mongoose.connection.db.dropDatabase().then(function() {
      mocks.generateAuthorAndPosts(3);
      mocks.generateAuthorAndPosts(3);
```

```
      mocks.generateAuthorAndPosts(3);
      mocks.generateAdmin()
    });
  }
}, function(error) {
  console.error('failed to connect to MongoDB...', error);
});

debugger;

export const mongooseConnection:ConnectionBase =
mongoose.connection;
```

3. We'll also update our `index.ts` file to include the debug module. We will set the debug namespace to `express:blog-app` so that we can see these events in the scope of our `express*` debug environment variable:

```
import app from './App'
import * as Debug from 'debug';

const name = 'express:blog-app';
const debug = Debug(name);
debug('launching %s...', name);

import { mongooseConnection } from './Database';

const port:number = Number(process.env.PORT) || 3000;

app.listen(port, (error:Error) => {
    debug('listener registered on port %s', port);
    if (error) {
        return console.log(error)
    }

    return console.log(`server is listening on ${port},
mongodb:${mongooseConnection.db.databaseName}`)
});
```

4. Finally, we will build and run our application in the debug mode:

```
npm run build
npm run debug
```

5. We will be able to see the application stop on the first line of our express application's webpack-compiled bundle. Note the current line of execution and a prompt waiting for input:

```
nmcclay@NMCCLAY-MBP Sat Aug 26 01:59 PM — ~/WebstormProjects/my-express-project
(master|*) ∴ npm run debug

> my-express-project@0.0.0 debug /Users/nmcclay/WebstormProjects/my-express-project
> DEBUG=express* node debug ./dist/express.bundle.js

< Debugger listening on [::]:5858
connecting to 127.0.0.1:5858 ... ok
break in dist/express.bundle.js:1
> 1 module.exports =
  2 /******/ (function(modules) { // webpackBootstrap
  3 /******/    // The module cache
debug> cont
```

6. The application will pause here until we enter the command cont or c for continue. This will then run the application until we reach our declared debugger command in Database.ts:

```
< Sat, 26 Aug 2017 17:59:01 GMT express:router use '/' session
< Sat, 26 Aug 2017 17:59:01 GMT express:router:layer new '/'
< Sat, 26 Aug 2017 17:59:01 GMT express:router use '/' router
< Sat, 26 Aug 2017 17:59:01 GMT express:router:layer new '/'
< Sat, 26 Aug 2017 17:59:01 GMT express:router use '/api' router
< Sat, 26 Aug 2017 17:59:01 GMT express:router:layer new '/api'
< Sat, 26 Aug 2017 17:59:01 GMT express:router use '/' <anonymous>
< Sat, 26 Aug 2017 17:59:01 GMT express:router:layer new '/'
< Sat, 26 Aug 2017 17:59:01 GMT express:blog-app launching express:blog-app...
break in dist/express.bundle.js:1118
 1116     console.error('failed to connect to MongoDB...', error);
 1117 });
>1118 debugger;
 1119 exports.mongooseConnection = mongoose.connection;
 1120
debug>
```

7. When you finish debugging, you can escape by typing ctrl+c twice to escape the debug utility and close your Node process.

How it works...

The DEBUG environment variable provides a namespace key for which debug namespace logs will be displayed, as follows:

```
DEBUG=express*
```

Using the express* namespace, we will be able to match a wide range of available express process namespaces, including express:router, express:router:layer, express:application, and our own custom express:blog-app.

The built-in debugger allows us to stop the execution of our application and interact with it to help determine the source of issues. The debug utility command line supports a number of commands and shorted aliases for commands to make working with the debugger easy. The following table presents Node.js debug utility commands and aliases:

Command	Alias	Description
next	n	Executes the current line and goes to the next line
step	s	Steps into the current function
out	0	Steps out of the current function
pause		Pauses code execution
help		Lists the available debug utility commands
setBreakpoint()	sb()	Sets a breakpoint on the current line, a provided line number, or at the start of a specific script file
clearBreakpoint()	cb()	Clears a given breakpoint using the same details as provided to setBreakpoint
breakOnException		Allows debug utility to pause when an unexpected exception occurs
breakpoints		Lists the currently enabled breakpoints
backtrace	bt	Lists a logical stack trace for the current execution context
list()		Prints out the current execution context and the surrounding lines. Defaults to five lines above and below the current line, but can be provided any number of lines

watch()		Adds an expression (variable or function) to the watchers list
unwatch()		Clears a given expression using the same details as provided to watch from the watchers list
watchers		Lists the watched expressions and their values
repl		Creates a new Node Read–Eval–Print Loop execution context
exec		Executes a given expression
run	r	Runs the current script
restart		Restarts the current script's execution
kill		Stops the current script's execution
scripts		Lists the available script files
version		Prints the current V8 engine version

This set of tools allows you to debug a Node application as it is running with V8's JavaScript engine. This means that any changes to source code will not be automatically applied to the debugging context, because your application source code is not the code you are currently debugging. This can be confusing at first when debugging, but makes sense if you consider the manner in which Node executes its code. If you need to make changes to your source code, you will need to completely restart the debugging process.

There's more...

Even though the command line-debug has been replaced in Node 8, this doesn't mean that you can't use it. Attempting to run the same debug command in Node 8 will simply display a deprecation warning, asking you to use the inspect instead:

```
[DEP0068] DeprecationWarning: `node debug` is deprecated. Please use `node inspect` instead.
```

Otherwise, this feature works in the same fashion as it does in Node 6, with the same debug utility commands available. If you want to remove the deprecation warning, simply update your debug script in your `package.json` to use the `inspect` command instead:

```
"debug": "DEBUG=express* node inspect ./dist/express.bundle.js",
```

The documentation for the inspect command and the deprecated debugger is virtually identical; however, if you are interested in learning more about the options available when using this type of command-line debugging, you can learn more about it from the following official Node.js documentation: `https://nodejs.org/api/debugger.html`.

Debugging Node.js using node-inspector in Google Chrome

Debugging in the command line has never really been something that most JavaScript developers have much experience with. By far, the most common debugging tool for JavaScript is the browser's developer toolkit and its associated debugging tools. These tools, popularized with utilities such as Mozilla's *firebug* or Chrome's own developer toolkit, allow developers to set breakpoints, inspect values, and evaluate expressions all within their web browser.

Wouldn't it be great to use this same debugging toolkit for the Node.js application? Until recently, the only way to accomplish this feat was by including a module called node-inspector into your application. However, since Node 8, this feature is actually a fully integrated feature of Node.js debugging. Let's explore how to debug our Node.js application using Chrome's developer tools.

Getting ready

In order to streamline this process as much as possible, I highly recommend that you download the **Node.js V8 Inspector Manager (NiM)** Chrome extension from the following link: `https://chrome.google.com/webstore/detail/nodejs-v8-inspector-manag/` `gnhhdgbaldcilmgcpfddgdbkhjohddkj`.

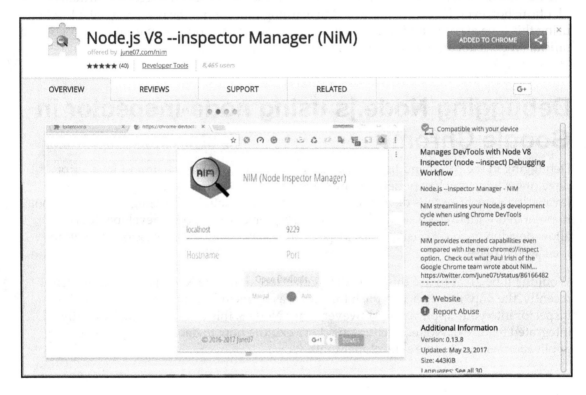

This extension adds an incredibly useful auto-open functionality whenever a new debugging session is started using Chrome. This makes it trivial to transition from starting an inspector debug session in Node.js to actually getting the developer tools loaded and waiting for you.

How to do it...

Let's follow these steps to add Chrome developer toolkit debugging to our Node.js application:

1. First, we will update our debug NPM script in our `package.json` file to simply pass the `--inspect-brk` flag. This flag will replicate the same behavior as the Node.js debugger utility that pauses the execution context when the application starts. This is useful so that the asynchronous launching of the Chrome developer toolkit won't miss any important events that might happen on startup that you might want to debug:

```
{
   ...
  "scripts": {
    "clean": "rimraf ./dist",
    "start": "node $NODE_DEBUG_OPTION ./dist/express.bundle.js",
    "debug": "DEBUG=express* node --inspect-brk
./dist/express.bundle.js",
    "build": "webpack",
    "watch": "npm-run-all clean build --parallel watch:server
watch:build --print-label",
    "watch:build": "webpack --watch",
    "watch:server": "nodemon ./dist/express.bundle.js --watch
./dist --on-change-only"
  },
   ...
}
```

2. After that, simply build and run your application:

```
npm run build
npm run debug
```

3. If you have the Node.js V8 Inspector Manager installed, and Google Chrome is running in the background, you will note a new tab has been opened, which shows the source of your Express application's bundle in a paused state. Simply press the play button in your developer tools to continue:

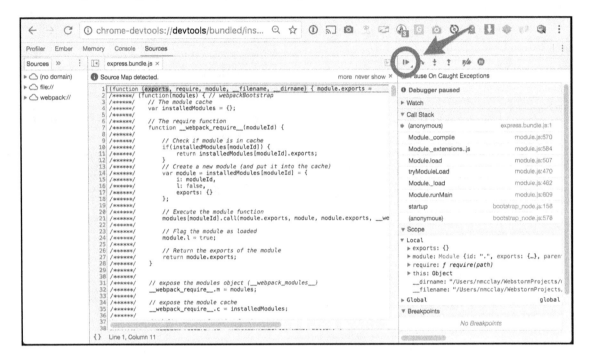

4. The debugger will stop at the next breakpoint which is inside our /src/Database.ts file. What is so interesting about this file is that it actually shows us the source map representation of this file instead of the actual compiled source in our WebPack bundle. This is very helpful to try to identify issues without the abstraction of looking at transformed source code, and this is possible due to Chrome's great source map support:

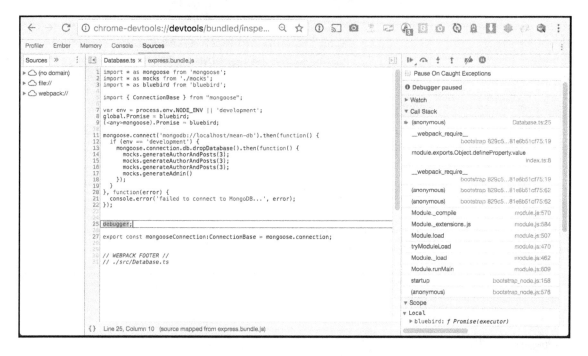

5. Attempting to close this browser tab will automatically reopen the tab to the current debug context. Similarly, restarting the process will automatically reload the tab. To leave this tab, first close the Node.js debug process and then close the tab within your browser.

How it works...

In Node version 6.3, this sort of debugging was made available as a preview for how debugging would eventually work in Node 8. Before Node 6.3, the only way to use this sort of developer tool inspection was to use the node-inspector module.

You can refer to the following link for more information:

```
https://github.com/node-inspector/node-inspector.
```

This module has some limitations in terms of its ability to report on long and asynchronous stack traces. Now, this feature is a fully supported and robust part of Node.js's debugging toolkit.

The `--inspect` and `inspect-brk` flags are signal hooks into V8, which allow a debugger to connect to an active Node.js process, and to send and receive debugging information. Google Chrome version 55+ simply leverages its existing robust JavaScript developer toolkit to support working with these messages. The main difference between `--inspect` and `inspect-brk` is that `--inspect-brk` will stop the main application context and wait for a debugger to tell it to proceed, whereas `--inspect` will simply run and allow a debugger to connect to the process. This can potentially lead to breakpoints being skipped in startup processes, so this is why we used the `--inspect-brk` version.

There's more...

There is another way to access Node.js debugging contexts within Google Chrome--simply enter the URL `chrome://inspect` into your browser, as follows:

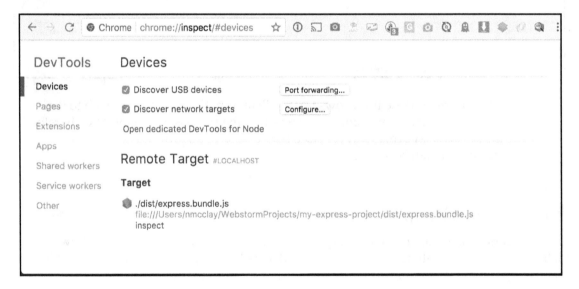

You will land on Chrome's DevTools Device inspection configuration page, with a set of remote debugging targets listed below the *Remote Target* section of the page. From here, you can simply click on **inspect** for your process, and it will launch the same debugging context that the Node.js V8 Inspector Manger does. You can learn more about how these contexts connect to Node's inspector by checking out the official documentation for inspector on the Node.js website: `https://nodejs.org/en/docs/inspector/`.

Debugging Node.js using JetBrain's WebStorm IDE

The inspector feature of Node.js is actually the process that virtually all debugging tools use to communicate with Node.js. It supports a wide range of different tools, including many popular integrated development environments (IDEs). In this section, we'll explore how to apply the same approach we used for debugging with our Google's Chrome browser developer toolkit, and instead connect it to the popular JavaScript developer tool, JetBrain WebStorm.

IDEs offer many advantages; perhaps one of the most handy is the ability to add breakpoints to code without actually modifying the source code directly. Let's explore how to set up debugging support in JetBrain WebStorm.

Getting ready

WebStorm is a professional developer tool and has a cost to acquire a full license. However, you can download a free 30-day evaluation version that you can use to try out with this section. You can visit the following link for it: `https://www.jetbrains.com/webstorm/`.

1. Click on the **Download** button to download the latest version of WebStorm for your operating system. After downloading, you will need to launch WebStorm and select the **Open** option from the start up screen. Then, navigate to your project and open it:

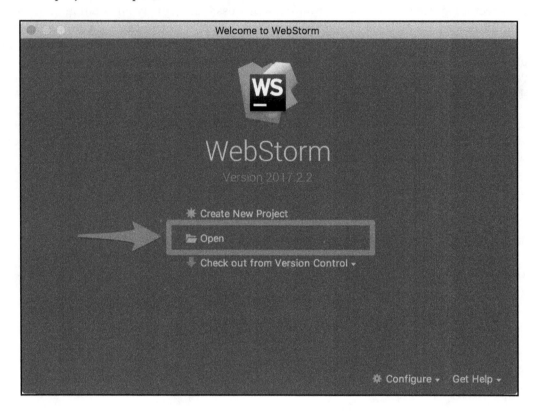

2. Inside your new project, you will first need to configure WebStorm for your version of Node.js and JavaScript. To do that, find the **Preferences** section in WebStorm's taskbar:

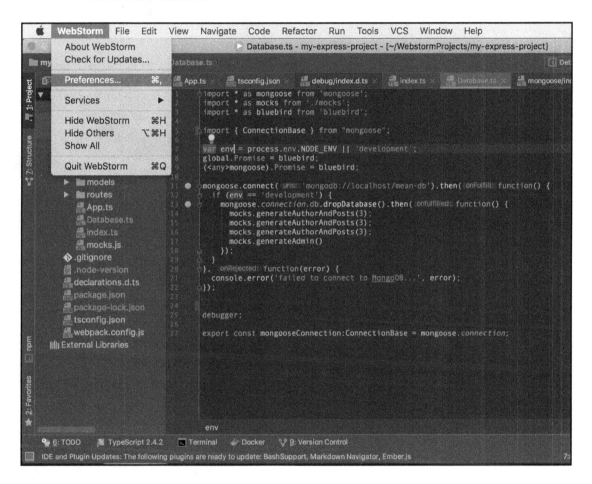

3. Search for Node.js in the Preferences search input and find the **Languages & Frameworks > JavaScript** section. Here, you will want to change your current JavaScript language version to *ECMAScript 6* and click on **Apply**:

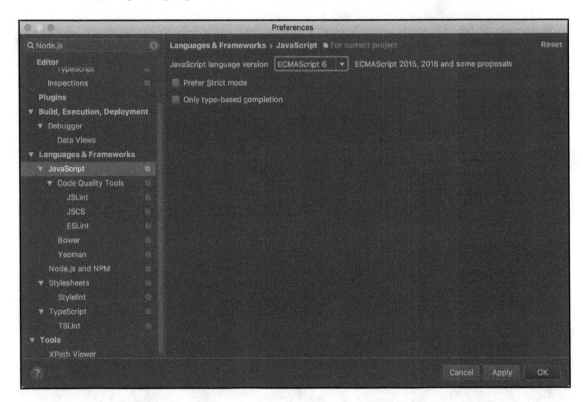

4. Next, go to the **Languages & Frameworks > JavaScript > Node.js and NPM** section and make sure that you select your active Node interpreter. If you are unsure where your node interpreter is on your machine, you can run `which node` on Linux machines:

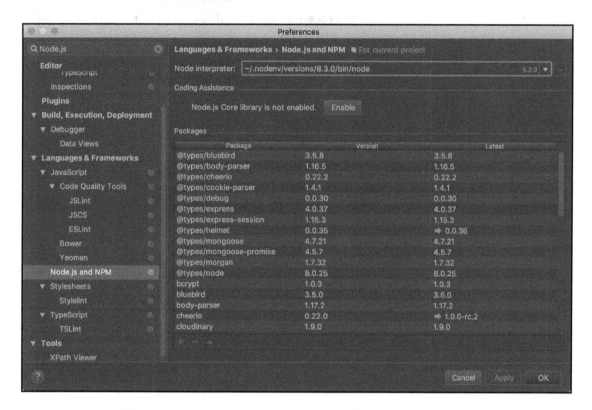

5. Now that our IDE is properly configured to work with the right version of Node and JavaScript, we can do the rest of the setup to perform debugging with it.

How to do it...

Let's perform the following steps to set up debugging for our Express application with Jetbrain's WebStorm IDE:

1. First, we will update our NPM debug script in our project's `package.json` configuration. This time, we will simply add a `$NODE_DEBUG_OPTION` placeholder to our configuration. This placeholder will be populated by WebStorm based on its own Debug configuration when it launches the process:

```
{
  ...
  "scripts": {
    "clean": "rimraf ./dist",
    "start": "node $NODE_DEBUG_OPTION ./dist/express.bundle.js",
    "debug": "DEBUG=express* node $NODE_DEBUG_OPTION
./dist/express.bundle.js",
    "build": "webpack",
    "watch": "npm-run-all clean build --parallel watch:server
watch:build --print-label",
    "watch:build": "webpack --watch",
    "watch:server": "nodemon ./dist/express.bundle.js --watch
./dist --on-change-only"
  },
  ...
}
```

2. Next, we will need to create a Configuration for debugging our application. Click on the drop-down arrow beside the play and bug icons in the top-right corner of WebStorm. From there, select **Edit Configurations**...:

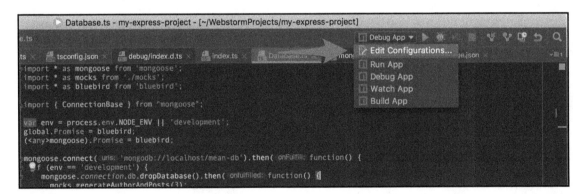

3. In the Edit Configurations dialog, create a new configuration by clicking on the +
   icon in the top-left corner of the dialog, and choose **npm** as the configuration
   type. Name this configuration **Debug App** and provide with it the path to your
   `package.json`, the `run` command, the `debug` script, and copies of any of your
   environment variables that need to be passed to your application. Then, click on
   OK to close the dialog:

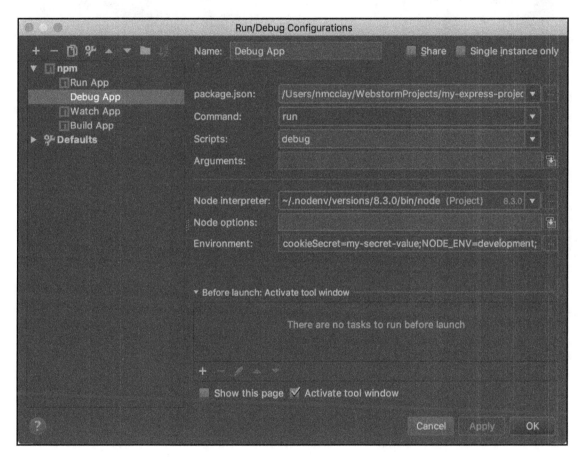

4. Now that our debug process is configured, we can start adding some breakpoints to the application we want to debug. Let's add two breakpoints at line 11 and 13, by clicking in the gutter region between the line number and the source code. This will add a red dot that indicates an active breakpoint:

5. To run our debugger, we will simply click on the green bug icon in the top right of WebStorm with our Debug App process selected in the dropdown. The application will start up and immediately pause its execution at the start of our express application's WebPack bundle. Click on the green arrow **Continue** button in the bottom left side of the WebStorm debugger panel to have the application process run until it hits our first WebStorm defined breakpoint at line 11:

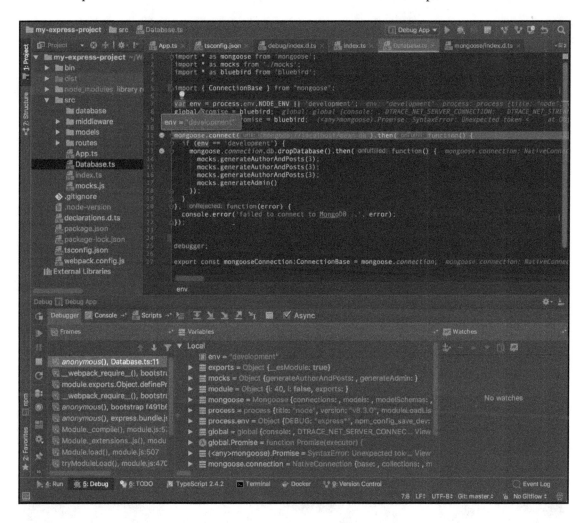

6. Clicking on continue again will move the debugger forward to line 25 where we left our debugger line. Pressing it again after that will resolve it in line 13 after Mongoose connects. Whenever the debugger pauses at a breakpoint, the variables section and the source code itself will intelligently display previews of values and state as they currently exist in the code. Hovering over elements can provide even more details about the state of expressions.

How it works...

WebStorm's debugger connects to the same Node inspector process that Chrome's developer toolkit does. It leverages this process to communicate with the running Node.js process and send messages, including application state and debugging instructions back and forth with Node and V8. The big enhancement here from Chrome is that code is being debugged directly beside the source code. So, making changes to code directly is very easy to do while inspecting values. However, this doesn't change how Node as a process runs and makes edits to source code, and debugging will not be swapped inside V8. The only way to change source code in a running Node.js debug session is to restart the process.

The main debugging interactions in WebStorm are managed through the debug panel, with the main operations for managing the process being aligned on the right side, and the debugger operations being listed in the top of the panel, beside the different view tabs. Hovering over icons in the debug panel will reveal a tooltip describing what action they represent.

The debug panel in WebStorm has many different features based on which tab you are looking at. The default tab of the panel is the Debugger tab, and it contains the current stack-trace, accessible variables and their values as inspectable drop-downs, and a watch list that allows you to track specific expressions:

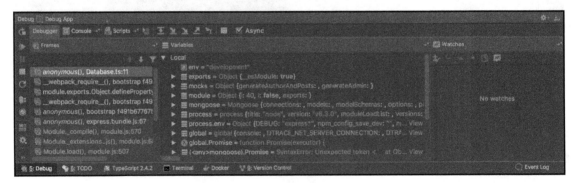

The **Console** tab contains the current logs from the console of the process, including any debug logs, and also features an interactive console to interact with your application in its current, paused execution state. This can be very handy for experimenting with potential changes that you might be considering to your source code when resolving an issue:

The last tab is the **Scripts** tab, which provides a list of logical scripts that are accessible by the Node process. These are mapped via source maps to project files as well. If you are curious where the source for this file is after it was complied, you can see that file path listed beside the project file in light gray text:

The WebStorm debugger provides a robust conventional developer environment for Node.js that many software developers will appreciate. The ability to simply interact and work with the Node.js application in the same manner as other development environments that JetBrains products support can bring a sense of comfort and confidence when debugging your application that other debugging tools might not satisfy.

Production error tracking and debugging with Sentry.io

Having solid debugging tools available in your development environment is great, but what about after your web application is released? Keeping tabs on unexpected behavior in your application can make responding to customer issues much quicker and less stressful than attempting to reproduce an error from a first-hand account. It can also help give insight into the frequency of issues in your application to help triage the fixes that effect the most customers first.

There are many tools available for monitoring errors and issues in production websites. One option that is easy to use and free to get started is **Sentry**, a multi-platform error tracking and monitoring service that is easily integrated into an existing Angular web application. Let's explore how to add production tracking and debugging support to our Angular blog application using Sentry.

Getting ready

Before we can start integrating our application with Sentry.io, we will need to create a free account to acquire an API key, very similarly to integrating with the Stripe API earlier in this book. A free Sentry account is good for up to 10,000 errors a month, which is very likely more errors than any single developer would ever want to see. Navigate to `https://sentry.io/welcome/` to get started:

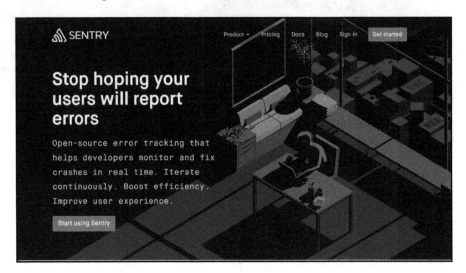

After clicking on the **Start using Sentry** button on the home page, you will be asked to provide some basic information about yourself and accept Sentry's terms of service:

Account Information

Name:

> Your Real Name

Email:

> you@example.com

Password:

> something super secret

Organization Information

Organization Name:

> Your Company's Name

If you're signing up for a personal account, try using your own name.

Billing Email: (optional)

> billing@example.com

If provided, we will send all billing-related notifications to this address.

Promo code: (optional)

>

☐ I agree to the Terms of Service and the Privacy Policy

☐ Sure, send me a monthly product update

Continue

Start for free

Get things off the ground with Sentry's free plan, and when you're ready to expand usage you can simply pay as you go.

No contracts

You can upgrade or downgrade at any time, and we'll automatically adjust your rate at the beginning of your next billing cycle.

Questions? Comments?

Looking for more information? Contact our sales team.

After creating your account, you will be directed to a very easy-to-use on-boarding experience that will allow you to choose the framework you want to integrate Sentry with. **Angular** is the third option in the popular frameworks list, so choose that option and give your project a name before clicking on **Continue**:

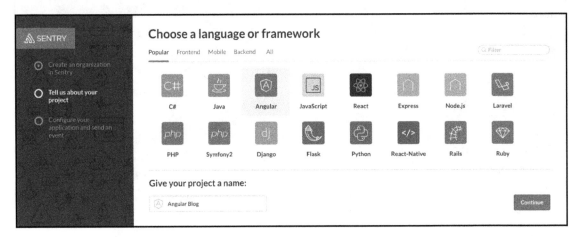

After choosing your framework, you will land on a page of documentation covering how to configure your Angular application. While this documentation is similar to what we are covering in this section, there are some important tweaks not covered in this minimal quick-start. Instead, search and click on the **Project Settings** button in the top-right corner and navigate to the **Client Keys** (DSN) section.

There, you will find the **DSN (Public)** API Key that you will need to integrate Angular with Sentry:

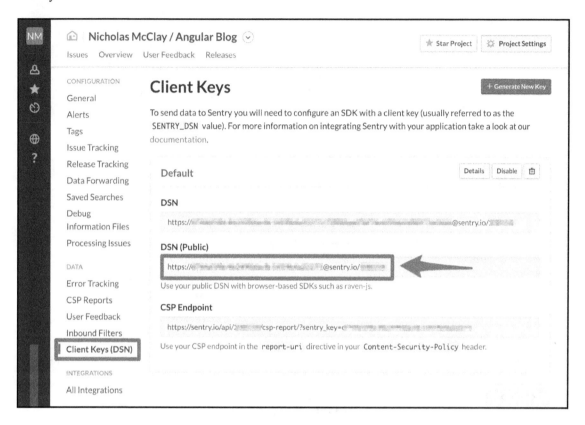

Finally, before we get started with coding, you will also need to install Sentry's client side logging module called `raven-js` to your application's `package.json` dependencies:

```
npm install raven-js --save
```

How to do it...

Let's perform the following steps to add production tracking and monitoring to our Angular application with Sentry:

1. First, we will need to add our Sentry DSN API key to our application's `/src/environments/environment.ts` and `/src/environments/environment.prod.ts` configurations. The main difference here is the production flag, which we can set to true for simplicity with testing our integration, for now:

```
export const environment = {
    production: true,
    sentryDSN: 'https://xxxxxxxxxxxxxxxxx@sentry.io/xxxxx'
    ...
}
```

2. Before working with any new library in Angular, it's a good idea to add the type definitions to your project's `tsconfig.json` configuration. `raven-js` includes its own typescript definitions inside its typescript directory. We'll simply include that in the `typeRoots` declarations under `compilerOptions`:

```
{
  "compileOnSave": false,
  "compilerOptions": {
    ...
    "typeRoots": [
      "node_modules/@types",
      "node_modules/raven-js/typescript"
    ],
    ...
  }
}
```

3. To integrate Sentry, we will create a `/src/app/sentry.provider.ts` provider configuration to set up Sentry. This provider will override Angular's default ErrorHandler with a custom one that will bubble up any exceptions or errors to our Sentry service so that we can be notified about them and analyze them later. One important adjustment we want to make is to use `Raven.captureException` only if we are indeed in the production mode. We do this by simply checking the production flag in our imported environment configuration:

```
import {ErrorHandler} from '@angular/core';
import * as Raven from 'raven-js';
```

```
import { environment } from '../environments/environment';

const SENTRY_DSN:string = environment.sentryDSN;

Raven
  .config(SENTRY_DSN)
  .install();

export class RavenErrorHandler implements ErrorHandler {
  handleError(err:any) : void {
    if (environment.production) {
      Raven.captureException(err);
    } else {
      console.error(err);
    }
  }
}

export default { provide: ErrorHandler, useClass: RavenErrorHandler
};
```

4. We will import and add our provider to our main `/src/app/app.module.ts` module configuration:

```
...
import SentryProvider  from './sentry.provider';

...
@NgModule({
  ...
  providers: [
    { provide: LOCALE_ID, useFactory: getLocaleProvider },
    CurrentUserService,
    SentryProvider
  ],
  bootstrap: [AppComponent]
})
export class AppModule {}
```

5. Then, to properly test our error handling, we can introduce a bit of mischief and simply add a throw to our `/src/app/posts/create-post-form/create-post-form.component.ts` class. This way, whenever we open the modal dialog, it will throw an error that will be caught by `raven-js` and sent to Sentry:

```
...
@Component({
  selector: 'app-create-post-form',
  templateUrl: './create-post-form.component.html',
  styleUrls: ['./create-post-form.component.scss'],
})
export class CreatePostFormComponent implements OnInit {
  ...
  open(content) {
    this.model = new BlogPost("New Post Title");
    this.modalService.open(content, {backdrop: "static", size:
"lg"});
    throw new Error('fire!');
  }
  ...
}
```

6. If we build and load our web application with the production flag set to `true`, we can simply click on the **Create New Post** button and our error will be thrown. If you have any push notifications for your email on your computer while testing, you will be astonished at how quickly you'll be notified by Sentry that a new error has been discovered.

How it works...

Whenever an exception occurs in our Angular application, there is a global handler that processes it at the highest level of our application. This handler usually simply pushes the error through, to `console.error`, but in our case we can actually override this behavior to instead send the event to Sentry.

This approach has two major advantages over traditional error handling. One is a user facing change: the error itself is invisible to the user. Even if they pull open the developer console to inspect, there is no indication of a stack trace or other error when the exception occurs. Of course, if the error breaks functionality for the user, this point is moot, but if the user doesn't notice any issue, such as a failed background request or an asset not loading, then this is an optimal solution.

The other major advantage is that the errors, along with their stack-traces, user behaviors, and the various conditions surrounding it are persisted to Sentry for a later analysis. Sentry will automatically notify you of new errors as they occur, and aggregate similar bugs together to help determine the issues that are most in need of addressing:

Since so many of the details surrounding the bug can be reviewed in detail, it's much easier to address customer issues through real data about the issue instead of asking someone to explain exactly what they did and what happened. This can be a true lifesaver for difficult-to-hunt-down production bugs:

The breadcrumbs section in particular is incredibly helpful. It details a tracked series of user events leading up to the error. This includes any network requests, console logs, user interactions, and, of course, the exception itself:

BREADCRUMBS			Q Search breadcrumbs...
↻	xhr	**GET** https://www.googleapis.com/blogger/v3/blogs/715947053740	00:41:11
↻	xhr	**GET** https://www.googleapis.com/blogger/v3/blogs/715947053740	00:41:12
>_	console	[object Object]	00:41:12
👤	ui.click	div.row > div.col-3 > app-create-post-form > button.btn.btn-block.btn-primary	00:41:17
>_	console	handle!	00:41:17
>_	console	error?	00:41:17
⚠	exception	Error: fire!	00:41:17

With this much detail ready for recall when investigating issues, the process of resolving bugs that are difficult to reproduce can be considerably mitigated. At the very least, it can provide critical data to inform whether a reported customer issue is actually occurring as described in production or not.

There's more...

One of the coolest parts of Sentry is that it can be easily integrated into so many different kinds of applications. For example, if you really enjoy the features of aggregating errors and reviewing their details within Sentry's UI, why not add it to your backend applications as well? This is how you do it:

```
var app = require('express')();
var Raven = require('raven');

Raven.config(process.env.SENTRY_DSN).install();

app.use(Raven.requestHandler());
```

```
app.get('/', function mainHandler(req, res) {
    throw new Error('Broke!');
});

app.use(Raven.errorHandler());

app.listen(3000);
```

Integrating Sentry with Node.js is a great way to add backend monitoring to your MEAN stack web applications and maximize the potential of using a single tool for all your production monitoring and debugging. You can learn more about integrating Sentry with Node.js, including Express.js integration, in the official documentation: `https://docs.sentry.io/clients/node/`.

11
Automated Testing

As we come to the end of this book, we'll wrap up by discussing the details of working within an all JavaScript testing environment. While Angular-CLI features a robust built-in testing toolkit right out of the box, in this chapter we will explore how to use the Mocha test runner and Chai assertion library to run automated testing across the backend of our web application. We'll also explore how to hook additional testing tools, such as the ESLint JavaScript linter, into our testing framework.

The following are the recipes covered in the chapter:

- Creating unit tests for Node.js using the Mocha testing library
- Creating integration tests for Express REST APIs
- Integrating an ESLint test suite into your Mocha tests
- Cross-browser and device testing with BrowserSync

Introduction

The asynchronous nature of JavaScript has made testing a challenge for many application developers. However, the basic principles of why you should test software remain the same. Testing your code helps prevent unintended mistakes stemming from changes you introduce to your code. By providing test coverage to your application, it is much easier to feel confident that changes in features or functionalities won't result in undermining the existing applications' behavior.

As with most applications, testing for a MEAN stack web application can generally be thought of as a pyramid of three different levels of test abstraction: **Unit** tests, **Integration** tests, and **E2E** tests:

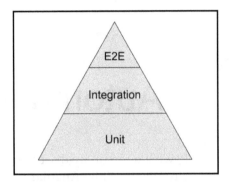

While there are many schools of thought when it comes to testing strategy, we will stick to some of the most common types of testing you may want to do in a MEAN stack web application. We'll be simplifying our focus to unit and integration tests.

End-to-end testing for web applications requires considerable configuration and setup of specialized tooling, such as *Selenium* and *WebDriver*, to be accomplished. While this sort of testing can be incredibly powerful, it can also be much more brittle and temperamental to maintain. This is why you should have fewer end-to-end tests proportionally to the quantity of integration and unit tests for your application. For this reason, instead of spending considerable time covering all the intricacies of end-to-end testing with JavaScript, we'll focus on the much more plentiful unit and integration testing levels of abstraction.

 If you are especially interested in using **end-to-end testing** for your JavaScript application, I recommend checking out WebDriver.io, and learning about how to use WebDriver and Selenium together for testing Node.js applications.
`http://webdriver.io/`

Creating unit tests for Node.js using the Mocha testing library

The base of our testing pyramid is made of unit tests. These tests are highly componentized, individual functionality tests that simply ensure that a unit of code, such as a route or some middleware, conforms to its expected API and handles failure cases as expected. Unit tests don't generally rely on other aspects of our application, and rely on extensive mocking of application states and data structures to test functionality instead. Testing individual methods and business logic in our application, such as our Express application middleware, makes for great unit tests.

Getting ready

Let's explore how to apply unit testing using the popular `Mocha` and `Chai` Node.js libraries to our Express web server. Before we start, we'll want to ensure that we install these libraries and their TypeScript type definitions to our application's `package.json` file:

```
npm install mocha chai @types/mocha @types/chai --save-dev
```

In keeping with our convention to use TypeScript consistently, we will need to add some additional libraries to assist with creating unit tests in Mocha with TypeScript:

```
npm install mocha-typescript ts-node node-mocks-http --save-dev
```

These libraries provide a range of tools for testing with Mocha in a TypeScript friendly Node.js environment:

- `mocha`: A Node-based test runner that supports asynchrous testing in JavaScript
- `chai`: A test assertion library for Mocha
- `mocha-typescript`: A helpful set of TypeScript decorators that make writing TypeScript tests easier
- `ts-node`: A utility for loading TypeScript resources for node processes
- `node-mocks-http`: A mocking utility for Node.js applications that makes testing Express middleware without running Express directly much easier

With these dependencies installed, we are now ready to start writing our Mocha unit tests in TypeScript for our Express web server.

How to do it...

Let's perform the following steps to create a Mocha unit test for the authentication middleware of our Express web server:

1. First, we'll need to create a new /test directory in the root of our Express project where we will keep our test files. We will also need to update our project's tsconfig.json TypeScript configuration file to include our test directory and any .ts files within it:

```
{
  . . .
  "include": [
    "src/**/*.ts",
    "test/**/*.ts"
  ],
  . . .
}
```

2. Next, we'll create a new Mocha unit test file, called /test/unit/test-middleware-auth.ts. Note that we created another subdirectory called /test/unit to denote this file as a unit test. We also named the file in a way that represents its logical path in our application, which is /src/middleware/auth.js. Simple and consistent organization like this can make tracing test failures back to source code in our application much easier. Our test file simply imports the @suite decorator from mocha-typescript, which we will use to stub out a new test class:

```
import { suite } from 'mocha-typescript';

@suite class AuthMiddlewareUnitTest {

}
```

3. Now, we can write our first Mocha test using the @test decorate from mocha-typescript. For this test, we will import the /src/middleware/auth.js middleware all on its own, and use Chai's assertion library to test that the various types and properties of the middleware are what we expect them to be. This sort of generic method testing is common in unit tests, but as we'll see, it isn't limited to that:

```
import { suite, test } from 'mocha-typescript';
import * as chai from 'chai';
const expect = chai.expect;
```

```
import * as auth from '../../src/middleware/auth';

@suite class AuthMiddlewareUnitTest {

    @test("middleware exists")
    public middlewareExists() {
        expect(auth).to.be.a('object');
        expect(auth).to.respondTo('logger');
        expect(auth).to.respondTo('requireRole');
        expect(auth).to.respondTo('unauthorized');
        expect(auth.logger).to.be.a('function');
        expect(auth.requireRole).to.be.a('function');
        expect(auth.unauthorized).to.be.a('function');
    }

}
```

4. Next, we can extend our test to confirm that our middleware acts as we expect.
   Instead of running our whole Express application, we will use `node-mocks-http` to create a mock Express application that we can feed to our middleware to
   check its behavior. The main benefit of this is that our test is much more
   lightweight and very isolated to this particular middleware's behavior. We'll also
   need to extend the `Session` interface slightly to support providing a user object
   to it, as in our real application. As our `requireRoleAllow` test suite is testing
   Express middleware, it is naturally asynchronous and requires a callback to be
   completed. In order to test asynchronous behavior in Mocha, all we need to do is
   manually call the `done()` method passed into the test context in our callback:

```
import { suite, test } from 'mocha-typescript';
import * as chai from 'chai';
const expect = chai.expect;

import * as auth from '../../src/middleware/auth';
import { createMocks, RequestOptions, ResponseOptions, Session,
Mocks } from 'node-mocks-http';
import { EventEmitter } from "events";

interface UserSession extends Session {
    user: any;
}

@suite class AuthMiddlewareUnitTest {
    private createExpressMock(reqOptions: RequestOptions): Mocks {
        let resOptions:ResponseOptions = {
            eventEmitter: EventEmitter
        };
```

```
                return createMocks(reqOptions, resOptions);
        }

        @test("middleware exists")
        public middlewareExists() {
            expect(auth).to.be.a('object');
            expect(auth).to.respondTo('logger');
            expect(auth).to.respondTo('requireRole');
            expect(auth).to.respondTo('unauthorized');
            expect(auth.logger).to.be.a('function');
            expect(auth.requireRole).to.be.a('function');
            expect(auth.unauthorized).to.be.a('function');
        }

        @test('requireRole allows valid user session role')
        public requireRoleAllow(done:MochaDone) {
            let role:string = 'super-admin';

            let options:RequestOptions = {
                session: <UserSession>{ user: {
                    role: role
                }}
            };

            let expressMock:Mocks = this.createExpressMock(options);

            auth.requireRole(role)(expressMock.req, expressMock.res,
    function() {
                expect(expressMock.res.finished).is.false;
                done();
            });
        }
    }
```

5. We want to test more than just the expected outcome of our application as well. We should ensure that failure cases for our middleware also fail as they are expected. This can be accomplished by registering an event listener for the end event broadcast by node-mocks-HTTP's response mock object. This behavior perfectly mimics the expected Express behavior in a much more lightweight fashion. Now, we simply need to inspect the state of the response data to assert that it matches our failure conditions:

```
...

@suite class AuthMiddlewareUnitTest {
    ...
```

```
        @test('requireRole denies invalid user session role')
        public requireRoleDeny(done:MochaDone) {
            let role:string = 'super-admin';

            let options:RequestOptions = {
                session: <UserSession>{ user: {
                    role: 'user'
                }}
            };

            let expressMock:Mocks = this.createExpressMock(options);
            expressMock.res.on('end', function() {
                expect(expressMock.res.statusCode).to.equal(403);
                expect(expressMock.res._isJSON()).is.true;
                let responseJSON =
    JSON.parse(expressMock.res._getData());
                expect(responseJSON).has.property('errors');
                expect(responseJSON.errors).to.be.a('array');
                expect(responseJSON.errors).to.have.lengthOf(1);
                done();
            });

            auth.requireRole(role)(expressMock.req, expressMock.res);
        }
    }
```

6. Finally, we need to add a `test` command to the project's NPM scripts section of
   our `package.json` file. This command will simply invoke Mocha with the `ts-`
   `node` compiler so that Mocha can use TypeScript. We need to provide the `--`
   `recursive` flag so that our `/test/unit` directory is included as well:

```
{
  ...
  "scripts": {
    "test": "mocha --compilers ts:ts-node/register,tsx:ts-
node/register --recursive",
    "clean": "rimraf ./dist",
    "start": "node $NODE_DEBUG_OPTION ./dist/express.bundle.js",
    "debug": "DEBUG=express* node $NODE_DEBUG_OPTION
./dist/express.bundle.js",
    "build": "webpack",
    "watch": "npm-run-all clean build --parallel watch:server
watch:build --print-label",
    "watch:build": "webpack --watch",
    "watch:server": "nodemon ./dist/express.bundle.js --watch
./dist --on-change-only"
  },
```

```
        . . .
    }
```

7. Running our Mocha tests is now as simple as invoking the script from the command line:

```
npm test
```

How it works...

The Mocha test runner uses `ts-node` to load our TypeScript test files, compiles them to JavaScript, and executes them. The files are then evaluated for their suite context, and each test within the suite is evaluated in sequence. The actual test is incredibly fast itself due, in large part, to the extensive mocking we are doing for the Express application request and response behaviors.

Our test assertions are written using the `expect` keyword from Chai, followed by a series of very readable chain methods for what the expected values should be. These assertions are very useful and flexible for composing the test criteria you want to assert. The Chai assertions library includes dozens of different assertions that can be composed in many different ways depending on the needs of your application. The Chai Assertions APIs are illustrated in the following table:

Assertion	Example	Description

`to`, `be`, `been`, `is`, `that`, `which`, `and`, `has`, `have`, `with`, `at`, `of`, `same`, `but`, `does`	`expect({a: 1, b: 2}).to.have.all.keys(['a', 'b']);`
	`expect([1, 2]).to.be.an('array').that.does.not.include(3);`
	`expect({a: 1}).to.not.be.an.instanceof(Array);`
		While not assertions in their own right, these are chainable getters that can be used in conjunction with all the other assertion methods to improve the readability of your test assertion.

`equal`	`expect('foobar').to.equal('foobar');`	Asserts that the target is strictly equal to the provided value.
`deep`	`expect({a: 1}).to.deep.equal({a: 1});`	Used to extend assertions such as `equal`, `include`, `members`, `keys`, and `property` to evaluate deep object equality.

`eql, eqls`	`expect({a: 1}).to.eql({a: 1});`	Nearly identical to the `deep.equal` assertions, with the difference that it doesn't cause chained assertions to use deep evaluation.
`not`	`expect({a:1}).to.not.have.property('b');`	Negates all assertions that follow in the chain.
`property`	`expect({a: 1}).to.have.property('a');`	Asserts that the target has a property with the given key name.

`ownPropertyDescriptor,`
`haveOwnPropertyDescriptor`
	`expect({a:3}).to.have.ownPropertyDescriptor('a',{`
	`    configurable: true,`
	`    enumerable: true,`
	`    writable: true,`
	`    value: 3`
	`});`
		Asserts that the target has a property with the given key name and a property descriptor matching the provided values.

`include`	`expect([1, 2, 3]).to.include(2);`	Asserts that the target contains the provided value. This assertion work across strings, arrays, and simple object properties.
`members`	`expect([1, 2, 3]).to.have.members([2, 1, 3]);`	Asserts that the target array has the same members as the given array.
`oneOf`	`expect(1).to.be.oneOf([1,2,3]);`	Asserts that the target is a member of the given array list.
`keys, key`	`expect({a: 1, b: 2}).to.have.all.keys('a', 'b');`	Asserts that the target object or array has the given keys. It will almost always be used in conjunction with the `all` and `any` assertions.
`any`	`expect({a: 1, b: 2}).to.not.have.any.keys('c', 'd');`	Causes all keys assertions that follow in the chain to only require that the target has at least one of the given keys. It does the opposite of the `all` assertion.
`all`	`expect({a: 1, b: 2, c: 3}).to.include.all.keys('a', 'b');`	The opposite of the `any` assertion, it requires any key assertion on a target to have all of the given keys.

nested	`expect({a: {b: ['x', 'y']}}).to.nested.include({'a.b[1]': 'y'});`	Enables dot-and-bracket notations in all property and include assertions that follow in the chain. It cannot be used in conjunction with the `own` assertion.

own	`Object.prototype.b = 2;`
	`expect({a:1}).to.have.property('b')`
	`.but.not.own.property('b');`
		Causes property and include assertions to ignore any inherited properties. It cannot be used in conjunction with the `nested` assertion.

ordered	`expect([1, 2]).to.have.ordered.members([1, 2]);`	Causes all `members` assertions that follow in the chain to require that members be in the same order.
a, an	`expect('foobar').to.be.a('string');` `expect(new Error).to.be.an('error');`	Asserts that the target's type is equal to the given value as a string.
ok	`expect(1).to.be.ok;`	Asserts that the target's value is loosely equal to `true` (==).
true	`expect(true).to.be.true;`	Asserts that the target's value is strictly equal to `true` (===).
false	`expect(false).to.be.false;`	Asserts that the target's value is strictly equal to `false` (===).
null	`expect(null).to.be.null;`	Asserts that the target's value is strictly equal to `null` (===).
undefined	`expect(undefined).to.be.undefined;`	Asserts that the target's value is strictly equal to `undefined` (===).
NaN	`expect(NaN).to.be.NaN;`	Asserts that the target's value is strictly a `NaN`.
exist	`expect(0).to.exist;`	Very similar to the `ok` assertion, but works only for `null` or `undefined` values.

empty	`expect([]).to.be.empty;` `expect('').to.be.empty;`	Asserts that the target's string or array length is strictly zero.
arguments	`function test () { expect(arguments).to.be.arguments; }` `test();`	Asserts that the target is an arguments object inside a function.
above	`expect(5).to.be.above(3);`	Asserts that the target is a number or a date greater than the given number or date.
below	`expect(2).to.be.below(5);`	Asserts that the target is a number or a date less than the given number or date.
least	`expect(2).to.be.at.least(2);` `expect(2).to.be.at.least(1);`	Asserts that the target is a number or a date greater than or equal to the given number or date.
most	`expect(2).to.be.at.most(2);` `expect(2).to.be.at.least(5);`	Asserts that the target is a number or a date less than or equal to the given number or date.
within	`expect(3).to.be.within(3, 5);`	Asserts that the target is a number or a date greater than or equal to the first provided number or date start, and less than or equal to the second provided number or date finish.
closeTo, approximately	`expect(2.5).to.be.closeTo(2, 0.5);`	Asserts that the target is a number that's within a given delta range of the given value expected.
lengthOf	`expect([1, 2, 3]).to.have.lengthOf(3);`	Asserts that the target's length property is equal to the provided number.

instanceof	`function Foobar () { }`
	`expect(newFoobar())`
	`.to.be.an.instanceof(Foobar);`
		Asserts that the target is an instance of the provided constructor.

match	`expect('foobar').to.match(/^foo/);`	Asserts that the target matches the provided regular expression.

string	`expect('foobar').to.have.string('foo');`	Asserts that the target string contains the provided substring.
throw	`var error = function() { throw new Error('Error!'); };` `expect(error).to.throw(); expect(badFn).to.throw(TypeError);`	Asserts that the target is an exception.
respondTo	`function Foobar() {} Foobar.prototype.method = function() {};` `expect(new Foobar()).to.respondTo('method');`	Asserts that the target has a method with the provided name.

itself	`function Foobar () {} Foobar.prototype.functionMethod = function() {}; Foobar.objectMethod = function() {};`
	`expect(Foober).itself.to.respondTo('objectMethod')`
	`.but.not.respondTo('functionMethod');`
		Causes all respondTo assertions that follow in the chain to behave as if the target was an object, even if it's a function.

satisfy	`expect(1).to.satisfy(function(number) { return number > 0;` `});`	Invokes the provided matcher function with the target being passed as the first argument, and asserts that the value returned is true (==).
change	`expect(Foobar.addOne).to.change(Foobar.getTotal);`	Asserts that the target value will change the response of the provided value.
increase	`expect(Foobar.addTwo).to.increase(Foobar.getTotal);` `expect(Foobar.addTwo).to.increase(Foobar, 'total');`	The same as change, but only when the result is greater for the provided value.
decrease	`expect(Foobar.removeOne).to.change(Foobar.getTotal);` `expect(Foobar.removeOne).to.decrease(Foobar, 'total');`	The same as change but only when the result is lesser for the provided value.
by	`expect(Foobar.addTwo).to.increase(FooBar.getTotal).by(2);` `expect(Foobar.addTow).to.increase(Foobar, 'total').by(2);`	Specifies the expected delta in change for the increase and decrease assertions.
extensible	`expect({a: 1}).to.be.extensible;`	Asserts that the target is extensible, which means that new properties can be added to it. Primitives are never extensible.

sealed	`var Foobar = Object.seal({}); expect(Foobar).to.be.sealed;`	Asserts that the target is sealed, which means that new properties can't be added to it, and its existing properties can't be reconfigured or deleted.
frozen	`var Foobar = Object.freeze({});` `expect(Foobar).to.be.frozen;`	Asserts that the target is frozen, which means that new properties can't be added to it, and its existing properties can't be reassigned to different values, reconfigured, or deleted. Primitives are always frozen.
finite	`expect(1).to.be.finite;`	Asserts that the target is a number, and isn't NaN or positive/negative Infinity.
fail	`expect(Foobar).to.fail();`	An assertion that will always throw an error.

In reality, this unit test isn't fully complete. There are additional unit behaviors we may want to assert in our test, such as if `logger` creates a log file successfully, or if `unauthorized` returns the correct error state. However, now that we've covered the process of implementing successful mocks of Express application behavior, these tests should be possible for you to flesh out fully on your own.

There's more...

The `expect` assertions within Chai are known as **Behavior Driven Development** (BDD). This style of assertion is completely oriented around the behavior of your application's state, and is written in a manner that makes it very easy to understand which behavior is being tested for. Chai also supports another BDD style assertion keyword, the `should` assertion:

```
let should = chai.should();

Foobar.should.be.a('string');
Foobar.should.equal('foobar');
Foobar.should.have.lengthOf(6);

http.get(123, function (err, data) {
```

```
    should.not.exist(err);
    should.exist(data);
    data.should.be.an('object');
  });
```

The `should` assertion is an alternative way in Mocha to write the same types of Chai `assertions` as the `expect` assertion keyword, but with what some consider a more naturally readable BDD style.

You can learn more about assertion styles in Chai though the official Chai documentation website at `http://chaijs.com/guide/styles/`.

Creating integration tests for Express REST APIs

The next level of testing abstraction is integration tests. Unlike unit tests, which rely on only mocks to derive their behavior, integration tests usually introduce some level of real application integration with other services, connections, and dependencies. These tests can be highly important as they can be much more behaviorally realistic in their definition than unit tests. They are excellent for testing full behaviors of your application while still being very focused on individual parts. Testing functionalities such as our Express REST APIs and checking their expected results make for great integration tests.

Getting ready

Let's explore how to add some API integration tests to our Express web server's REST API. In order to work with our API, we'll need to install a Chai plugin called `chai-http`, which will work as a lightweight request library to make `HTTP` request assertions in our tests:

```
npm install chai-http @types/chai-http --save-dev
```

Another detail we need to address is that the `/src/routes/Angular.ts` module of our application relies on our Angular source files being inside the `/dist` directory. We can circumvent this by simply making this route optionally provided via an environment variable:

```
...
const angularBuildPath = process.env.angularBuildPath ?
process.env.angularBuildPath : path.resolve(__dirname, 'angular');

class AngularRoute {
    public route: Router;
    private angularBuildPath: string;
    private indexPage: CheerioStatic;

    constructor() {
        this.route = express.Router();
        this.angularBuildPath = String(angularBuildPath);
        this.indexPage = this.getIndexPage(this.angularBuildPath);
        this.enableGzipCompression();
        this.route.get('*', this.serveRoute.bind(this));
    }
    ...
}

export default new AngularRoute().route;
```

This way, all we need to do is export this environment variable the same way we do for any of our environment variables, such as our cookie secret or API keys:

```
export angularBuildPath /Users/nicholas/my-projects/my-express-
project/dist/angular
```

This will now allow us to run our project fully, without relying on the source built into the `/dist` directory.

How to do it...

Let's follow the given steps to create an API integration test for our Express web server's `/api` endpoint:

1. First, we will create a new test file, called `/test/integration/test-route-api.ts`. This new integration folder helps us keep our tests organized logically in terms of their level of abstraction, while the naming convention reinforces the relationship of the tested content to the project's source code:

```
import { suite, test } from 'mocha-typescript';
import * as chai from 'chai';
const expect = chai.expect;

@suite class API {
}
```

2. Before we can start writing integration tests, we need to instantiate our application to the state that we will need in order to run the test. For this API test, we will need to configure our application to start up and run at a predetermined host and port. We'll configure our server in a `before` method. It's important that this method is declared as a `static` method so that `mocha-typescript` will only invoke it once before all our test contexts run. Similarly, we'll declare an `after` method to close down our server when all our tests have finished running:

```
import { suite, test } from 'mocha-typescript';
import { Server } from "http";
import * as chai from 'chai';
const expect = chai.expect;

import app from '../../src/App';

@suite class API {
    private static port:number = 3000;
    private static host:string = 'http://localhost';
    private static connection:string;
    private static server:Server;

    public static before(done:MochaDone) {
        this.connection = this.host + ":" + this.port;
        this.server = app.listen(this.port, done);
    }

    public static after() {
        this.server.close();
```

```
        }
    }
```

3. We're now ready to write our first test; a simple status check of our /api REST API endpoint. We will need to import chai-http in order to connect to our API to assess its behavior. This is as simple as providing the location of where our web server is running, and using the built-in get method to make a request to our endpoint. Then, we can simply evaluate the response using Chai's assertion library:

```typescript
import { suite, test } from 'mocha-typescript';
import {Server} from "http";
import * as chai from 'chai';
const expect = chai.expect;

import app from '../../src/App';
import chaiHttp = require('chai-http');
chai.use(chaiHttp);

@suite class API {
    ...

    @test("responds with status 200")
    public status200(done:MochaDone) {
        chai.request(API.connection)
            .get('/api')
            .end(function(err, res) {
                expect(res).to.have.status(200);
                expect(res.text).to.equal('API is running');
                done();
            });
    }
}
```

4. This particular endpoint doesn't do much; it only allows GET requests. So, we can write two different error tests to assert that POST requests will be served either a 415 or a 404, depending on the POST request's Content-Type header. With these tests, it is easy to see how we can quickly and easily set up a new request context in a new test without having to restart or tear down our application context again:

```typescript
    ...

@suite class API {
    ...
```

```
@test("responds to POST with status 415")
public status415(done: MochaDone) {
    chai.request(API.connection)
        .post('/api')
        .end(function (err, res) {
            expect(res).to.have.status(415);
            done();
        });
}

@test("responds to JSON POST with status 404")
public status420(done: MochaDone) {
    chai.request(API.connection)
        .post('/api')
        .set('Content-Type', 'application/json')
        .end(function (err, res) {
            expect(res).to.have.status(404);
            done();
        });
}
```

5. To run our integration test, we simply need to call our `npm test` script, and our test will run along with our existing unit tests:

```
npm test
```

How it works...

Our integration tests are very similar to our unit tests, with the major difference being that our integration tests actually launch our application. Due to this, these tests run considerably slower than our unit tests:

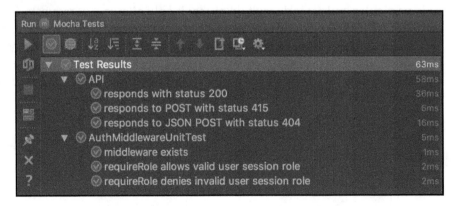

WebStorm's detailed Mocha test logging shows that our integration tests suite runs about 12 times slower than our unit test suite. At this point, this time difference is clearly negligible, but as we scale up, it can easily became a bottleneck if our integration tests are taking too long. It's important to consider this hidden time cost of higher-level testing, and reinforce why it's a good idea to have more unit tests than integration tests in your application's testing strategy.

The `chai-http` library we used for writing these integration tests provides two key enhancements that make working with Express REST APIs much easier. The first is the micro `HTTP` request library built into `chai-http`, which is actually its own project called **Super-Agent**. Super-Agent is an ultra lightweight Node.js-based request library that we are using when we are configuring our request:

```
chai.request(API.connection).get('/api').end();
```

The Super-Agent API provides many useful ways to configure your integration test for a particular endpoint of your REST API:

Method	Example	Description
get, post, head, delete, put, options, patch	.get('/api')	Sets the request HTTP type and target URL for an upcoming request. Only one HTTP type method may be used in a request chain.
end	.end()	Sends the currently configured request.
send	.send({foobar: 'foobar', total: 12})	Attaches content to the body of the currently configured request. Can accept either a JSON object or a string value.
set	.set('Content-Type', 'application/json')	Sets a header by key and value on the currently configured request.
query	.query({ order: 'asc' })	Sets a query parameter by key and an optional value on the currently configured request. Will also accept multiple parameters at once.
sortQuery	.sortQuery(function(a, b) { return a.length - b.length; })	Provides a sort function for determining whether the order query parameters should be serialized to the currently configured request.
type	.type('form')	Shortcut for setting the type of HTTP request content. Accepts string values such as *json, form, png,* or *xml.* Will also accept any valid Content-Type header value.

retry	`.retry(2)`	Sets a maximum number of retries for requests that fail to connect due to latency issues. `Retry` does not trigger for failure or error responses that are not network-related.
redirect	`.redirects(2)`	Set the maximum number of redirects to be followed by the request before failing. Defaults to five redirects.
accept	`.accept('application/json')`	Sets the `accept` header value for the currently configured request.

ca, cert, key, pfx	`let cert = fs.readFileSync('cert.pem');`
	
	`.cert(cert)`
		Sets a certificate authority, certificate file, and private key or encoded key to the currently configured request.

responseType	`.responseType('blob')`	For browse usage, this allows for handling of binary response bodies in the currently configured request. Not necessary when running inside Node.js.
abort	`.abort()`	Aborts the currently configured request.

timeout	`.timeout({`
	`    response: 3000,`
	`    deadline: 40000`
	`})`
		Sets timeout parameters for the currently configured request. These parameters will trigger the `retry` operation when reached. Values are measured in milliseconds.

auth	`.auth('username', 'password')`	Allows for the passing of basic `auth` parameters to the currently configured request.
attach	`.attach('cover', 'path/to/cover.png', 'cover.png')`	Sets a resource to be attached to a multipart file upload for the currently configured request. Can be used multiple times to attach multiple files to the same request.
field	`.field('user[email]', 'nmcclay@nickmcclay.com')`	Sets form field values for the currently configured request.
buffer	`req.buffer(false)`	Configures the current requests setting for handling buffered requests. Providing false will disable the default buffering for text to allow you to manually control file buffering.

withCredentials	withCredentials()	Enables CORS support through the ability to send cookies from the origin. Only works when Access-Control-Allow-Origin is not a wildcard (*), and Access-Control-Allow-Credentials is true.
on	.on('error', handle)	Sets an event listener for the currently configured request events. Supports common request events such as error, progress, response, send, and end.
use	import * as nocache from 'superagent-no-cache'; .use(nocache)	Adds a *Super-Agent* plugin to the currently configured request.

The Super-Agent official documentation also covers many additional details for advanced configuration options you might find useful for writing your integration tests, and is available at http://visionmedia.github.io/superagent/.

The other useful part of chai-http is the additional plugin assertions it adds to the Chai core assertion library. These assertions are oriented around the types of details you are most likely to want to assert with a response from a REST API:

Assertion	Example	Description
status	expect(res).to.have.status(200);	Asserts that the target has a status with the provided value.
header	expect(req).to.have.header('Content-Type', 'text/plain');	Asserts that the target has a header with the provided key and value.
headers	expect(req).to.have.headers;	Asserts that the target has any HTTP headers.

ip	`expect('127.0.0.1').to.be.an.ip;`	Asserts that the target represents a valid IP address.

json, html, text	`expect(req).to.be.json;`
	`expect(req).to.be.html;`
	`expect(req).to.be.text;`
		Assert that a `Response` or `Request` object has the provided Content-Type header.

redirect	`expect(res).to.redirect;`	Assert that a `Response` object has a redirect status code.
redirectTo	`expect(res).to.redirectTo('http://example.com');`	Asserts that a `Response` object has a redirect status code that matches the provided value.
param	`expect(req).to.have.param('orderby', 'date');`	Asserts that a `Request` object has a query string parameter with the given key and optional value.

cookie	`expect(res).to.have.cookie('session_id', '1234');`	Asserts that a `Request` or `Response` object has a cookie header with the given key and optional value.

There are many other plugins for Chai, similar to `chai-http`, that can further extend the power of your testings assertions within Chai.

> You can learn more about the available plugins and what they do from the official Chai plugins web page at `http://chaijs.com/plugins/`.

One final detail worth noting is that we are launching our Express application without any database functionality. This is partially because this particular integration doesn't require it, but more than that, it's so that we can control that aspect of our tests directly instead of requiring our application to be aware that we are in a testing mode. You can very easily include the database configuration as well as the application, and set any mocks needed in the same hook we used to set up our Express application earlier. Try experimenting by adding this database configuration file back to any other integration tests you might want to create.

There's more...

Your Chai `assertion` library can do more than just providing utilities for assertions in your tests; it can also provide you configuration for them. These configuration options let you decide how you want your assertion failures to be presented to you by Chai. For example, the `chai.config.includeStack` flag is `false` by default. However, by configuring it to `on`, you can influence whether a stack trace is included in the assertion error message:

```
chai.config.includeStack = true;
```

The `chai.config.showDiff` flag is `true` by default, and it controls whether a difference of the expected value from the received value is displayed for the assertion:

```
chai.config.showDiff = false;
```

Finally, the `chai.config.truncate` threshold flag sets the number of lines in a function, object, or array that will be presented in the assertion error before being truncated. The value is set to `40` by default, and you can set it to `0` to completely disable truncation in the assertion:

```
chai.config.truncateThreshold = 0; // disable truncating
```

With these configuration options, you can tailor your expected output from Chai to what is most useful for you.

Integrating an ESLint test suite into your Mocha tests

Having JavaScript on the backend of our web server allows us to have consistent code formatting across our whole stack if we wish. While not your usual sort of application behavior testing, linters are an important tool in automated testing to ensure that your code is consistent with your own code conventions and style guide. When working in a team environment, or when allowing others to contribute to an open source project, having an objective source of truth for what standard the code is expected to conform to is incredibly beneficial. It's amazing what mistakes a simple linter can help point out without having to directly scrutinize or code review someone else's work.

Tools such as **ESLint** will help us keep our code uniformly formatted, while still having robust configuration options that we can use to custom tailor edge cases of our application source code. It also allows easy hooks into automation to run our linter whenever we run our tests.

Getting ready

Let's explore how to add ESLint to our Express web server application. We'll start by installing ESLint globally to NPM as well as the `mocha-eslint` library to our project's `package.json` file:

```
npm install mocha-eslint --save-dev
```

The `mocha-eslint` library allows us to integrate ESLint directly into our Mocha test runner as its own suite. This way, our linter will automatically run whenever we run our other test suites.

How to do it...

Let's follow these steps to add an ESLint linter test suite to our Express web server:

1. First, we will create a new test file, called `/test/test-eslint.ts`, in our test directory. We won't need to include `mocha-typescript` since `mocha-eslint` configures our suites and tests for us. Instead, we'll simply configure which directories we want to lint and what the output format should be:

```
import * as lint from 'mocha-eslint';

let paths = [
    'src',
    'test'
];

let options = {
    formatter: 'stylish',
    strict: true,
    contextName: 'ESLint'
};

lint(paths, options);
```

2. Next, we'll need to create an ESLint configuration file, called `.eslintrc.js`, in the root of our project. This file is a configuration file for how ESLint should run in our project. As our application is using TypeScript, ES6 modules, and Node.js, we will need to tweak this configuration. Express's middleware pattern can also be an issue with ESLint as it can be interpreted as including unused variables. Instead of changing our Express middleware convention, we will simply tell ESLint to ignore these variables in our application. Similarly, we will ignore `console.error` messages as they can be genuinely quite useful to have in Node.js applications:

```
module.exports = {
  "env": {
    "browser": true,
    "commonjs": true,
    "es6": true,
    "node": true
```

```
    },
    "extends": "eslint:recommended",
    "parserOptions": {
      "sourceType": "module"
    },
    "rules": {
      "indent": [
        "error",
        2
      ],
      "linebreak-style": [
        "error",
        "unix"
      ],
      "quotes": [
        "error",
        "single"
      ],
      "semi": [
        "error",
        "always"
      ],
      "no-unused-vars": [
        "error",
        {
          "argsIgnorePattern": "res|req|next"
        }
      ],
      "no-console": [
        "error",
        {
          "allow": ["error"]
        }
      ]
    }
  }
};
```

3. Sometimes, you will have files that are bit different than your usual linter standards. For instance, our /src/mocks.js file uses console logging to inform us of actions that it's taking in generating mock models. Instead of removing these, we can simply tell ESLint that this convention is okay for just this file. We do so by adding a comment at the top of the file with this instruction. When ESLint runs, it will check for these local rule adjustments before running the file through the linter:

```
/*eslint no-console: "off"*/
```

```
...
module.exports = {
  generateAuthorAndPosts: function(postCount) {
    ...

    user.posts = posts;
    user.save().then(function(user) {
      console.log('created new author: ' + user.email);
      return Post.insertMany(posts).then(function() {
        console.log('created ' + postCount + ' new posts');
      }).catch(function(error) {
        throw error;
      });
    }).catch(function(error) {
      throw error;
    });
  },
  ...
};
```

4. Now, we simply need to run our NPM test script, and we will see any files that don't match our linter configuration output as failures to Mocha:

```
npm test
```

How it works...

When you first implement a linter in a project with existing source code, it's very likely that there will be issues in your project. These errors are summarized in the output of the linter, and can help gauge how much effort is needed to bring your code into compliance. One really interesting aspect of ESLint is that it has some support for automatically fixing some types of common linter errors.

For example, here is an the output from ESLint after adding it to our Express project:

```
38 problems (38 errors, 0 warnings)
26 errors, 0 warnings potentially fixable with the `--fix` option.
```

These errors are usually limited to whitespace and formatting issues, but can be a big help when bringing a code base into compliance with your linter. Simply run the `--fix` command through the global `eslint` command-line utility in order to apply these fixes to your source code:

```
eslint . --fix
```

What will remain are the errors that will require direct intervention on your part to resolve. Sometimes these errors are simple mistakes, such as leaving unused variables in your code, or unnecessary `console.log` statements you had forgotten about:

```
12 problems (12 errors, 0 warnings)
```

With your linter in place, its now much more difficult to forget these simple mistakes and guarantee that your application's source code is tidy and consistently formatted through your entire code base.

There's more...

ESLint, much like WebPack and TypeScript, is a configuration-driven tool that provides excellent, best-in-class documentation for how to use it. There are many plugins, tweaks, and configuration options available for tuning your linter to your exact preferences.

 You can learn more about how to configure ESLint for your application from the official documentation website at `https://eslint.org/`.

Cross-browser and device testing with BrowserSync

A modern twist to testing in application development is the emergence of mobile devices as platforms for web applications. The challenge, of course, with mobile applications is in testing the application across a wide range of device form factors and browsers. One tool that can be very helpful in this endeavor is using a utility such as **BrowserSync**, which uses web sockets to synchronize interactions in your application across multiple browsers or devices.

This may seem abstract at first, but the idea is that it allows you to run your application from one central location, and have multiple devices follow your user interactions simultaneously. This can help reveal browser-vendor specific compatibility problems in your web application. This sort of multidevice testing itself isn't automatic; however, the setup with BrowserSync can lend itself well to future acceptance testing automation driven through utilities such as **WebDriver** and **Selenium**.

Getting ready

To use BrowserSync, we will need to install the BrowserSync client and the `browser-sync-webpack-plugin` to integrate BrowserSync with our WebPack build process. Run the following command to install them as `devDependencies` to your project's `package.json` file:

```
npm install browser-sync browser-sync-webpack-plugin --save-dev
```

How to do it...

Let's perform the following steps to add BrowserSync integration to our application's WebPack build process:

1. First, we will need to add the `browser-sync-webpack-plugin` to our project's `webpack.config.js` WebPack configuration. We'll set it up to work as a proxy for our normal application web server that is running on port 3000:

```
. . .
const BrowserSyncPlugin = require('browser-sync-webpack-plugin');

. . .
module.exports = {
  . . .
  plugins: [
    . . .
    new BrowserSyncPlugin({
      host: 'localhost',
      port: 3100,
      proxy: 'http://localhost:3000/'
    })
  ]
};
```

2. Now, we need to start a WebPack `--watch` process to enable synchronization with BrowserSync. We can do that using the `watch:build` NPM script in our project's `package.json`:

```
npm run watch:build
```

3. Now, WebPack and BrowserSync will automatically start running in the background. We can now start our Express web application as a separate process that the proxy will rely on:

```
npm start
```

4. With our application running, we can visit the BrowserSync client on our local machine. Visit `http://localhost:3001`, and you will be greeted with the BrowserSync **Overview** page. Click on the **NEW TAB** link under **Local** `http://localhost:3100`. This will launch a new tab that will seem identical to our Angular application running `http://localhost:3000`, except that you will see a black banner saying **Connected to BrowserSync**

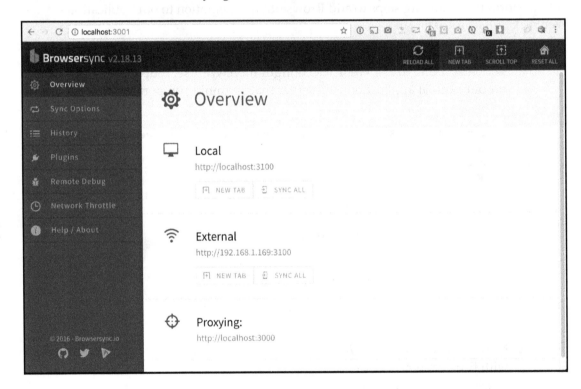

5. Now, return to the BrowserSync overview page and copy the external URL to open it in another browser. If you have a mobile phone on the same internal network as your laptop, you should be able to even use that device's web browser. After connecting, you will see the same screen as your other browser, except for any differences in screen size or other vendor styling differences. Scroll your screen on one browser, and the screen on the other, will also scroll. Navigate to different pages of your application and watch as your interactions are mirrored over to your other browser in real time.

How it works...

BrowserSync sets up a proxy to our Express application's static file server and injects additional logic that configures a web socket connection between it and BrowserSync. When multiple devices are connected to the same BrowserSync server, interactions are mirrored and sent to the other devices. This allows interactions such as scrolling, clicking, and page navigation to stay in sync across multiple devices.

You can configure which types of interactions you want to see synchronized across devices under the **Sync Options** section:

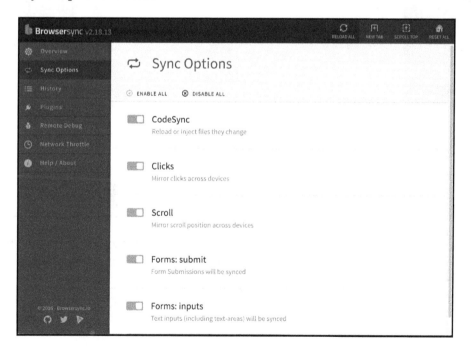

The real potential of a utility such as BrowserSync comes from being able to run multiple browsers through the same set of interactions and quickly see what works and what doesn't. It can also serve as an integration utility for doing automated cross-browser testing when you start creating acceptance tests for your application.

There's more...

BrowserSync also offers many other utilities to make testing your applications easier. For instance, you can use the built-in **Network Throttle** control to set up a server that mimics limited network connection speeds, including 3G and 2G cellular network speeds. This can be useful for determining how your application behaves on networks with limited connectivity speeds:

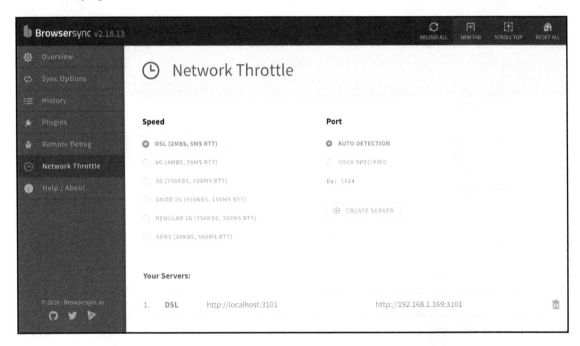

There is an abundance of documentation available online for BrowserSync on the official website, including recipes and tips for configuring BrowserSync for different application frameworks and environments; visit https://www.browsersync.io/docs.

Whats new in Angular 4

Angular 4 is the latest release of Google's popular web application framework. Already considering a robust JavaScript web application framework, the changes in version 4 are geared towards making applications smaller, faster, and with a more predictable upgrade cycle. These changes represent a turning point in Google's overall strategy with Angular.

A big part of that strategy shift is actually in the name of the framework itself. The primary reasoning for the name **Angular 4** from **Angular 2** is related to a decision the Angular core team made in September 2016, to shift to **Semantic Versioning,** for the Angular project and its core libraries. This means that the version numbers for Angular have strict meaning in terms of the content within any specific version.

As described in the official documentation for Semantic Versioning, or **semver** for short:

Given a version number MAJOR.MINOR.PATCH, increment the:

- MAJOR version when you make incompatible API changes,
- MINOR version when you add functionality in a backward-compatible manner, and
- PATCH version when you make backward-compatible bug fixes.

Additional labels for pre-release and build metadata are available as extensions to the MAJOR.MINOR.PATCH format.
`http://semver.org/`

What this means in practice for Angular is that Angular 2 was a semver major version, Angular 3 was another major version (although as a beta and largely unused), and Angular 4 is the newest major version. Angular 3 is just a footnote underscoring the significance of the changes from Angular 2 to 4 in terms of its semver version progression:

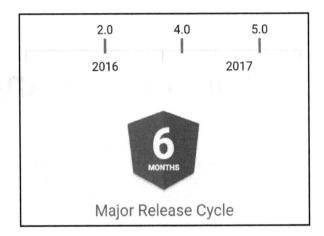

`http://angularjs.blogspot.com/2016/10/versioning-and-releasing-angular.html`

Ultimately, Google wants developers to not sweat about major versions notations and instead use **Angular,** generically, to be the latest major semver version of the **Angular Framework**, with Angular 1.6.x being denoted with the legacy name **Angular.js**. This doesn't mean Angular 2 won't be getting major bug fixes or security fixes, but it does mean that all new API enhancements and improvements will be channeled into Angular 4 and beyond, in order to align with the semvar specification. Google's goal is for the major version numbers to just be a point of conversation with developers about the contents of each release, and the upgrade to Angular 4 is the first time we will get to try this new approach.

How exciting! Let's get started!

Angular 4 Improvements and New Features

Let's look into the improvements and the new features that come with upgrading to Angular 4. According to the semvar specification, major upgrades come with API changes that may be incompatible with legacy versions of the API. These API changes can be a large source of concern for developers worried about deprecated features causing their app to stop working as expected. Thankfully, another huge strategy change with Angular 4 from 2 was a much more predictable & reliable upgrade experience for developers.

Packaging and Modules

Many of the big changes in Angular 4 are largely opaque to developers and include changes to the packaging and build system that Angular uses. The newest version of Angular's core libraries is packaged in what is known as **Flat ES Modules**. This change is a performance optimization to help reduce the size and increase the speed of generated builds in Angular.

Generated File Size Optimizations in Angular 4
Slimming down the generated file size of your application can improve the startup time and responsiveness of your web application. There is an additional experimental option in Angular 4's package system for using **ES2015 Flat ES Modules** which can save up to an additional 7% of your final bundle size. However, at this time Angular-CLI does not expose Webpack configuration options to developers, so, unfortunately, you can only take advantage of this feature with a fully custom build toolchain.

Major version updates also mean new features and enhancements to APIs, to make building your application easier and more powerful.

A newly optimized view engine

Angular's **ahead-of-time** (AoT) view compilation was up until Angular 4 generated a considerable amount of boilerplate that could result in considerably larger than expected application file-size. However, thanks to updates to the view engine in Angular 4. You can now enjoy considerably more optimized views with smaller file-sizes.

This upgrade is a replacement for the existing view engine and comes with no configuration changes or updates needed to your Angular application to take advantage of the enhancement. Google touts that many developers will see over 60% generated file-size savings over the previous generation of Angular's view engine. Those file-size savings can directly translate into a faster loading web application user experience in your application.

Added TypeScript 2.2 support

Angular 4 has upgraded from TypeScript version *2.0* to version *2.2*. TypeScript is a super-set language of JavaScript that adds additional language features including strict type checking that will compile to normal JavaScript. Updates in TypeScript includes considerable amount of changes in specific language features, digging into which is beyond the scope of the book. However, one new feature in TypeScript 2.2 that Angular developers may find very useful, is the new support for the **ECMAScript 2015 mixin class pattern**. **Mixins** provide a new way to compose shared behaviors and functionality on classes without them needing to inherit from a base class.

For example, consider you have multiple Angular components that you want to have a shared interaction behavior such as a right-click context menu. The functionality would simply show a menu when a user right-clicks on the component, but the contents of the menu would be slightly different for each component. With a mixin, you could create the underlying functionality of having a context-menu that responds to the right-click and shows a menu in a single place. Then, each component could simply include it without having to share an underlying class relationship and override the context-menu contents part of the mixin without disturbing the right-click triggering behavior.

This sort of compositional functionality in Angular can be very flexible and powerful, and lets you bring enhancements to your web application without duplicating functional boilerplate code.

ngIf directive added support for else statements

In the previous generations of Angular, if you wanted to have an alternative view for an `if` statement, one common approach was to use a switch statement. For example:

```
<div [ngSwitch]="isToggled">
  <span *ngSwitchCase="true">On</span>
  <span *ngSwitchDefault>Off</span>
</div>
```

This approach works reasonably well but if you implemented the same sort of logic in a template or controller you would likely choose to use an **else statement** instead. Now in Angular 4, we can set an *else* condition in our `ngIf` directive:

```
<div *ngIf="isAdmin; else normal_user">
  <p>You are an Admin</p>
</div>

<ng-template #normal_user>
  <p>You are a normal user</p>
</ng-template>
```

We simply provide an else statement with a view reference that will be shown if the logic in our `ngIf` directive evaluates to false. We can even supplement this new `else` case with the `then` non-inline template condition:

```
<div *ngIf="isAdmin; then admin_user else normal_user">
  <p>This will be hidden</p>
</div>

<ng-template #admin_user>
  <p>You are an Admin</p>
</ng-template>

<ng-template #normal_user>
  <p>You are a normal user</p>
</ng-template>
```

With this new feature, you can see how we can uniformly format different states of the template driven from the same `if` statement.

Support for assigning local variables

Sometimes in a template, it can be useful to assign the value from a particular piece of logic to a local variable to use in the template itself. This is especially useful when the value of the logic is looking at, is an **observable** which has to resolve asynchronously before data is made available to the template. For example, consider the case of loading the details for a movie in Angular. The user selects a movie title and the app will fetch additional details via an API request:

```
<div *ngIf="movieDetailsObservable | async; else loading; let movie">
    <h1>{{movie.releaseDate}} - {{movie.director}}</h1>
    <p>{{movie.description}}</p>
</div>
<ng-template #loading>Loading...</ng-template>
```

The template has a conditional check for the movie details that resolves asynchronously and provides a reference for the movie details once they are loaded. In the mean time, we use the new `ngIf else` statement to display a loading state to the user.

New email form input validator directive

When handling email inputs in Angular you usually want to validate the format of input before doing anything else with it. This validation could be handled in several ways but one of the most common was simply adding a regular expression match to the input with the pattern directive:

```
<form #form="ngForm">
    <input type="email"
           ngModel
           name="email"
           required
           pattern="^\w+([.-]?\w+)*@\w+([.-]?\w+)*(.\w{2,3})+$">
    <button [disabled]="!form.valid">Submit</button>
</form>
```

This approach works, but obviously, introduces a very ugly **regular expression** right into the middle of our template. If we had many different instances of email input fields in our application, we would quickly find ourselves duplicating this regular expression in multiple places as well. Thankfully, Angular 4 introduced a simple built-in email directive that does the same thing:

```
<form #form="ngForm">
    <input type="email"
           ngModel
           name="email"
           required
           email>
    <button [disabled]="!form.valid">Submit</button>
    <p>Form State: {{form.valid ? "Valid" : "INVALID"}}</p>
</form>
```

This provides a much cleaner and more elegant way of validating simple email address inputs in Angular.

Source maps for generated templates

Angular already has relatively sophisticated template error messaging that does a good job of explaining the source of most template errors. However, there are sometimes when highly nested templates can return errors in Angular can be quite tricky to track down because the templates are compiled into a generated format. Angular 4's addition of source maps for generated templates will make it easier to trace template errors back to a meaningful context in your application.

Here is an example of a template related router error in Angular 2:

```
Can't bind to 'routerLink' since it isn't a known property of 'a'. ("
<ul>
 <li router-active>
 <a [ERROR ->][routerLink]="['Index']">Home</a>
 </li>
</ul>
"): AppComponent@6:7
```

This error correctly identifies the line, and component responsible for this error, however, it doesn't disclose any more detail about the source. Here is the same error in Angular 4:

```
Can't bind to 'routerLink' since it isn't a known property of 'a'. ("
<ul>
 <li router-active>
 <a [ERROR ->][routerLink]="['Index']">Home</a>
 </li>
</ul>
"): ng:///AppModule/AppComponent.html@6:7
```

We can see that, with source maps, we get a fully qualified resource path that leads us back to the exact module and template file responsible for this exception. This sort of enhanced error handling makes working with templates in Angular much more friendly for developers and quality assurance engineers in a team environment.

As with any major framework upgrade, new features come with changes to how legacy features work as well. In the next section we'll dive into the changes and deprecations we have to be aware of when upgrading to Angular 4.

Angular 4 Deprecations and API Changes

In theory, updating your Angular application is simply a matter of updating the `package.json` Angular core library dependencies. However, depending on the features your legacy Angular 2 web application uses, there are a handful of changes in Angular 4 that must be addressed if you upgrade your application.

Following Angular Changes

The Angular team releases detailed change lists for every release of Angular on their GitHub repository. These changes have links to detailed documentation and explanations for the changes. It's recommended that you read through the change list before upgrading your Angular application to make sure you understand you are aware of any deprecations or major changes between your version and the version you are upgrading to.
`https://github.com/angular/angular/blob/master/CHANGELOG.md`

Template tags and attributes have been deprecated

The `template` tag and attribute have been renamed in Angular 4 to `ng-template`. While not a fully removed from Angular 4 yet its usage will throw a single exception in your application the first time it is encountered:

```
The <template> element is deprecated. Use <ng-template> instead ("
</div>

[WARNING ->]<template #normal_user>
<p>You are a normal user</p>
</template>
"): ng:///AppModule/AppComponent.html@7:2
```

This change may seem strange at first, but it's actually part of a long-term plan in Angular to allow support for the web components standard which may use the template tag as a generic web component template definition. In any case, updating your application to use `ng-template` instead is a relatively easy update since the underlying APIs and usage have not changed. This upgrade will become mandatory by Angular 5 when the template tag and attribute is planned to be fully removed by Angular 5.
`https://developer.mozilla.org/en-US/docs/Web/HTML/Element/template`

Animations are now an optional library

The animation library much like the `router`, `http` & `forms` library is now an optional dependency in Angular. This means if you are using animations in your Angular application you will need to import them from this separate package in Angular 4:

```
import {Component} from '@angular/core';
import {
  trigger,
  state,
  style,
  animate,
  transition
} from '@angular/animations';

@Component({
  selector: 'app-root',
  templateUrl: './app.component.html',
  styleUrls: ['./app.component.css'],
  animations: [
    trigger('activateState', [
      state('inactive', style({
        backgroundColor: '#eee',
        marginLeft: '0'
      })),
      state('active',   style({
        backgroundColor: '#cfd8dc',
        marginLeft: '50px'
      })),
      transition('inactive => active', animate('100ms ease-in')),
      transition('active => inactive', animate('100ms ease-out'))
    ])
  ]
})
```

Functionally, this separate animation package works the same as the previous core package. However, if your application doesn't need animations that you don't need to include it in your `package.json` as a dependency.

Enabling Animations in Angular
It's worth noting if you haven't included animations into your application
before you will also need to include the `BrowserAnimationsModule` in
your `app.module.ts` imported modules list. Angular-CLI by default
doesn't include this module, so you will have to add it yourself if you
want to use the animation package in your application:

```
import { BrowserModule } from '@angular/platform-
browser';
import { BrowserAnimationsModule } from
'@angular/platform-browser/animations';
import { NgModule } from '@angular/core';
import { FormsModule } from '@angular/forms';
import { HttpModule } from '@angular/http';

import { AppComponent } from './app.component';

@NgModule({
declarations: [
AppComponent
],
imports: [
BrowserModule,
BrowserAnimationsModule,
FormsModule,
HttpModule
],
providers: [],
bootstrap: [AppComponent]
})
export class AppModule { }
```

ngFor class is deprecated

This may seem alarming if you are used to using this `ngFor` directive in Angular to
template lists of items in your application. This deprecation is specifically only for the
`ngFor` class, not the `ngFor` directive itself. You will still want to use `ngFor` for any loop
templating needs in Angular and this will not throw any sort of warning or exception.

However, if you have a custom class or directive implementation that previously extended the `ngFor` class, you will want to make sure to update that reference to use `NgForOf` instead.

Renderer class is deprecated

The `Renderer` service in Angular is useful for doing direct user interface manipulation while still taking advantage of Angular's sophisticated event handling and data-binding. For example, this component uses the `Renderer` service to add a style to our component's element that will turn all our text blue:

```
import {Component, Renderer, ElementRef} from '@angular/core';

@Component({
  selector: 'app-root',
  templateUrl: './app.component.html',
  styleUrls: ['./app.component.css']
})
export class AppComponent {
  constructor(private renderer: Renderer, </span>private element:
ElementRef) {};

  ngOnInit() {
    this.renderer.setElementStyle(this.element.nativeElement, 'color',
'blue')
  }
}
```

This feature will continue to work in Angular 4 for now, but it has been officially deprecated and will likely be removed in Angular 5. Instead, we should upgrade our application to use this class's successor `Renderer2`.

```
import {Component, ElementRef, Renderer2} from '@angular/core';

@Component({
  selector: 'app-root',
  templateUrl: './app.component.html',
  styleUrls: ['./app.component.css']
})
export class AppComponent {
  constructor(private renderer: Renderer2, private element: ElementRef) {};

  ngOnInit() {
    this.renderer.setStyle(this.element.nativeElement, 'color', 'blue')
  }
```

```
    }
```

It's worth noting that there are some minor API differences between `Renderer` and `Renderer2` such as the method name change of `setElementStyle` in `Renderer` to `setStyle` in `Renderer2`, but it generally fulfills the same role and functionality.

Component lifecycle hooks are now interfaces

If you have any custom components in your Angular application that implement class method overrides to any of the component lifecycle hooks in Angular you will need to update your implementation to use the `implements` keyword instead of `extends`:

```
@Component()
class MyComponent extends OnInit {}
```

In Angular 4, because these lifecycle hooks are defined as interfaces instead of abstract classes you must use the `implements` keyword:

```
@Component()
class MyComponent implements OnInit {}
```

Index

NPM
  used, for upgrading Angular 2 to Angular 4 11

O

object document mapper (ODM) 242
object-relational mapping (ORM) 238
objectId references 291
Observables 83

P

Postman 162
pre-save hooks
  using 287, 291
private use areas
  reference link 341
production error tracking 368, 369, 370, 371, 372,
    374, 375, 376, 377
programmatic page redirection, in Angular 36
promises
  about 105
  used, for creating asynchronous services 101,
    103, 104
  working 105

R

reactive forms 92, 93
regular expression 416
Representational State Transfer (REST) 161
REST APIs
  building, with Express 162, 163, 165, 167, 168,
    169
RESTful APIs 161
routes, in Express
  working with 128, 130, 131
RxJS 110

S

salted hash 287
salted password hashing
  reference link 287
Sass nesting
  using 50, 51, 52, 53
Sass partials
  using 53, 54

working with 54, 55
Sass variables
  using, for style reusability 48, 49
Sass
  Bootstrap, working with 56
  configuring, in Angular 42
SchemaTypes API
  about 280
  reference link 282
Selenium 406
Sentry 368
Sentry.io
  debugging 368, 369, 370, 371, 372, 374, 375,
    376, 377
  URL 368
service-oriented architecture (SOA) 106, 161
services, Angular
  about 96
  creating for data 96, 97, 99, 100
sibling routes
  creating, in Angular 34
single-page application (SPA) 123
singleton 96
Stripe 199
Stripe customer API 230
Stripe payment processor
  working with, in Express 225, 226, 228, 230
structured query language (SQL) 237
sub-documents
  about 283
  creating, in Mongoose model 283, 284, 285
Super-Agent
  about 397
  reference link 399

T

template forms 92
tests
  running, in Angular-CLI 39
typescript library 307
Typescript
  with Express.js 306, 307, 308, 312, 313
  with Node.js 306, 307, 308, 312, 313

www.ingramcontent.com/pod-product-compliance
Lightning Source LLC
Chambersburg PA
CBHW060646060326
40690CB00020B/4537